MARMALADE ME

JILL JOHNSTON

E. P. DUTTON & CO., INC. · NEW YORK · 1971

ACKNOWLEDGMENT

Almost all the essays in this book
appeared in *The Village Voice* in the decade 1960–70.
I acknowledge with gratitude the opportunity
the paper afforded me to develop my style and ideas
and especially to Diane Fisher
who permitted and encouraged the most radical shift
in my work when it began to occur in 1966.

CONTENTS

PART 5

PART 6

ILLUSTRATIONS

INTRODUCTION

It would be fun, and quite tempting, to use this introduction to tell stories about Jill Johnston's behavior at parties, art openings, and on various travels. However, Jill spends considerable effort in enlivening her own writings with tales of outrageous encounters and preposterous incidents, leaving no room for competition.

When she visits me on West 99th Street, Jill Johnston insists that I come out to the street (carrying the drinks), and we sit in her Volkswagen camper so that she can "keep an eye on things." The camper is always doubleparked, and she sometimes does her washing there, dumping the soapy water into the street.

Such stories accompany Johnston wherever she goes, but they shouldn't give the reader of this book the impression that her work is merely entertaining and without considerable significance. It is quite possible that Jill Johnston is one of the most important, radical, and innovative writers of her time.

In April, 1969, a panel including Charlotte Moorman (musician), Andy Warhol (filmmaker), John De Menil (collector), Ultra Violet (actress), Bridgit Polk (photographer), and David Bourdon (critic), met in New York City to discuss Jill Johnston's writings. The event was entitled "The Disintegration of a Critic." It could have been called "The Disintegration of Criticism," for, in fact, this was the real subject of the discussion. It has recently become apparent that Jill Johnston is the foremost exponent of a new criticism, offering a methodology for criticism that rejects the prevailing doctrine that sees criticism as a secondary art form. Johnston, however, does not seem particularly concerned with the destruction of criticism; rather, she is attempting to establish a new form.

Her career in criticism began conventionally enough. She wrote art reviews for *Art News,* and dance articles on performances by Yvonne Rainer, the Royal Ballet, and Robert Morris. They were constructive pieces that were illuminating and interpretive. But her style gradually shifted. The earlier pieces on art and dance no longer seemed to satisfy Jill Johnston the artist. Mere evaluation and explication of artworks seemed a somewhat hollow—if not an outright patronizing endeavor. So Johnston introduced, by her writings, a new vision for criticism *without apology,* and for criticism claiming its own identification in the world of artistic expressions. It is a vision of enormous scope and one that offers considerable potential. She wrote: "I'll take a plot of level territory and stake out a claim to lie down on it and criticize the constellations if that's what I happen to be looking at. I also stake out a claim to be an artist . . ." [1]

The most difficult path for an artist to tread is one that doesn't exist. Yet it is the only possibility for an artist involved in the initial identification of a new idiom. Obviously, a lot of new material will be rejected later on. In so doing, the artist assumes considerable risk. But there is an interesting view from this wild, uncharted path. From its vantage point the well-worn routes seem quite absurd: "Is Fred Asparagus the only guy

[1] "Critics' Critics," *The Village Voice,* September 16, 1965.

who is long and green and dances beautifully?".[2] And the big, standard "questions" appear particularly stupid: "Maybe the great thing about life is a bag of popcorn in a lady's room." [3]

A major discovery by Jill Johnston is, simply, that criticism is a unique form that does not necessarily depend upon another specific object or phenomenon for its own existence and worth. However, that criticism does possess a unique identity has not yet been sufficiently demonstrated. Before it can be demonstrated, the *possibility* needs to be conceived and the new, potentially vital form must be envisioned.

Thus, if we glean from Johnston's writings only the vision of a new possibility for artistic expression, then her contribution to art is secure. Yet there is more to be found. It seems sadly typical of our academic, philosophical method, when approaching the new, that we overlook some of the obvious (and important) characteristics of our subject. In Johnston's case, it is her beautiful style, her terse, witty playing with words, and the confident, delightful enthusiasm she brings to every subject.

One result of Johnston's critical preoccupations has been a turning inward from art as subject to the critic herself as subject: what she refers to as "confessional literature." This might appear narcissistic, as an almost total devotion to person, but should not be misread as a simple ego trip. The art historian can recall many instances of artists turning to the subject of man (and self) in order to demonstrate a new approach that is without apparent precedent. The ancient sculptor relied upon the image of man as the vehicle for his explorations into the identification and viability of an abstract, three-dimensional language. It was in the field of portraiture that the Renaissance artist offered some of his most revealing and significant insights concerning the nature of man and the geometry of the surface. In the field of literature the examples of authentic innovation coupled with exhibition of private and personal subjects are numerous.

Nevertheless, many will ask whether Johnston's writings can properly be called criticism. There have lately been several indicators that popular criticism as a discipline is broadening its scope and claiming new responsibilities. Shortly before her death Ivy Compton Burnett remarked: "The critics are becoming boyish. They only write about themselves." In the area of art criticism the new trend—which involves writing about subjects, opinions, and happenings not directly or "logically" connected to the art object—is spreading widely. In the pages of the formalist *Artforum* magazine, in academic art columns like those of *The New York Times,* and in the sensationalist quasi-political art pieces in *New York* magazine, critics are sneaking personal, political, and poetic material into their criticism, thus reflecting their dissatisfaction with interpretation, formal reportage, qualitative value judgments, and publicity functions. In 1970 a special issue of the newspaper *Culture Hero* was entirely devoted to the subject of Jill Johnston, and virtually all of the twenty-five contributors assumed a highly subjective approach in their articles.

Johnston's work, therefore, represents a radical departure from existing notions concerning the role and function of art criticism. If formal distinctions between various art forms have become increasingly blurred, the boundaries that formerly delineated the guidelines for proper criticism have similarly been obscured. It is to Johnston's credit that her work is several things all at once. It is poetry. It is criticism. It is history. It is self-revelation. While the chief purpose of this series of volumes in modern art criticism is to enlighten and publish percipient art writing, it also should assume a vanguard position in the area of new commitment and identification for criticism itself.

GREGORY BATTCOCK

PREFACE

This selection of work from the decade 1960–70 represents two distinct styles of life and writing. The transition is recorded in Part 3. Until 1965 I was a dedicated critic of dance, painting, sculpture, Happenings, and all forms of intermedia. I became a critic in 1957–58 just when the entire art world was entering a convulsion of dissolving boundaries. The rebelliousness of the times suited my temperament and I became a champion of the new dance which was often as intermedia oriented as the Happenings by painters sculptors and composers. Still, I remained attached to my original ideal of pursuing an interpretive descriptive analytical approach to the "old dance" which was still alive (for me), and of applying such standards to anything new. Thus the writing is enthusiastically academic and labored and Part 2 comprises a small selection of all that work. In Part 4 three of the pieces are left over from that era.

During those wild times I was leading the wild personal

life of the parties and openings while consigning myself otherwise to the rigors of my academic career as thinker and critic.
In August, 1965, both lives exploded in a conflagration of work
and personality. I became what Timothy Leary has called a
revelatory casualty and all seemed lost. What had happened
seemed very unclear actually except that I had a new career
opened up to me as a "mental case" and eventually I decided
to exploit it instead of burying it because I had become privately convinced that the society which had stigmatized me as
crazy was itself crazy and that through the purgatorial fires
of a mind-exploding experience I had, without warning or
preparation, become a rather healthy person. I was frightened
but delighted and secretly conceived a scheme for explaining
myself to the universe. Clearly it would do no good to wag my
finger. A case for a defense is naturally a prosecution of the
causes for the defense and ergo self-defeating. Besides, I had no
ready vehicle for such a defense. I had a column in *The Village
Voice* called "Dance Journal." But of course a defense was in
order since I felt destroyed and humiliated, so my strategy was
to convert my column into confessional literature without anybody noticing. By exposing myself I would exonerate and redeem
myself and hopefully plead the case for a visionary life. How to
subvert my own friendly newspaper toward this end became a
great crossword puzzle to be solved by secret omissions and
hazardous adventures with the language. My precedents for the
styles I developed can be found in all so-called stream-of-
consciousness writing of this century, in all confessional autobiographical literature, and in the poetry of the French Dada
Surrealists, wherever automatic and *non sequitur* in character.
My project was to shatter and reorganize the language for myself. I developed a passion for "found" fragments—statements
and exclamations heard or read—and for arranging them in
the bizarre continuity of the *non sequitur* linked by some personal need or system of association. Two pieces, "The Grandest
Tiger" and "Danscrabble," are totally collaged in this way.
Others include the method as introductory and/or closing remarks and throw-in or throw-away fragments to break up certain linear continuities. Also I took to punning and compounding words and breaching rules of syntax and projecting time
dislocations by intercutting, and writing all pieces in a single

paragraph for an open-ended and blending structure that the reader could stop and start, pause and begin, as his own choice or requirement. "Fluxus Fuxus" was an early fluke in containing almost all methods that I later advanced self-consciously. "Critics' Critics" may not be of any special interest formally, but was my first statement of complaint at the critic's role— having finally recognized the power invested in the critic to further or hinder the careers of other artists who themselves seemed not to recognize the artistry of the critic but only the political function, which later I completely revoked in making myself the subject of my work and turning my own life into the theatre I had previously restricted myself to writing about in its formally announced locations. Thus the conflagration of work and personality I had experienced in 1965, again in 1966, gradually united in an autobiographical column in which to love and travel and exult and dream and complain and project my fantasies for saving the world. The key piece in the book is the "Robert Whitman" review of a Happening he made in a swamp on Long Island in August, 1966. It was written in a gushing ten minutes or so and in the eye of my second tornadic transformation of consciousness when associations were rampant and happily I was unable to distinguish myself and dreams from the dream of those events in the swamp. There is very little writing thereafter for a year since once more I became a "revelatory casualty" and succumbed to the social judgment of my deficiency and uselessness as a human being in a "normal society." But a year later, fall of 1967, I picked up the pieces again and tentatively remembered what I had unlearned and began that slow methodical search for the stylistic oddities that would reflect my disintegration and reintegration and affirmation of the visionary experience they call insane if not drug induced or church defined. I became a champion of my own psychology as the model of a once-normal neurotic striving American spontaneously breaking through the curtain layers of our functional limited consciousness to the deep archaeological ruins of the numinous egoless self where we unite in the total transcendent One.

JILL JOHNSTON

PART 1

UNTITLED

Somebody I know can't stand reading a thing like Norman Brown's *Love's Body* where "everything means everything else." Someone just told me about people who go to the trouble of tracing back their genealogy and find everybody in it, or a broken link that's unaccountable. All those skeletons in the closet. Every genealogy is a fiction. There's no such thing. There's only one genealogy. It takes place in our dreams. Every specific genealogy is a fiction. I just reread *Moses and Monotheism*. I like it that a Jew such as Freud should have put himself out so much as to prove that Moses was an Egyptian. But everyone knows that Moses was a Mexican immigrant. And Malcolm X said Jesus was a black man. And they still don't know who Shakespeare was. I think he was an American Indian posing as King James. For myself, I had three fathers and they were all illustrious. Moreover, my mother's three fathers and mine were one and the same, further elaborating the incestuous project. Anyhow, try figuring out your origins some balmy night on hash and saki or the likes. How many of those flying carpets have taken to the air in the course of luminous Oriental nights? Where were we when we last met? It must have been a memorable occasion.

I had a brief conversation with Diane, my editor, which in some corporate board meeting might have added up to a momentous decision. Actually it was a simple agreement. We agreed that a new column in these pages headed "Intermedia" or "Cross-over" would be an absurdity compounding an already absurd situation of medium categories which are becoming increasingly difficult to contain and define, much to my delight. This column is itself a joke. Any other name for it would be equally amusing. My model is the title of that ridiculous book by Havelock Ellis—*The Dance of Life*. No doubt I'm saying the already obvious. What does it mean to name something? Where do we come off giving everything a legal identity? The genealogy of language is the same as for persons. It ends up in the paramecium, one of the most illegal of organisms. What do we do with language after accepting it as a practical expedient? In a real or pseudo-etymological exercise you can uncover the hoax of a frozen legal identity which finds its way into that mausoleum called the dictionary. The dictionary is the language equivalent of the doomsday book. Yet it's one of my favorite books. I use it all the time. I use it for work and for pleasure. It's utterly confusing. You can get a terrific high on the dictionary. What does it mean to encircle something and paste a name on it and qualify the name with adjectives born in somebody's hysterical manifesto and then say well now that it has a name and it means this and that it's all over baby. We're dead as soon as we're born with a name. We make ourselves new again by changing our names, by dreaming ourselves back into our real or pseudo genealogies. Or we make ourselves new not by changing the name but by repeating and repeating it into a magical transcendence of itself. It becomes meaningless by becoming so much itself.

This is a complex subject. I want to be clear and obtuse about it at the same time. The occasion is an orgy of poetry and intermedia thinking generated by three Poetry Events in Central Park, September 27–29, organized by John Giorno;

followed by a heady discussion with John Perreault, who contributed one of the events. Perreault restates the ancient purpose of poetry, all art. "Poetry breaks up the ordinary use of language to let more reality come through." Until recently poetry was never traditionally just naming things (excepting the primitives). Traditionally our Western poetry has made language new by altering the context of words within a grammatically correct syntax. In the recent tradition (Dada, Surrealism, Symbolism, etc.) the context of words was radically altered by the shattering of the conventional syntax. E. E. Cummings, for instance. Syntax is linear. Its breakup is a collusive synthesis. Poets and artists had been doing this a long time before McLuhan delivered it to an unsuspecting public. Intermedia is the ultimate realization of a synthesis that's been taking place all century in each medium. Cubism was one of the first radical manifestations of it in painting. Prophets of the new intermedia are the likes of Cage, Artaud, and Schwitters, to name three if I must. Each medium is now transcending itself by emphasizing or extending each aspect of itself which relates to every other extension of our senses. The traditional legalized medium (i.e., painting) projects the stimuli for one of our senses as supreme. Environmental sculpture, painting, etc., is one sort of intermedia attempt to put the object back in the forest where it's a tree among trees. In the forest every sense is equally supreme.

The artists are making a last-ditch stand to re-integrate what the child and the savage do naturally. Words are pictures are sounds are sights are touch are smell are the altogether forever. The artists are rampaging through the graveyards of the file cabinets to throw the alphabetized cards into the beautiful chaos of the altogether from whence they were so painfully extracted to make a mess called civilization. Intermedia is as old as the hills, as Emmett Williams said of the new kind of picture poem called Concrete Poetry. Our oldest ancestors were the great intermedia people. The new intermedia developments are not an indication of progress but of regression. To regress is to progress. If there's such a thing as progress it means to go back. To find again the child and the savage in us. To cure ourselves by finding again the all at once altogether. By naming things we separated things. By naming things in logical syntax we separated the subject, verb, and object—the actor, the action, and that which is acted upon. Somehow it came about that even artists, among the best of children in a childless society, called themselves poets or composers or dancers or painters or sculptors. The new synthesis is a hallucination and McLuhan rightly pointed out that the opening of all our senses to all the data would result in hallucination.

Perreault dates the recent intermedia activity of poets from 1965. He says he himself took courage from John Giorno who at that time was beginning to put his "found" poems on tape and project them in an environmental situation of black light. Giorno was inspired by William Burroughs and Brion Gyson. Perhaps the only poet whom people identify as a poet who was earlier pushing the performance aspect of poetry into a deeper extension of itself was Jackson Maclow. Jackson was the only poet, considered a poet in the formal sense, associated with the Fluxus exploration of the late fifties and early sixties in which everybody was everything. If you asked me what George Brecht is today I couldn't tell you. If you say artist people think painter, etc. The last time somebody asked me what I did I said I was an archaeologist. Having said it I believe it. A jolly new profession. They asked me then if I'd done any exciting digging lately and I said yes absolutely all the time. I think the guy who dug up Troy was one of my ancestors. But about Jackson. He was one of the poets in the Central Park evenings. With the exception of slides projected on the back wall of the bandshell he was doing what he's been doing for a decade or more, in this case: a poem made by chance (he too was a student in Cage's 1957 course at the New School) and delivered by a chorus of five as a superimposed overlapping etc. simultaneous exposition of a simple story about "the turtles embark upon a journey to the sea whose course is a mystery . . . no one knows where the turtle goes . . ." The text is both chanted and spoken. The story is heard in fragments as well as in a syntactical sentence.

As a poet connected with and emerging from the New York School of Poets (led by the older Ashbery, Koch, O'Hara) Perreault had no tradition for moving into a performance situation beyond a straight reading. His friends in fact initially opposed the move. The New York School of course overlaps with the beat poets (Ginsberg, Corso, Ferlinghetti,

Burroughs) and the Black Mountain School of Olson, Creeley, Duncan, et. al. With perhaps an exception here and there, including the well known disrobings (Ginsberg) in the fifties, the readings were always straight podium deliveries. Excepting a fiery prophet like Ginsberg, Perreault thinks they're all a great bore, the readings. He says that if the standard device of poetry is to involve all the senses through words by suggestion, the next logical step is to actually do it. As a poet turned performer, in the broadest sense, he's involved in the making of a new tradition in his medium, at the moment shared by Giorno, Maclow, Anne Waldman, Michael Benedikt, Hannah Weiner, Emmett Williams (all on the Central Park events), and probably others I don't know about or slipping my mind. As such they merge with all the other artists whose particular mediums (a habit they can't or don't want to shake) may appear to remain the paramount aspect of an intermedia situation but whose concerns are expressing the great longing and project of an era running short on survival time.

Re-integration. The everything as everything. The organism as totally illegal. The legality of nothing but pleasure in an orgy of self-reproduction (the paramecium). The end of importance. The end of politics. The end of hierarchies. The end of families. The end of groups. The end of the earth as a penal colony (Burroughs). —No end to what there can be an end of in the great re-integration: the intermedia of the cosmic village; the intermedia of the genealogy as a vast prolific dream; the intermedia of language as the gurgling of happy infants; the intermedia of hordes of artists (all the people) making sand castles and other important inanities inside and outside their heads, or doing nothing at all. Intermedia is the world before and after we chop it up into bits of pieces and stash it away in a filing cabinet labeled MINE, YOURS, THEIRS.

I'll have to continue this next week. I want to say a few concrete things about the actual performances, including observations about the language itself, in part inspired by the discussions with Perreault.

Meanwhile, off the subject (or on I think) I wish to add my salute to those of my friends (and everybody) to Marcel Duchamp whom I have often saluted and met only twice and talked with just once. He has always lived and will continue to live. He made us and he was everything we made him. He was made long before and ahead of his time. We should be happy.

October 10, 1968

MARMALADE ME

I thought to write last week on a bunch of poetry events I saw one afternoon, November 17, at Longview Country Club. About twenty-one two-minute events by poets, organized by Hannah Weiner. But the ivory tower has become the control tower as the naked ape speeds toward the moon. If the flight for the moon overshoots its mark the announcers will go off the air immediately, the families of the astronauts will be notified in person instantly, the President will simultaneously be informed and will then go on the air to advise the population of the disaster. The operation will take twenty minutes exactly. Presumably the control tower will continue to communicate with the astronauts as they speed toward infinity, sipping their final meals out of their final plastic bags. That might be the ultimate poetry. If all philosophy since 400 B.C. has been a footnote to Plato, possibly all poetry since Sappho has been a preparation for astronautical communications during operation sayonara. But I don't really believe it (although I believe everything). The handwriting on the wall is the first mark made by a delighted infant. When did the human animal begin to notice its own footprint as a mark of pleasure, a visible imprint on its environment, another autoerotic involvement, having no functional design (i.e., the bear follows the tiger to the water's edge, etc.). Putting it another way, when did the human animal make a sand castle out of its own shit after how many eons of dropping it and forgetting it like the horses at the circus. Did the human animal become human when it called itself human? It doesn't matter. I'm thinking of the calling as an invisible mark, the handwriting as current in the air, as the sound that became a fury. The sound (and motion) came first. The sound was the noise of an infant's disapproval at separation from its cave of blood and water. When did the sound become so specified as to signify a particular object? Other animals make such sounds, but so far as we know they don't get very deep into grammatical complications. (Can you write a simple declarative sentence with seven grammatical errors?) But I presume all animals enjoy the sounds they make. Do you think that when someone talks just for the sake of talking he is saying the most original and truthful thing he can say?

The sound is a current is a heartbeat is a footstep is a footprint is a handshake is one thing you do dead and alive whenever you do anything and whenever you make a sound you do everything else too, even eating your words. I suppose the origin of human poetry as it's classically defined means the transition from essential sound (expressing a pain or a pleasure, or signifying a need and later the object who might gratify the need) to the sound made for the sake of making a sound as a pleasurable extension of body sense not thinking about the next meal or the fine feathers on a new peacock. But I don't believe this either. The ultimate poetry might be that first noise of a shocked infant spilling out of a bloody canal. Moreover, I think it's impossible to separate the pure pleasure of making a play on a bodily extension (sound, motion, etc.) from the expressions of the so-called functional needs of food, shelter, affection. The ancient primitive rites demonstrate the wedding of the two in the totality of living which we compartmentalize through language. Still, we have this thing called art. I have an image of an animal turning back on its tracks to examine the shape of one of its footprints. Maybe he compares the shape to a memory of a footprint he once followed to the water's edge. Maybe he goes home and makes a lot of footprints around the campus just to go back and notice how he made them and how they look alike or different according to the texture and firmness of the ground. Maybe he examines the bottom of his foot to correlate the shape of the foot with the imprint he's making. Exhausting these possibilities he might really freak out on directional extensions. The campus begins to look like a study in

Jill Johnston lecturing. Ralph Crane, LIFE Magazine © Time Inc.

advanced geometry. Pretty soon he's making the same marks inside on the walls and floors and he's using a piece of bark he brought in from a tree and he's got an object between his toes or fingers looks like a cock he's using for a pencil he fashioned with his teeth out of a piece of slate. Next thing you know he's doing a doctoral dissertation on the shadows cast by abominable snowmen. Now, there isn't any ultimate poetry. It begins and ends with a scream on the way in (or out) and a conversation on the way out (or in). The astronauts could be screaming in their conversation on the way out and the infants could be talking in their screaming on the way in.

Maybe the animal with a pencil outlining his foot on a piece of bark made the first human poem. Making a mark, writing, and drawing, were originally one. The image as a representation of foot also becomes the image sent abroad to a relative to convey some information about a foot. A bunch of other symbols (sun for hot, straight lines for fast action, five circles for repetition) convey the information that "hot foot is on the move again." One of the biggest head trips you can take is thinking backward and forward and in circles on the subject of writing and drawing, or painting. A lot of observers have described Franz Kline's paintings as "calligraphy." And Mark Tobey's painting as "white writing." Not to mention Pollock, although the word they liked for that was "drip." Not to mention Cy Twombly, whose abstracted script paintings have been mistaken for handwriting exercises in chalk on a blackboard. But quickly, think backward (or ahead) to modern pictograph paintings by Torres Garcia, by Gottlieb, by Bradley Walker Tomlin, even some early Pollock, whatever looks like hieroglyphs in rows of compartments. Could you say the same for Jasper Johns's number paintings? But quickly, think on to the Pop Art fascination with whole words or fragments of words (done all century by the Cubists, Dadaists, Surrealists, etc., or an American like Stuart Davis) mixed up with the pictures of things and the pigmentation or acrylics or what, and the crap thrown in to confuse the definition of painting finally (i.e., Wesselmann). Thinking on poetry, as writing, the terms "poem painting" (O'Hara plus Rivers) and Concrete Poetry are a contemporary way of restating the synonymity of writing and drawing, and drawing naturally as painting. Dylan Thomas made Concrete Poetry too. So did Cummings. And Mallarmé. And I like all the picto-typing effects of the recent stuff. But I never saw a printed page in any case as anything less than a picture plus a sound plus a drawing plus a symbol or symbols and all the meanings the symbols seem to want to mean and/or whatever I'm wanting them to mean too. All these things at once. I also eat my words. I get very sexy on reading.

What is prose and if you know what prose is what is poetry? (Stein). I asked Hannah Weiner how her twenty-one poets qualified as poets. She said she just knew them as poets who also did things. But Peter Schjeldahl, I asked, did he ever do anything? No he didn't. At Longview's, Peter's two-minute event featured himself shaving while several friends shot at him with cap pistols. Beautiful poem. I'm serious. And Jim Carroll murdered a cockroach with a can of roach spray. And Ron Padgett did "In the Audience," which involved Mr. Padgett being in the audience from the beginning and staying until the end (he said). And Hannah Weiner had her two events you couldn't say what exactly anymore. And the most recent organizations by post-Judson people were called Spring Gallery or Fall Gallery Concerts, including poets and painters as well as choreographers just like in the early middle late days of Judson Dance Theatre; but the official designation at least does away with a conventional medium identity. I'm sure the poets realized the excellent ironies of their November 17 presentation. Supposing Hannah had included Steve Paxton's Tiny Event of two or so years ago which consisted of a taped reproduction of pilot and hostess instructions in flight called "A. A." But Steve is a choreographer!—And for me the Tiny Events were concluded with funny fetching finesse in my own house after the Longview performers doing a tango inside a small taped-off area after she announced the event as an "MZWT," meaning Mike Zulu Whisky Tango in the International Code (signal system for ships at sea). And Eduardo Costa of Argentina showed "Fashion Fiction" slides and taped commentary on gold accessories molded to fit the ears, fingers, or toes. And Jackson Maclow climbed a ladder to slowly unfold the number "one," seen as "1" in red corduroy on a silver ground, then roll it back up again. And Ronald Gross distributed a few dozen roses to the audience in memory of Gertrude Stein. And Michael Benedikt put fake tears on Carolee Schneemann's face. And Vito Hannibal Acconci read a poem about walking, while he walked. And Bici Hendricks distributed one-line poems curled up in transparent pill capsules. And John Perreault Xed out three windows with black masking tape. And Lewis Warsh and Anne Waldman played being "at home" on a blanket, with grass, television, and taped conversation. And John Giorno got everybody out of the place at the end with tear gas bombs and I didn't wait to hear his taped poem which occurred when he set the bombs.

Stein's question about prose and poetry (which I once applied to dance) might now be put thus: What is poetry and if you know what poetry is what is an event? Anyhow, I like to see the poets, or whoever calls himself a poet these days, doing events. As I said or implied in the *Voice* (October 10), the poets have been joining with all the other artists whose identities are blurring. The solution to the problem of identity is, get lost. These Tiny Events were like a lot of Fluxus and Yam occasions of the late fifties and early sixties. Two old Fluxus Yam people were even included: Maclow and Emmett Williams. Even the choreographers, traditionally the last to catch up, have been further out than the poets. Many dances by the Judson Dance Theatre were affairs by Mark DeVestele, who announced an event without title, crouched in the middle of the floor, removed a shoe and sock, and displayed a red bubble on one toe acquired that morning he said in an accident of something falling on it the toe. But naturally lots more events followed before Mark and his pals left. I wonder if I'd have thought to mention his toe event here if he'd just told us about it or if he'd displayed the toe without announcing it as an event and assuming a spatial position proper to an event of more consequence than the table talk we were also enjoying so much. What is of more consequence than something else? I like tangerine trees and marmalade skies and I think I should inform somebody that Deborah Hay is now taking belly-dancing classes.

A lot of people are seeing the ultimate poetry in all the signs from coast to coast. I forget when I first really turned on to the signs. It might've been a trip back to the city from George Segal's house in New Brunswick, on Route 1 at night and after a mind bending table twister about death and related non-subjects. Every sign, neon or otherwise, turned into a fantastic put on. For the "meaning" aspect of words I'm reminded of what a man recorded of a ten-day "psychotic episode" (insanity) in Ronald Laing's *Politics of Experience.* He said he couldn't read the newspapers because everything he read had a large number of associations with it. Just the headlines, for instance, would have much wider associations in his head than normally. He was tuning in to the metaphorical monster in us. In the so-called normal state we look for the Surrealist compounds to do that kind of work for us. But it's always available, without a good Surrealist to show us it's there. Remy Charlip has a tiny little drawing in his new book of an "octopuss." It's a cat with eight legs. Driving to New Hampshire last week I saw a Massachusetts license plate reading: MATER. On the trip home a huge billboard: BRING AUNT MILLIE HOME AGAIN. But perhaps the ultimate in road poetry was a trip two years ago down from Rhinebeck, at night with a friend. My friend had some good stuff up there in Rhinebeck and I was high on myself as usual and we were much into a verbal trip, laughing I didn't think we'd make it etc., when we got really freaked on that endless white line coming and going down the center of the road. You mightn't believe it but that line was coming right through the car and through our bodies. It must've been because we both said it was. I've never been the same since. I don't know a verb from a house. Sometimes I see an object on the table I can't recognize, I can't find a name for it, I can't imagine what kind of name it could have. I've also been looking for some time, without finding it, for a pencil on my cluttered table.

The handwriting on the wall as a mark on the road made by an unwitting highway employee. If he went back to notice his line, he too would be on his way to infinity sipping his last meal and making poetry with the control tower. At that point who needs to make a line? I can't afford to have any more ideas or I'll need another head for the rest of my brain. When your carburetors are in tune your pistons are in love with your spark plugs.

What about sky writing? What about words made by human bodies by the Living Theatre and by football coeds on the football field? What about scribbage and scrabbage and alphabet soup and ticktacktoe? The alphabet soup people must've been very hip to how we eat our words. I understand the school system is beginning to wise up to the absurdity of the alphabet. They teach by whole words now. No need to teach anything actually. Television is sufficient. I was happy about the school strike, knowing my kids were at home getting "conditioned" and "brainwashed" by television. I take McLuhan seriously when he says why should the children go to school now to interrupt their education. My last story here is about a beautiful teen-age boy who is supposed to be retarded, meaning he can't read or write. But he's been looking at television a long time. One day I watched a program called "Camp Runamuck" with him. (Is or was there such a program?) I knew then he must know how to read. The boys had "Camp Runamuck" written on their T-shirts. They were obviously at camp. They were clearly running amuck. And they were always talking about it. Now I ask you, can my retarded friend read or not? His mother says he picks out his favorite brands of whatever at the supermarket by himself.—What I figure is that this boy is too goddam smart for the school system. Lucky for him they say he can't read or write. I couldn't care less myself. He's extraordinary. And he's always writing, never mind reading. His mark in the world is very apparent to me. I should've known me when I was you, then I would've been me. I wish I'd known you when I wasn't me and I would've been you. If there are as many minds as there are heads, there are as many loves as there are hearts. Riding the image as though it were a breaking wave.

December 12, 1968

THERE IS NO SILENCE NOW

Silence is the book by the man who might qualify for "best known, least understood" of contemporary artists. The collection of lectures, essays, and anecdotes by John Cage, if read both freely and carefully, should provide an experience of the man, his ideas, and inventions, that could be an occasion for expanding discoveries. Cage has pushed contemporary art beyond its thinkable limits by the breadth and strength of his intellect and the daring of his imagination, so much so that those who read *Silence* should find it difficult to curl up inside any comfortable box made before picking up the book. If that sounds discouraging I would add that John Cage is a cheerful existentialist and as such he suggests a view of the landscape more varied and changing than any afforded by squinting through the peepholes of a box.

For those who may not know, the title of the book is not a joke. In some important sense, Cage has reversed all traditional practices of composing music by making silence the material of music as well as sound. This seeming contradiction in terms is made possible by redefining the nature of silence. In the past, silence served music only to punctuate a phrase; it was, in other words, the invisible servant in the form of a pause that gave dramatic emphasis to an otherwise constant stream of sound (the ever-present directives of the master) or provided the space in that stream between the melodically continuous notes. It is well known that Cage has been prominent in upsetting this traditional practice (of melodic and harmonic structures) by working directly with sound—letting sounds be themselves, as he has often said, so that each sound may be heard only as itself and not depend for its value on its place within a "system" of sounds. It is not so well known that the key to this revolution is silence. Cage may be the first composer in history to say that there is no such thing as silence. He quotes, as personal proof, an experience in an anechoic chamber, a room made as technologically silent as possible, in which he heard two sounds: his nervous system and his circulatory system. In terms of music, this means that the conventional "pauses" of the past are as filled with sound as the music made by performers from a notated score. This sound is what happens to be in the environment, and it is "called silence only because it does not form part of a musical intention."

Silence means the whole world of sound, Life; and its entrance into the world of music means the end of that exclusive activity called Art whereby the composer makes a separate act meant to "illumine the darkness" of the chaos of everyday life. What is our life that it must be so informed by these rarefied man-made structures?

The admission of life into music originally meant noise, and, in a short article on Edgard Varèse published in 1958, Cage describes the present nature of music as "arising from an acceptance of all audible phenomena as material proper to music." (I note the parallel to the "found object," or "readymade," in painting and construction.) Cage has extended this acceptance by making himself, so far as possible, like a man who might do nothing more (as a composer) than give a slight initial impulse to a stack of blocks, stones, cards, and watch the resulting configuration with the pleasure of experiencing something new. "Form is what interests everyone and fortunately it is wherever you are and there is no place where it is not."

One might also imagine how the same man could mastermind the most complex conjunction of events enacted by a number of people without knowing in advance what those events would be and how they would converge or separate in space and time. Such a situation is precisely what preoccupies Cage at the present time. In 1950, as a result of his already advanced ideas and actions, as well as his studies in Zen, he moved into an era of "chance operations" by implementing methods established in the *I Ching* (*Book of Changes:* a Chinese Book of Oracles dating from pre-Christian times), establishing sounds and continuities by tossing three coins six times. Any such method, though leaving a wide margin for the occurrence of events outside the intention of the composer, is still the "work" of that composer and permits little determination by the performer. By 1955, Cage had launched new techniques designed to eliminate this dictatorship over the performer and make him the creator of what he does (under the most fragmentary specifications), thus introducing what Cage calls indeterminacy—a truly experimental state of mind and action because it produces events "the outcome of which cannot be foreseen."

One of the most difficult lectures in *Silence* is "Indeterminacy" (given in Germany in 1958), set like his other lectures, in a unique structure and typescript (in this case, "intentionally pontifical": small print) and examining in concise detail the degrees to which he finds each of several compositions (by Bach, Stockhausen, Earle Brown, Christian Wolff, Morton Feldman, and himself) to be "indeterminate with respect to its performance."

Cage's heresy, of course, is his partial, sometimes total, abdication of will. The pride of the West is bound up in the "profundities" resulting from the application of mind over the brute forces of nature. Now that this pride has been shattered by so many instances of irrationality in human nature and by discoveries pointing to the finitude of human knowledge, the most advanced thought and art of our time brings man back to his proper situation within nature. Cage achieves this position through external (as distinct from subconscious or "automatic") techniques—methods of chance and indeterminacy—which release him from his own psychology, taste, and permit the natural flow of impermanencies as they impress themselves on a mind empty of memories, ideas, and preconceptions; in short, empty. "If one maintains secure possession of nothing (what has been called poverty of spirit) then there is no limit to what one may freely enjoy."

Cage views the tradition of art in the West as an imposition on the viewer—forcing him to respond in a special way rather than making a situation of many possibilities. Particular emotional responses are inevitable, and, when the situation is indeterminate, each viewer will make his own experience out of it. The question, as always, arises: What is the point of making anything at all, since at any moment the world is teeming with possibilities for experience? For Cage, the answer is that there is no point, it is simply something to do, which means that living and making a thing are not two separate acts. And if everybody can do it, then let everybody, "for the more, as is said, the merrier."

Cage's adventurous intellect has brought him beyond the necessity of doing anything (in the Western sense of "striving"), and, in some sense, his music propounds the necessity of doing nothing. His silent piece, *4′ 33″,* is an expression of that necessity. It is a piece "in three movements during all three of which no sounds are intentionally produced. The lengths of time were determined by chance operations but could be any others." In this piece, Cage makes everybody present (audience) the creator and the performer. It is doubtful that too many people would be interested in paying their money to listen to themselves (coughing, chair-creaking) for an entire evening. But Cage made an important point about the nature of the "new music" that must have been well taken, by some at least, at the performance of his silent piece. Regarding the extreme result of silence in music Robert Ashley, a composer, made a striking statement at an interview with Cage in Ann Arbor, Michigan. He said: "It seems to me that your influence on contemporary music, on 'musicians,' is such that the entire metaphor of music could change to such an extent that—time being uppermost as a definition of music—the ultimate result would be a music that wouldn't necessarily involve anything but the presence of people. That is, it seems to me that the most radical redefinition of music that I could think of would be one that defines 'music' without reference to sound."

The influence of John Cage, in the thought and action of many corners of contemporary art, is immense. One reason for this influence, I'm convinced, is his command of language. He has spoken eloquently for advanced music, his own ideas, and methods; for dance; for those who also enjoy life and like to hear somebody like Cage talk about it; for those who are also stimulated by the Eastern philosophies, Zen in particular; and for those who also sense the need for a life based on experience rather than judgment. There is no logic in Cage's lectures (unless it be the logic of style, which is everywhere in evidence); he merely describes situations, or gives spontaneous voice to convictions and insights, or rambles coherently about nothing, as he does in "Lecture on Nothing"—and, in so doing, he brings us some of the most crystal-cut prose of contemporary writing; that which comes close to, if it is not, poetry, because of its lucid condensation, its quicksilver transaction between thought and word.

RAINER'S *MUSCLE*

Latest expanded coverage of Yvonne Rainer's *The Mind Is a Muscle,* presented at the Anderson Theatre April 11, 14, and 15 in its latest expanded form. The work began in 1965 as a little snowball (four and a half minutes called *Trio A*) which was slowly pushed over familiar and unfamiliar territory to its present state as a huge ball containing the history of its journey. The process was accretive rather than protean. I'm sentimentally attached to it as one might be toward a baby whose birth

Steve Paxton (left) and Merce Cunningham (right).
Photograph by Richard Rutledge.

Yvonne Rainer. Photograph by Al Giese.

you attended and subsequently watched in its expanding versions of itself. *Trio A* was the germinal origin of the dance. The woolen underwear, a pretty tough fabric, to be covered (though never obscured) by a multifaceted garment made of the same sturdy stuff with certain additional embellishments. I've seen *Trio A* a number of times and still think I haven't really seen it. The underwear metaphor isn't a good one from the view that you've never seen such intricate underwear. The trio is actually one solo. The three dancers perform the solo simultaneously but are almost never in unison since each performer moves at his own speed. The solo seems to consist of innumerable discrete parts or phrases. The intricacy lies in the sheer quantity of diverse material presented in a short space of time. Yet all this detail is assimilated by a smooth unaccented continuity rendering some illusion of sameness to the whole thing. Each phrase receives equal emphasis. "The end of each phrase merges immediately into the beginning of the next with no observable accent. The limbs are never in fixed still relationship and are stretched to their fullest extension only in transit, creating the impression that the body is constantly engaged in transitions." One could view the entire solo as a single phrase. Here's the crux of a departure from conventional phrasing. Traditionally a phrase is identified as a distinct entity by its plotlike structure of a beginning, a middle, an end—more technically translated as a preparation, a climax, and a recovery. Ballet and modern dance are full of variations on this dynamic alternation of energy output. It means of course that certain moments are more important than others, which is, in microcosm (in the phrase), an expression of the whole hierarchical structure of traditional dance. Rainer's polemic is to undermine this tyrannical arrangement. Since she remains in some dialectical relation to the tradition (both *Trio A* and *Trio B* require a technical background for performance), I construe her position to be of the first magnitude (the first since Cunningham's radical alterations) in advancing the medium within a context of movement still understood as "dance." *The Mind Is a Muscle,* I hasten to say, is a hybrid of this dance-based movement and the ordinary anybody-can-do-it action with which several of her peers are more exclusively concerned. It's all dance to my way of seeing it, but for now it's convenient to refer to something that's "still understood as dance" to help clarify positions.

In the early days of the Judson movement Rainer generated excitement chiefly as an original eccentric with a powerful personal projection. As early as 1964 she began to reevaluate her situation to begin moving away from accessible forms by purging the work of idiosyncratic (emotion-laden) gesture and dynamically varied movement. *Trio A* was the first fully realized expression of a new position. The shift is most emphatically toward neutrality: toward the matter-of-fact "doing" of a thing rather than the "performing" of a thing, toward a "work-like rather than an exhibition-like presentation," toward a removal of seductive involvement with an audience. The performers of *Trio A,* for instance, never confront the audience; the gaze is constantly averted as the head is in motion or deflected from the body if the body happens to be frontally oriented. In the section called "Film" a view of the seven dancers is partially obstructed as they operate behind a screen about eight feet by eight feet placed downstage center. Another tactical withdrawal underscored by an introspective self-involvement is the solo walk skip jump leap activities and the group messing around—hoisting and carrying each other and playing a hand game in transit. Still, I see Rainer reacting somewhat to her own stringency. As Paxton said, it's impossible to repress yourself. A gesture in "Film" looked like right out of *Terrain* (1963), arms awkwardly spread, head pressed into a hunched shoulder. Not to mention the intimate personal material in a marvelous stylization of the choreographer's gastrointestinal illness: two dancers all over the place limping, lurching, staggering, clutching the abdomen with one hand. Yet the more personal stuff is presented as always with factual detachment. In her hottest referential material, the love duet in *Terrain,* the pressure was on getting the beauty of it cold. And here, in the *Muscle* are a few bits, comically lifted out of a love context, reminiscent of the old lascivious duet. In "Stairs" three dancers are engaged in much play activity on a mobile staircase of five steps: climbing up and down, jumping off, scrambling and sliding, etc., and getting a foam rubber mat involved in it. There are several "assists"—at breasts, buttocks, crotch, like cuts in a surreal movie, or better just having your ass pinched in an elevator, all out of whack and much to some pertinent polymorphous bodily point. No member outstanding.

Muscle as it stands now in its one hour and forty-five minute length is in some sense a compendium of all Rainer's formal interests. One I haven't mentioned here, among others, which is crucial to the tone and look of the piece, is an old interest in playing things off against each other. Like the simple repetitive action in *We Shall Run* (1963) accompanied by the grand heroics of a Berlioz "Requiem"; or the same simplicity of a section of *Three Seascapes* attended by a Rachmaninoff. Ironic exposure of an antiheroic dance. In *Muscle* there are nine interludes. Two of them, a taped dialogue (conversation) and a pornographic poem (John Giorno), function as verbal equivalents to the dance, albeit embellishments of a sort. But the musical divertimentos: "Dial M for Murder"—"The Pink Panther" (lush corny movie music)—"Amelia Earhart's Last Flight"—"Strangers in the Night"—"She Has Funny Cars"— plainly throw the flat neutrality of the dance into relief and offer an ironic concession to conventional theatrical expectations. The juxtaposition is terrific. Then there are the guys hawking candy during the piece (America hurrah). And the charming juggler (Harry De Dio) who entertains us on one side of the stage with his battery of tricks while the dancers on the other side alter their configuration as a group in a procession of still lifes or tableaus of a quiet desultory beauty. I found them both equally distractive.

Additional physical properties to the dance are both corroborative and extraneous. A backdrop of reflective polystyrene silver lowered during *Trio A;* a carpet of bubble-wrap (packing material) rolled out in *Trio B;* the quantity of sticks thrown out one by one in the final solo; the yellow fluorescent light fixture lowered in "Film"; the huge impressive looking white lattice or grid structure lowered briefly in the solo. There's a nod in this toward her sculptural compatriots ("Minimal" essentially) from whom she's found support and guidance in common interests. And there are the barbells, mattresses, staircase, and swings which . . . wow this has become a complicated dance. For all that and all the interludes the fundamental issue of the work is the muscle. "My body remains the enduring reality." Or as R. Drexler said, "My last resort is my body." The other cool collected handsome straightforward and dedicated bodies in the dance belong to Becky Arnold, Gay Delanghe, Barbara Lloyd, William Davis, David Gordon, and Steve Paxton.

April 18, 1968

CAR CRASH

Writing in 1920, Kurt Schwitters, who was associated with the Dadaists but who called his own theory of art "Merz," outlines a fantastic scenario for a stage event that would embrace all branches of art in an artistic unit. "Merz," he said, "stands for freedom from all fetters," and the Merz work of art par excellence would be the Merz drama in which all parts are inseparably bound up together. "It cannot be written, read, or listened to, it can only be produced in the theatre." In conclusion he exclaims with wonderful petulance: "I want the Merz stage. Where is the experimental theatre?"

Mr. Schwitters should be alive to see and participate in the realization of his vision which the Reuben Gallery on Third Street is now promoting for the second year. Jim Dine's *Car Crash,* the first in a series this year, is not the kind of wild combination that Schwitters had in mind—everything here relates to the car crash—but it embodies the essential idea of a composite form, and it goes an important step further. Mr. Dine has included the audience itself as an active component in the Happenings—active by their situation right in the middle of it.

If much modern theatre has sought to break down the separation between audience and actors, this is the supreme seduction. But painting also has been luring the observer into close identification with its materials and subjective states; and at the Reuben Mr. Dine literally encloses everyone within a collage room. It includes objects relating to cars and crashes, and one side consists of large hunks and rolls of cork and cardboard strewn about in shelves. Everything is drippingly whitewashed. A mess, yet ghostly pristine. The set is the scene of the crash, its aftermath, and its eternal persistence.

The moving events are an exclamation mark. Cars and humans are indistinguishable, except for the Big White Woman (Pat Muschinski), a high immovable figure who is like a monotone chorus barely remembered, but still powerful, from a human drama of the past. She might be an immortal victim, rigor-mortised in the collage, lately an angel, stupefied with memories.

The first action is a searching ride about town by the White Man Woman Car (Marcus Ratliff), the White Woman Man Car (Judy Tirsch), and the Aluminum Car (Jim Dine), accompanied by recorded honky motor noises. The Aluminum Car makes off with frightened grunts, leaving the road to the other two who build an erotic dance to the point of car-human, or human-car intercourse.

Blackout. The Aluminum Car reenters, howling. A crashing racket behind one side of the collage. The Big White Woman utters her car poem

> *The car in my life is a car*
> *with a pole in the harm of*
> *my soul which is a pretty*
> *clank.*
>
> *My car is my hertz spot of love*
> *to zoom through the whole*
> *transmission of my lovely*
> *tire . . .*

She begins a litany of "Help, help . . ." while Aluminum Car runs down a tape that spells out Help many times over.

Another blackout and Aluminum Car takes command of some big chalk and a blackboard. He outlines a red car with a monster jaw for the front end. He rubs it out and draws another like an earthworm. With increasing frenzy, spurred on by his own incredulous grunts, he super-poses one after the other while the two car-humans and the Big White Woman stammer a chorus of recognition, disbelief, and devastation in choking half-syllables.

November 10, 1960

"ENVIRONMENTS"
AT MARTHA JACKSON'S

The "terrible children" invaded Martha Jackson's Gallery last May and June with more of those baffling noncommercial commodities, things you can't use or sell or label even, which nobody could be too clear about why they should be encouraged or endured much less considered the prestige items they obviously are, or else why would Miss Jackson (whose commercial acumen is well known) clutter up her fashionable yard with a bunch of junky car tires that she permitted Allan Kaprow to put there?

I don't know what Miss Jackson thought about those tires. I didn't think much myself, I mean I perceived a bunch of tires there in the yard and then asked my son if he wanted to stay and play around in them while I went upstairs to see the rest. I know Mr. Kaprow is against people finding dark serious meanings, commentaries on the state of the union, etc., in these situations, and I agree, there seems no pressing reason to find anything other than what you see; in fact the cultural references are usually a dodge and a distraction right off, a way of trying to account for what seems incomprehensible—how, say, Art and a mess of old tires could possibly be related. (And I don't mean to imply that they are, although they might be.)

Well, this was an unusual show. The gallery put out a fine brochure, tall and thin, called "Environments, Situations,

Spaces," containing "statements" by each artist preceded by their handsome autographs. George Brecht is always clean as a clipped wing, airy, cheerful, and self-disappearing. He has a little white room just off the yard with a nice white chair in it, comfortable for a Cape Cod porch and adjoining Jim Dine's *Spring Cabinet*. Brecht's autograph in the brochure is an inch wide. His first two statements are: a. nothing-special; b. no theory.

Whereas Claes Oldenburg sears his page with a mud-luscious Whitmanesque catalogue of the materials of art, and for Oldenburg the list is inexhaustible because he is for an art that is everything, everything that is "that does something other than sit on its ass in a museum," and preferably everything that is *not* self-consciously refined, in other words that is raw, quick, smelly, holy, many small "sweet and stupid" acts of ungracious side-splitting, nose-blowing living that are supposed to be left for keeps in dirty abandoned corners. Oldenburg's *Store* has that unkempt look; the items hang in blobbish disregard for civilized order; the store articles are sculptured in relief with muslin strips dipped in plaster and placed over chicken wire, then painted with enamel to give the business a high dripping festive gloss.

These environments, situations, spaces are not going any place; they're not on the market for immortality; they're just not negotiable at all, except for tempting traffic with the eye and heart that is looking for more or less anything, or ready to stumble on something; and even that is saying too much, or too little, and no doubt Robert Whitman is right when he says that "this whole business has been complicated by people who say all smart things . . ."

ON THE HAPPENINGS—
NEW YORK SCENE

The term Happenings was coined in 1959 after an event given in New York at the Reuben Gallery by Allan Kaprow titled "18 Happenings in 6 Parts."

In 1952 at Black Mountain College in North Carolina, John Cage gave an experimental performance with the audience seated in the middle of it. Cage lectured from a podium, David Tudor played the piano, Charles Olson talked or laughed on cue from the audience, Robert Rauschenberg the painter played a wind-up victrola, Merce Cunningham danced, and other activities took place more or less simultaneously. One might take this as a starting point for the recent flow of events, or Happenings, in this country, in Europe, in Japan.

John Cage was the most likely person to pioneer the new movement. His own experimental music, based on letting "sounds be themselves rather than vehicles for man-made theories or expressions of human sentiments," led him to a music in which sounds, like events in nature, would occur without premeditation. At any moment you might hear a number of sounds issuing from known or unknown sources, occurring in spontaneous continuities and combinations. To create an art based on this way of looking at things is to give oneself up to the possibility of anything; and this means at least a partial relinquishment of the artist's conscious intentions. It certainly means giving up the idea of art as usually practiced in the Western world. And in the end it leads inevitably to *theatre:* a field of action where anything may happen. Cage's *Water Walk* consists of three minutes of sound, but the sounds are made by so many objects and with so many actions by the performer that it is impossible to speak of the piece as music in any conventional sense. Nor is it a matter of art picking up where life leaves off, for the piece includes sounds and actions from mundane activities; and its start and finish are as arbitrary as anything that happens in it. It, like life, simply goes on.

It is difficult to make quick sense of the complex origins of any eventuality, but as for the immediate forerunners of Happenings, one might mention three sources.

In *The Theatre and Its Double* (which the poet, Mary Caroline Richards, was translating in the early fifties, and from which she read a chapter each week to a group of interested friends), Antonin Artaud proclaimed the necessity of a theatre brought back to its *physical* essentials. Without pinpointing the exact forms these essentials should assume, Artaud was demanding a return to the primary function of a theatre: the exercise of magic through the combined force of all the physical properties that the stage in its decadence had relegated to the role of "support." He says:

> . . . *the theatre* [*must be*] *contained within the limits of everything that can happen on a stage, independently of the written text.*
>
> . . . *to link the theatre to the expressive possibilities of forms, to everything in the domain of gestures, noises, colors, movements, etc., is to restore it to its original direction.*
>
> . . . *the spectator is in the center and the spectacle surrounds him* . . . *in this spectacle the sonorization is constant: sounds, noises, cries are chosen first for their vibratory quality, then for what they represent.*

From the revolution in art posed by Cubism and collage came the voice of Kurt Schwitters. Writing in 1920, Schwitters, who was associated with the Dadaists but who called his own theory of art Merz, outlines a fantastic scenario for a stage event that would embrace all branches of art in one artistic unit. "Merz," he said, "stands for freedom from all fetters," and the Merz work of art par excellence would be the Merz drama in which all parts are inseparably bound up together. "It cannot be written, read, or listened to, it can only be produced in the theatre."

The Dada demonstrations, 1916–21, are the most obvious precedent for recent events. Georges Hugnet described a typical exhibition in Zurich:

On the stage of the cabaret tin cans and keys were jangled as music . . . Serner placed a bunch of flowers at the feet of a dressmaker's dummy. Arp's poems were recited by a voice hidden in an enormous hat shaped like a sugar loaf. Huelsenbeck roared his poems in a mighty crescendo, while Tzara beat time on a large packing case. Huelsenbeck and Tzara danced, yapping like bear cubs, or, in an exercise called "noir cacadou," they waddled about in a sack with their heads thrust in a pipe.

The Dada demonstrations were spontaneous and programmatic. The present Happenings, 1959–62, are more like serious extensions of paintings and construction. In 1956 Allan Kaprow converted an exhibition of collage into an environment, the *Penny Arcade*. Thereafter he experimented with environments, and with events as a natural result of the former. Then in 1957–58, along with several other artists (including a poet and a composer) he attended a class given by John Cage at the New School. Cage provided a new focus through the use of chance operations, stimulating the discovery of material and events through a liberation from personal habit.

But the painters, including Kaprow, who moved quickly to stage a series of events at the Judson and Reuben Galleries in early 1960, were more interested in a new dimension for their constructions in the form of personal expressive images. They were, in other words, not so interested in *letting* things happen as in *making* things happen. The convergence, then, of several personalities from different places at more or less the same time and with similar tendencies produced the new outbreak of events.

Before meeting any of the abovementioned, a young painter from Tennessee, Red Grooms, had done what he considered a "kind of play" in Provincetown and later the same year (1959) gave *The Burning Building* at the Delancey Street Museum. *The Burning Building* involved the action of a "pasty man," two firemen, a girl in white box, and another girl in top hat, moustache, and plastic covering. It was performed in front of and behind a curtain, which when pulled aside revealed a three-dimensional set of cardboard, canvas, sacks, cans, shoes,

wires, etc. forming the image of a fireman, a door; and a building through which Grooms (pasty man) dived at the end. It
concluded with a "grotesque" stomping dance by two real firemen, flashing lights, words yelled back and forth between
Grooms and the girl in top hat, cries of "Fire" shouted through
a slit, a chase, and a terrible racket.

By January, 1960, Grooms was active at the Reuben Gallery, showing *The Magic Train Ride* along with Kaprow's *Big
Laugh* and Robert Whitman's *Small Cannon*. And Claes Oldenburg and Jim Dine, two painters from the Midwest, organized
the Ray Gun Spex: three performances of six events by six artists at the Judson Gallery in February and March of 1960.

That same spring, out in California, LaMonte Young and
Dennis Johnson, two young composers, both students at
U.C.L.A., who had been giving simultaneous performances of
music and poetry, staged *Avalanche Number 1,* a three-hour affair which included, among other things: several poems recited
concurrently at different points in the audience; electronic
music; a thirteen-minute silence; and a *Poem for Tables, Chairs
and Benches,* being the moaning and scraping music made by
furniture being pushed across the floor.

The end of that year, 1960, Young came to New York
where he joined other composers and artists of similar interests.
Soon after he arranged a series of six concerts at Yoko Ono's
loft, becoming deeply committed to the kind of event that de-
volved on a single action or sound. His aim was to entice the
participant into an ever-increasing state of awareness of one
particular sound or action so that he became *one* with it—
which is what Young means when he says he likes "to get inside a sound."

He first did this in one composition when, for an hour he
sustained the sound of a gong scraping over cement. At this last
concert in Yoko Ono's loft he performed twenty-nine pieces,
each one titled *Draw a Straight Line and Follow It.* Young
thinks most artists are too busy trying to make their work interesting; to *make* something happen rather than to *let* it happen.

George Brecht is inclined to feel this way too. Brecht stud-
ied at the New School with Cage and became involved at the
Reuben Gallery with Kaprow, Whitman, and Lucas Samaras.
However, because of his interest in Zen and aspects of Dada

(Duchamp) as well as the music of Cage he continued, until recently, to use random operations and consequently did not make the kinds of Happenings the other painters were beginning to make. Before he came to do "less and less" he made several cabinets and "games" with "found" objects inviting manipulation and, by implication, removal or destruction. Thus he made participation in a work explicit, and again, the line between art and life dissolves. More recently he performed a *Comb Event* which consisted of engaging and releasing each prong of a comb with a fingernail. In the spring of 1961, he presented an Environment: a small white room with a white chair in it. Brecht likes to make something out of ordinary things (door bolts, coat hooks) usually considered "uninteresting, boring, unlovable."

Once the original excitement subsided, Dine, Kaprow, Oldenburg, and Whitman began to present their own respective Happenings at the New Reuben Gallery in the Winter season, 1960–61. The last evening at the old Reuben, in June, 1960, was the end of the first flush. You could hardly move for all the people who jammed in to have a good time. The spirit was excellent. And Robert Whitman's *E.G. Opera* was a serious crazy mess that satisfied some of the craving for blood hell nonsense and purgation that people were expecting.

At the new Reuben, Whitman gave *The American Moon* and *Mouth.* Both were elaborately executed Environments: the first in the shape of nine cubicles for the spectators opening on to a central "play area" where the action took place; silent films were projected in each cubicle; the second, an enormous papier-mâché mouth through which the spectators entered to sit inside. In *Mouth,* one event succeeded another in a quiet fantasy, ponderous and rhythmical, with a few scares. It might have been a forest scene. A large awkward shape of white cloth stretched on a frame of wire creaked side to side, as a pendulum, the heartbeat of the scene. A girl in heels came out running fast, staggering in a zigzag. She would start to fall, then catch herself and be off again. An arrow traveled slowly on a wire and pierced a cloth which made three people tumble out from behind it. A lovely "picnic car," a big paper and wood construction, drove patiently through the audience and disgorged two girls who sat down on the "ground" to eat a picnic lunch. A monster-like animal heaved slowly round from the back and nudged up to the girls. He left. One of the girls left too, got back in the car and drove it out. The other girl went to sleep near the pendulum. Four girls in costumes did a dance that had jumping and swaying in it. The girl in street clothes who had appeared first, as though escaping, climbed into the pendulum which turned into an elevator and rose, descended, rose again—and that was the end of the scene.

Claes Oldenburg's events are also rich in the possibility of new experience through association. He likes to present objects from everyday life, and transmute them by abstraction or by placing them in some unexpected context. Fake food served at a real table; real food in a false situation (a suitcase full of lemons); a girl in man's clothes; parts of the body appearing in fragments, therefore as objects (or fetishistic substitutions); a collection of objects, like those drawn from the pockets of an inert man (whose clothes are paint spattered so that he appears as an object himself); or those drawn and displayed from a suitcase: a yellowed book, fake rose, fake money, silverware, work glove, beat-up shoe, red sponges, mallet, tin cans, rubber hose, mousetrap, etc.

Oldenburg also often transforms his sphere of action into an environmental mess—a calculated rubble of paper, cardboard, stuffed burlap bags, dirty mattresses, tin cans, paint-spattered walls, and so on. He does this for several reasons. For one thing, he probably has a natural affinity for wrecks, the way most children do until they're "trained." For another, the use of found junk material is part of a contemporary tradition. Also, he lives in a proletarian neighborhood.

Which brings us back to the hard reality of "the thing in itself." No matter what happens in this kind of contemporary art, it is the physical, palpable substance of a thing that is its primary reality. When a word is spoken it is like the sound a person makes when he speaks. Its meaning, whatever it is for each person, is secondary, and it does not appear in a rational context. It has a quality, a vibration, a physical substance. When you see a woman drying and stacking dishes, or two girls making eggs at a hot plate, you see, feel, the body (its bulk in space, its special shape), the movement of the body in this particular action, the sounds issuing from this particular action, or, as in the case of the eggs, their smell. What does a woman drying and stacking dishes mean? It means a woman drying and stacking dishes. It looks and sounds a certain way. It looks and sounds different ways to different people. A woman in her own kitchen will look a certain way too, if you choose to look. So now we are speaking of theatre (art) in general, or life in general. Where one begins and the other ends is one of the interesting questions posed by Happenings. John Cage has said that "theatre takes place all the time wherever one is and art simply facilitates persuading us this is the case."

Encore, September / October, 1962

INSIDE *ORIGINALE*

There was Allan Kaprow at one of those Avant-Garde Festival performances at Judson Hall coproduced by Charles Moorman and Norman Seaman and he was carrying a big sheaf of script or score which he said was the score for Stockhausen's *Originale,* so somehow in a conversation during one number it was agreed that I might be an actor (one of five) since one of the actors was reluctant or out of town or indisposed. Next day Allan called me and said the actor was well or anxious or back in town and that therefore I might like to be a conductor. Next call I became an Actor again. But after Allan talked to Mary Baumeister, closely associated with the composer, he proposed as they agreed that I should be a free agent which later I discovered was what might have been called a "guest" since a personage called a "guest" was included in the score as an optional possibility by invitation of the director. As it developed there were several guests during the week of performances. Friday night the chimpanzee was ill and Mrs. X's daughter, who brought her two German Shepherds to the first performance, was out on Fifty-Seventh Street requesting the pleasure of an appearance of an elderly lady with her shaggy white dog to replace the chimp. The fourth night three unexpected guests made a rush on Nam June Paik, handcuffing him to a metal bar of the scaffolding. The three intruders were disposed of on the fire escape and locked out there. One of them was later found to be stuck head down in an apparatus on the roof. As a free agent I went to the last rehearsal just before the first performance to size up the situation. I looked at the score and asked a few questions about who was doing what when, etc. Stockhausen's score is that curious hybrid of control and indeterminacy common to works by many artists in the contemporary tradition of providing the possibility of unforeseen situations within a framework of instructions and temporal limitations. The framework for *Originale* consisted of strict time units for each action or performer. Thus an actor, according to specifications in the score, might have to appear at thirty minutes and depart at thirty-nine minutes (within the total time of ninety minutes). A further specification for an actor was that he choose selections from classical or modern drama to read or memorize for the performance. That left a wide margin of determination by the performer. Moreover, he could deliver his passages in whatever manner he desired. And I judged from the outfits, which changed night to night, that costume was similarly a matter of personal taste. Also, each actor had a bit of free time to do anything at all.

Along with the time structure, the sound score of the piece seemed absolutely determined. Stockhausen is best known in this country and abroad as an outstanding exponent of the new electronic music, produced on tape by a sinus generator. This technique was developed in the Studio for Electronic Music of the West German Radio under the direction of Herbert Eimert; and Stockhausen was one of five composers represented in the first performance of such compositions (1954). The electronic score for *Originale,* notwithstanding the included score for live piano and percussion ensemble, was the single dominant and pervasive element of the work. Considering the hodgepodge of properties, animals, and assorted activities in the piece, the time structure was not a unifying factor but a method of insuring a change of pace throughout a lengthy composition.

My own idea when I went to the rehearsal was to assess

the pace with a view to doing something when it seemed dynamically appropriate. As for what I would do exactly, I tried to be empty-headed about it in the spirit of improvisation, but I pondered the shape and footing of the scaffolding as one accessible instrument because I like to climb and hang on things. My only other thought was to interfere or make some relationship with the "painter" (time was allotted to a painter, who could do what he pleased), who made a big scene in a white outer-space gear standing on a ladder on the stage dropping raw eggs on the floor, shaking red pigment over the eggs, lying on a cot, laying a steamy stink bomb in a large can. I notified the painter of my intentions and he said to just be careful because he couldn't see very well through his cellophane visor; but if I had made some realistic account of the painter as the same fellow who walked around in regular clothes during the rehearsal flipping about the German Shepherds not being caged or leashed, I might have taken a quiet powder during his theatrical debut. The outcome, of course, after I had a good time crawling behind him into the recess under the stage, sitting on the floor pouring a little salt over his red pigment, adjusting a pair of white heels that happened to be there, and flailing the steam from the can with my hat, was that painter and wife, the following evening before the second performance, bore down on me with hot denouncements in the name of serious intentions and such jazz, which prompted Allan Kaprow to bear down on them in the name of grace and so on, while Allen Ginsberg, who had also been a subject of my happy interference the night before, sitting begoggled in gentle Buddhist indifference fingering some Eastern stringed instrument, remarked inaudibly that I could do whatever I liked with him, Jill. Well, what I decided about all this was that the psychology involved in indeterminacy is a complicated business. I recall somebody once asking John Cage, in a panel after a performance of new music, if he expected people to laugh at his piece, and Cage replied that he preferred laughter to tears. According to Mary Baumeister there was a fair amount of interplay or interference at the first performance of *Originale* in Cologne in 1961. Actually, I think more often than not in these compositions the performers are isolated in their respective activities. Indeterminacy in music has meant primarily the interpenetration of sound resulting from simultaneous juxtapositions of material from independent sources. In a typical indeterminate score by John Cage, each performer constructs his own program of action from the graphic notation accompanied by instructions. Such was his *Theatre Piece* (1960), an obvious precedent for *Originale*. As a piece of "theatrical music" the performers are expected "to be who they are (musician, dancer, singer, etc.) but the performer's decision as to what he is to do will often be determined by whether he makes a sound." Until recently, Cage's indeterminacy consisted of an unforeseen situation made possible by the simultaneous presentation of actions and sounds produced by performers who brought their own scheme to the performance after determining that scheme by submitting their choices to certain chance operations. Lately Cage has relaxed these controls to push indeterminacy into the realm of improvisation (on-the-spot decisions) more familiar to dancers and jazz musicians. In 1962 I performed as the "dancer" with Cage and Tudor in the former's *Music Walk*. I chose about forty-five actions mostly involving a load of household equipment, determining the sequence and time span for each action by the chance procedure indicated in the score. Armed with my forty-five cards I went to the rehearsal, but when I saw the lovely graphic designs on the cards of my colleagues and my own fell to the floor, dropped in the water, or some damn thing, I gave up on them and decided to move around from one coke bottle or frying pan to another during the performance. At that time such a course was not kosher in Cage's lexicon of behavior for the performer, who would do best to deliver himself from his own conventions (habitual preferences) by yielding to the external device of a chance procedure. However, it should be clear that habits are not so easily divested. One can force the issue by externally imposed strictures on time and sequence, but one is still left with that constant factor of the particular shape and volume of each body and the motion peculiar to that body. Cage looks like Cage to me no matter what he did beforehand to eliminate certain natural preferences in time and sequence. Moreover, the choice of equipment, determined by personal history, partially constitutes a "style," by which the composer is eventually identified. To be absurdly elementary about it, consider the fact that Cage goes on habitually making music. Life, in any case, is always a new mixture of habit and improvisation, and Cage is an inventor in a medium that he has made his habit. The "set" performances for a work like *Theatre Piece* make a set composition in a way as set as any traditional work. Cage's unique departure, of course, aside from the importance of extending music into a theatre of action, was to make the performer a composer in what amounts to a collective composition. Stockhausen's *Originale* is the same kind of work except that there is more freedom in certain respects and less in others. As mentioned above, the performer had no choice in the matter of time, a choice essential to Cage's position since Cage doesn't mind (philosophically) if the audience is bored, although he could conceivably depend on the law of averages to provide the pace that he refuses to set himself. In comparing *Theatre Piece* and *Originale,* I am struck by one overwhelming difference in the two works. Cage's score is absolutely consistent in that its simple instructions apply to all performers alike and there is no extraneous material obtruded by the composer. Stockhausen's electronic score and other determined factors are hardly extraneous in the sense that they are commanding elements in the work; yet the obvious desire for "free" action is countered everywhere by controls and restraints which make even much of what is free look like a setup, which indeed it is, as in the case of Nam June Paik, whose performance was a solo specialty act and whose plunge into a tub of water, following a breathless silence during which the Korean composer stood in a spotlight saturating his face, neck, and collar with shaving cream and rice, was accompanied by a Wagnerian burst of electronic thunder. I agree with Earle Brown, who described Paik as a "kind of Oriental Kammerkrieg" (in a letter called "Planned Panichood"). Paik's specialty is much more than an act. But I'm talking about context and disposition in a collective work. I think Stockhausen's idea was to make a great theatrical "combine" of sound, movement, lights, colors, properties, and players, and he figured it out like a playscript with parts for friends and acquaintances, with sections providing a simultaneous overlap of activities, other sections providing a focus for a single activity, with the constant presence of plant and animal decor, electronic equipment, and technicians. Some people said it was a terrible mess. They also said, as the *Times* critic did, that there was much to admire. I know that it was an exciting occasion in Germany in 1961 as the first German Happening. To some sophisticated New Yorkers, who have been through what Richard Bellamy refers to high-mindedly as the "classical" period of the Happenings, *Originale* looked like a soup of ingredients from any number of familiar events. Sherman Drexler, for one, thinks that nobody should want to see another Happening and that a sign at the exit should have read "This Way to the Egress," alluding to such a sign at the end of a Barnum and Bailey show of fake freaks. But *Originale* is not in the tradition of Happenings as we know them by the painters (Dine, Oldenburg, Kaprow, Whitman, etc.). It is possible to make clean separations between one kind of event and another in a movement of international proportions deriving from one or two common sources (e.g., Cage); yet Stockhausen's work belongs essentially to the new tradition of "theatrical music" realized on a more modest scale by certain American composers following Cage's suggestion. If *Originale* was a soup it was because Stockhausen mixed up three sizable components in his calculations. First, he wanted a Merz combine in which the Milky Way would have figured had it been feasible. Second, he is a composer, and his background as a composer is in a European deterministic tradition. The new electronic music offers a range of sound possibilities before unknown, but the composers in this medium have subjected their experiments to serial permutations traced back to the twelve-tone and serial techniques of Schönberg and Webern. Third, Stockhausen has been exposed to the attitudes and methods of Cagean indeterminacy and he wanted, as he has demonstrated in earlier compositions, some measure of free action by the performers. Thus the result was a weird triple exposure of chunks of set pieces (often having the mythopoeic quality of events in painterly Happenings), a muddle of indeterminate confusion, and a pressure from clock and director to keep within the bounds of a meticulous score. I don't know why the Fluxus people were picketing the concert (somebody told me Fluxus committed suicide recently), but it might have been interesting if the director had invited the picket line to participate as "guests." From one guest to another (real or optional): I felt superfluous enough to guarantee that any intrusion could be welcome and horrible at the same time. Beyond that, as

Duchamp once remarked and I have quoted before, perhaps the proceedings were "insufficiently lighthearted."

October 1, 1964

BILLY KLÜVER

Billy Klüver is a tall blond Swede who has lived in the U.S. since 1954. After five years at the Royal Institute of Technology in Stockholm, he went to the University of California at Berkeley and obtained a Ph.D. in Electrical Engineering. Since 1959 he's been a member of the technical staff of Bell Telephone Laboratories in Murray Hill, New Jersey. Klüver is one of three hundred Ph.D.'s at the Labs, each of whom occupies a room for independent research. First time I heard about Klüver it was in connection with Jean Tingueley's self-destroying machine called *Homage to New York,* which happened in the sculpture garden of the Museum of Modern Art on March 17, 1960. I heard that Klüver was a smart scientist and a friend of artists and that he was helping Tingueley assemble the materials for his machine. Klüver and Tingueley have been friends since 1952 or 1953. At that time Tingueley was making what he called "anti-tv sets" with motorized devices, "putting Malevich in motion." The two were friends of Pontus Hulten, who became director of the Moderna Museet in Stockholm in 1955. Later, in 1961, Klüver was to be responsible for the American contribution (twenty artists) to an exhibition of "Art in Motion" at the Moderna Museet. The following year he assisted in organizing a show of "Four Americans" there (Johns, Rauschenberg, Leslie, and Stankiewicz). In America, in 1961, he appeared in Claes Oldenburg's "Store Days I," a Happening in a series of ten that Oldenburg gave at his store on Second Street. In 1962 Klüver organized a Pop Art show in Philadelphia; in 1963 the Pop Art Festival in Washington, D.C.

Beginning 1961, Klüver and Robert Rauschenberg discussed a project for a "sound sculpture" that was not to be completed until spring 1965 in Rauschenberg's latest exhibition, called *Oracle,* an orchestral ensemble of five sculptures. Klüver says there was a difficult technical problem involved because Rauschenberg din't want any cords running from the objects to the control board. He wanted a maximum flexibility in the arrangement of the sculptures, that they might be moved in any relation to each other. Final scheme: the controls plus the five radios were placed in one sculpture and the four other sculptures contained a receiver and amplifier apiece, each one corresponding to a radio in the console sculpture. The manipulation of the volume and tuning speed of the five radios was up to the spectator, for whom the controls were available if he cared to see them and use them.

At Bell Labs Klüver's "room" is a rather small rectangular area, its floor space almost completely filled up by a big table containing instruments related to problems that presently concern him. The table "floats" on airplane tires in order not to be disturbed by the vibrations of the building. One thing he has been working on the past year or so is the measurement of the spontaneous emission of light in laser amplifiers. Klüver's assistant came in to pick up a box containing one of the vital instruments used by John Cage in his last performance of *Variations V* at Philharmonic Hall July 23. The assistant was taking the box down the corridor to another room to make some adjustments on the instrument before Cage arrived to take the box away on another round of performances. For *Variations V* Cage wanted sound to be generated by the motion of dancers who would be going on their own steam, according to choreography by Merce Cunningham. Cage discussed the project with his colleague, David Tudor. Tudor knew of a man called Robert Moog, who has a business in Trumansburg, New York, making electronic musical instruments. Last May Tudor and Cage went to see Moog, who agreed to provide twelve antennae (poles) with a triggering device based on the Theremin principle. In effect, the antennae would pick up sounds along their length by the relative proximity of a body. Cage wanted to know if the antennae would be sufficient to meet his purpose. Tudor thought there should be more mechanisms, or something at least that would be untraceable. If the visible antennae led the audience to link the sound with its source, another type of mechanism less detectable should also be provided. Tudor wanted a sonar device, but that was too expensive. Then he thought there might be somebody at Bell Labs who could tell them about photoelectric cells. In June they contacted Klüver and went to Murray Hill, first actually to talk to a man who made four designs that they decided were not practical. Klüver was present at the meeting and he offered to make photocells to test. Considered and discounted as an additional possibility was a device that might pick up currents in the skin and muscles that could be translated into sound. This was related to something Klüver worked out for Yvonne Rainer in 1963, a wireless microphone at the throat which amplified the sound of the dancer's breathing.

Anyway, Klüver made ten photocells (they vaguely resemble pistols) that would be scattered round the stage and would activate switches when the shadows of the dancers crossed their nozzles. The switches would in turn activate ten tape recorders and 10 shortwave radios. The system required a control console. Klüver found the man who could design a transistor circuit. C. H. Coker of Bell Labs designed the circuit and W. N. Wittnebert, the assistant mentioned above, made it. Cage and Tudor had previously decided to use the mixer designed by Max Matthews, director of Behavioral Research Laboratories at Bell, for the performance a year ago of Cage's *Atlas Eclipticalis* at the Philharmonic. The mixer is the central control board with sixty inputs by which Cage could control the volume and put the sound on one of six speakers around the hall. Whenever a dancer, by his shadow, triggered a radio or a tape recorder so that it became connected to the mixer (after passing through the convergent circuit), a connection that would last fifteen seconds, Cage "received" the sound and manipulated volume and speaker placement. Ultimately, he had great power, for although he couldn't control what was coming in, he could turn the whole thing off if he felt like it.

The mixer, by the way, was presaged in an aborted project that also involved Max Matthews. When Richard Lippold was commissioned to make a sculpture for the new Pan Am Building he heard that the building contractors were going to install

Muzak in the room where his sculpture would be. Lippold suggested that Cage supply this musical ornamentation instead. Cage contacted Matthews, who designed a circuit that would have controlled two hundred loudspeakers independently, and fragmented what was coming from them. The system as planned was similar to the one Klüver masterminded for *Variations V*. The sound sources were to be the material provided by Muzak and the people walking through the building. The people would activate photoelectric cells to stimulate the Muzak material to be distorted by Matthew's control system and sent out over the speakers. The automatic permutation of sound would never have repeated a pattern in a period of ninety-nine years. The management of Pan Am vetoed the project.

A visual conception for *Variations V* that might also have involved Bell Labs was a complement to the sound system. Television cameras were to pick up the dancers and send the images, distorted by Nam June Paik, onto huge television screens situated in the audience. This scheme, like the sonar device, was too expensive to go beyond the talking stage. Instead, Stan VanDerBeek provided films that combined predistorted TV images by Paik and shots of Cunningham and his company. The original idea would obviously have been more in keeping with the auditory system. As it was, VanDerBeek's film, projected onto an enormous screen conventionally located, was such a visual tour de force that it tended to dominate all effects. Ideally, no doubt, the dancers themselves should be disported in the round, either in the center of a peripheral audience or vice versa or both, and suspended on platforms as well. While the imagination is at it, maybe another world's fair or the like will produce an enterprising architect to construct something really fantastic in the way of a building to suit Cage's diabolical designs. The closest the fair has come to it was a Screamatorium suggested, probably not even considered, for the first New York fair, by a couple of nutheads with sound judgment.

Future possibilities of collaboration between scientists, artists, architects, etc., await only sanctions from private and official sources to support ambitious ideas. On a certain scale, more has been done than is generally known. Before leaving Bell Labs I saw the IBM Computer room. Klüver told me a little about the "computer music program" and the fact that James Tenney, New York composer, spent two years at Bell Labs making computer music. Coincidentally, a week later, I see the 1965 issue of *Impulse,* an annual of dance published in California, with two articles about a computer dance program at the University of Pittsburgh.

Klüver's idea about science in relation to art is that science and art have nothing to do with each other. As a collaborator he is interested only in providing the scientific unit that will make the artist's idea practically feasible. He is not interested in making a technical "process," an invention, like a new kind of musical instrument or any systematic machine, that could be used by artists for composition or execution of work. At the moment, he says, he continues to enjoy contributing a functional unit for one specific purpose. His most recent collaboration is with Andy Warhol, for an exhibition this fall at the Castelli Gallery. In 1963–64 he designed a circuit for Jasper Johns that would drive two neon signs on batteries. Probably the first portable neon sign. But Klüver is much more than designer and consultant in his involvement with artists. As friend and supporter and avid enthusiast of contemporary forms, as well as an engineer generous with his time and knowledge, he's a unique man behind and in front of the scenes. Klüver exemplifies the consciousness he described himself in a short article for the Hasty Papers in 1960, "Fragment on Man and the System." He said he thought man had the responsibility to shape the general systems in such a way that the general systems corresponded as closely as possible to the requirements of the individual realities. Klüver bridges both worlds for a mutual compact that is I guess, and I conventionally believe it, one big way out or ahead of the thing the newspapers are always scaring us about. He also said that "the system builder and the technology have the capacity of providing the individual with any type of system, involving any degree of uncertainty or change: a system could even be designed to disintegrate itself." I don't know whether he wrote that before or after the Tingueley affair at the Modern.

August 12, 1965

THE ROYAL BALLET

The Two Pigeons is a new ballet, an allegory in two acts and three scenes based on the fable by La Fontaine, choreographed by Frederick Ashton, and with music by Andre Messager. The Young Man (Alexander Grant) and his Young Girl (Lynn Seymour) are working out their problems in a "studio in Paris" assisted by a group of eight girl friends who flutter down the stairs in the studio after it becomes apparent that the young man is dissatisfied with the young girl's posing (he's a painter) and her subsequent attempts to humor him with kisses and tickles. He sulks around the studio while the girls flutter up the atmosphere and until Miss Seymour introduces the "pigeon" movements of the ballet—elbow-flapping, knee-prancing, head-pecking—at which time Mr. Grant joins her in a happy *pas de deux* establishing their position as pigeon-people lovers, symbolically reinforced by two real white pigeons who have been released from the flies. The eight girl friends then stop fluttering and coagulate into a climax of the pigeon idea. When they finish, the plot is advanced again as the young man recalls his original mood and droops with bad humor over the chair. Thereupon a bunch of handsome gypsies pour into the studio, and the young man arises from his torpor to become infatuated with a prototype of lust in the form of Georgina Parkinson, who dances with subtle extravagance (fiery black wig and all) in her role as the Gypsy Girl. Naturally Miss Seymour gets quite upset. She hangs on the young man; jostles between him and his weakness; pushes all the gypsies around; does an attractive shoo-fly solo; and engages her new competitor in a show-off duet of fast, nervous action in which the pigeon idea somehow stays intact, and the feet are important messengers of anger (the Royal feet are exquisitely trained).

The first act concludes as the young man follows the departed gypsies, mounting the stairs with a mixture of reckless abandon and traces of regret for his better half, who languishes below in romantic pigeon despair. The second act shows the Prodigal Son having a great time in the "gypsy encampment near Paris." With the girl friends and the early plot developments out of the way, the ballet becomes quite lively. The gypsy men make fancy, colorful patterns in a virile folk-stomping style, looking more masculine as a group than the boys over here. Mr. Grant and the gypsy girl display themselves with sporting fertility and wind up the orgy with proper lust as he pin-wheels her legs in a lift and circles around her with a serpentine torso to a bit of fanfare music that often emerges appropriately from this kind of confectionary score.

Well, so the prodigal pays for his merriment in hell. The gypsy boy takes him on, the rest join the assault (a rope is dramatically employed), and the young man is on his way back home, in front of a stockade scrim, bearing one of the white pigeons (again released from the flies), disheveled but chastened, back to Miss Seymour—who is happier to see the deserter than you might think, considering all she must have suffered. But as the fable goes ". . . Three days at most will give my whim its run / And then I shall be back to tell / All my adventures one by one / 'Twil cheer you up, and be the greatest fun." Actually, the choreography and performance of the reunion is rather touching, so I don't believe Mr. Ashton intended anyone to take this escapade lightly. In fact, reading between the lines (of both La Fontaine and Ashton), I see simply another enactment of the Christian cycle: apple, fall, atonement, redemption, purity— and where the devil are we after several thousand years? Would all these people get up and leave if the cycle were reversed? Or do they just go to see the Royal Ballet? I guess that's it. The story doesn't matter. It's just a game, a device to perpetuate the action. Nobody cares about those old stories anymore. Or do they? Maybe the British do. They can make pretty spectacles out of them, anyway. Next time I hope the pigeons fly out over the orchestra and up into the boxes and peanut galleries. And God Save the Queen.

May 2, 1963

MORRIS—CHILDS

On the third night of the concerts given by Yvonne Rainer and Robert Morris (March 23–25) at Judson, Morris presented *Waterman Switch*—a trio premiered at the Festival of the Arts in Buffalo in March and celebrated on the popular newsfronts as a "sensational attraction" for its nudity, which I agree can be quite sensational, especially in a place like Buffalo (the shock of the people there resulted in a twitter that crescendoed to a roar), but which can also be the occasion for an extraordinary work, and Morris rose beautifully to an idea that he had for an erotic dance.

The romantic beauty of *Waterman Switch* is absurdly simple. Have two nudes locked in an embrace walk very slowly the twenty-foot length of wooden tracks running from center stage into the wings, and have the walk accompanied by an aria from Verdi's *Simone Boccanegra* sung by the soprano Victoria de los Angeles, and you have a sound-image combo that knocks you out (as David Hockney said in an exchange with Larry Rivers about how he would rather have his painting thought beautiful than interesting because "interesting sounds on its way there, whereas beautiful can knock you out"). Morris's sculpture and choreography are often just interesting (e.g., the idea of *Check*) and he is one of the most interesting artists around, but for me at his best he is both interesting and beautiful, and with the new trio he outdid himself in the department of beauty.

The image described above was the obvious central attraction of the seventeen-minute work, but its placement, and the other elements of the dance, were crucial factors in the overwhelming total effect. The dance was in fact as much about water and string and rolling stones as it was about walking nudes. Typically Morris was the tape recording of rolling stones that ran uninterrupted from beginning to end, drowned out only by the soprano singing Verdi's aria. Typical also the conscious naivete of emphasizing the fact of duplication. First you hear the stones, then you see them as some foam rubber gray-painted facsimiles tumble onto the stage from the wings.

Lucinda Childs.

Robert Morris's *Waterman Switch*.
Ralph Crane, LIFE Magazine © Time Inc.

The stage is set, with strewn fake stones and the four ply-wood sections of track (visible to begin with in a downstage corner), which are then moved into position, one by one, for the "walk," by the third party of the dance, a girl dressed as a boy (suit, tie, hat), who then walks with the nudes, just upstage of them, holding a ball of twine stretched in a taut line over her shoulder into the wing from which you can imagine the distance, and unwinding into the wing toward which the three of them walk to emphasize a horizontal journey that takes four minutes and suggests an eternity. The girl-boy image (Lucinda Childs) is entirely functional for setup and support, but she is also a brilliant device as a neutral foil (familiar in various guises in Morris's sculpture) to the naked Morris and Rainer. Yet the two images seem scrupulously balanced. A girl obviously a girl dressed just as obviously as a boy can be an image no less striking than that public exposure which is immediately understood as vivid by any culture that undresses only in private.

In the third sequence of the dance, following the "stones" and the "walk," Childs holds one end of a long pole and Morris holds the other end (a red flag covering his parts) and runs round in circles (Childs the axis) while we hear a tape by Morris describing certain aspects of the dance that he suggests might appear out of sequence. Eventually, he says, he will have slides made of the dance and by means of the slides an aspect of the walking on the tracks sequence will appear here, in the circle-running sequence, and an aspect of the stones rolling on section will appear when the two nudes again walk on the tracks. He intends no such thing, but the suggestion is possibly a facetious commentary on the desirability of any "aesthetic" order and clarity, not to mention his own. And by way of countering the audience's anticipation of the unknown (or just to make another statement of fact) he says that the nudes will again walk on the tracks, which they do, and that the next section (after this circle-running) will consist of three people, two nude, one dressed, at the back of the stage, backs to audience, who will balance on stones, a long rope running between them that they will hold at chest height, which they do, and that the two nudes at either end near the wings will slowly move toward the one in the center by utilizing the roundness of their stones, which they don't, although they might if they were balancing in the water that Morris talks about as they stand there, the long rope between them. He reads, on tape, a short excerpt from the Notebooks of da Vinci, who made 730 conclusions about water. Morris's choice concerns mainly the effect of water on objects.

With the blackout on this scene a fine detail of the dance occurs in another duplication of fact. Ten slides taken from one of Muybridge's famous photo series of sequential action are projected in fast order on the back wall. The action involves a nude man, front view, lifting a rock and throwing it; another nude man, back view, lifting a rock and putting it down. Then, still pressing the issue, Morris moves quickly, holding a rock aloft, across the white rectangles of two "blanks"—illustrating the slides which illustrate Morris. Out of this blackout, as the lights come up, Childs again moves the tracks, one by one, so that they extend from center stage into the other wing, and finally Morris and Rainer again make the four-minute journey, with two differences in detail. Halfway across, Morris pours mercury from a small bottle over Rainer's shoulder to splat on the floor. And this time Childs with the ball of twine walks slowly from wing to wing further upstage of the nudes, such that the illusion of great time and distance is deepened and magnified.

With a dance like *Waterman Switch* the action-object idiom of the new movement assumes greater force and dimension. Another important dance made this year, in the same mode, was Lucinda Childs's *Geranium,* first presented in January at Alfred Leslie's studio as a twenty-five-minute solo and later revised as a fourteen-minute solo (performed in Boston and Richmond). *Geranium* is ostensibly about a football game. It is actually no more about a football game than, say, D'Arcangelo's highway paintings are about highways. I don't know if D'Arcangelo is crazy about highways, but asked if she likes football very much, Childs says not particularly. By now it should be old hat to observe that pop imagery is only as interesting as its "historical" moment (e.g., Johns's beer cans) or its possessor makes it, according to the cravings for aesthetic satisfaction that are first and final and always have been, be it Christ and cross, rocks and trees, or signs and stripes. So the football game of *Geranium* is a gambit for a series of incisive actions put together with that intuition of choice, time, placement, which leaves you saying "right" if you have to say anything at all.

The action is intricately coordinated with a tape recording combining a broadcast of a football game between the Baltimore Colts and the Cleveland Browns with the choreographer's voice (once taking over as broadcaster, another time listing the names of the players) and two snatches of rock 'n' roll songs. Right away the action alludes to the game as Childs sits still on a chair in shades and winter coat. More pointed is a reference to spectator in a slight brittle gesture of pulling sun glasses just below eyes and readjusting them. Removing coat, an extended slow section follows with a pole and a piece of tin foil. Pole and foil are like the instruments of measurement (the yardage of the game?), foil pulled very slowly down a certain length of vertically held pole; then the pole stretched horizontally across shoulders, the ends in either outstretched hand, and one end leaving a hand to arc overhead and finish diagonally upright at a close angle to body then turned in profile.

The sustained intensity of these two passages is beautifully broken as the tin foil becomes a floor object (the object of the game?) pinned by the pole, as by a broom handle, to be pushed, scraped, all around, in long random strokes, but only after an initial push accompanied on tape by the eruption of a rock 'n' roll bit and the subtle, if outright, suggestion of a "dance" as the choreographer steps, thrusts, forward about four times in time with the beat. Pole and foil are abandoned after the foil shifts from floor to flat (a rectangular board about six feet high) to move in another diagonal design, pushed upward by the pole in staccato abrasions against the flat.

The last three images are most strikingly related to the "game," yet no less effective in their greater dramatic impact. An old hammock on a long rope is employed as a lever as Childs leans way out from hammock and rope to describe a wide sweeping arc in what might be called a slow-motion run, to finish against the flat, lie down and pick up a hammer. Another sharp break occurs as she simultaneously cracks hammer on floor over the head and thrusts both legs up against the flat to hold in that position like a photo "still" of a player upended in combat.

The final image is a seriocomic distillation of the game in its physical essence of contact between foot and earth. The choreographer makes several footprints in dirt (or coffee grinds) by stepping in a small pile of it and using a brush to sweep off the excess to create the outline of foot and to push the dirt ahead for the next imprint. The dance closes with a blackout on the final "step" and the radio announcer blurting above the dinning crowd that "the clock has run out and the ball game is over."

Inserted between the hammock section and the footprint section is a curious break in which Childs puts on her coat and talks to the audience, explaining that she didn't have the equipment for this section, but she was going to do it anyway because she doesn't like to cut things out unless they're really impossible to do, and so on, which adds up to an episode of the dance consisting of an explanation, not unrelated to Morris's tape suggesting that certain sections of his piece might appear out of sequence, except that his talk is superposed on an actual sequence, and Childs's exposition becomes a separate entity. Both insertions, in their claims and cancelations, invoke "process" (something outside the closed and completed work) as a component within the work.

In both dances the common action by now very familiar in work by Judson choreographers has been rigorously controlled by an episodic structure of images tightly bound up by subject and by that economy of gesture where nothing is superfluous in each specific problem posed by handling an object. The problem is to do it and be straight about it, and Morris is a relaxed imperturbable performer and Childs projects a hard-edge concentrated impassivity, and the result of both performances is that action, object, and dancer merge in a single affective unit.

May 20, 1965

FALL COLORS

Possibly some people, like leaves, turn pretty colors when they begin to look old. Unlike leaves, the changing colors of people depend on states of mind. A mind in a terrible state produces odd changes. Advancing years can be a terrible state of mind. I know an elderly man, however, who isn't even changing colors. He looks new all the time. I saw an elderly lady on the stage of the Lunt-Fontanne Theatre who isn't changing colors either, but not for the same reason. She seems to be at the end of all seasons.

A former member of Martha Graham's company told me that he entered her company seventeen years ago. At that time she was not very young and she was "really something," and they were telling him how he should have seen her ten years before that, when she wasn't so very young either. Thinking thus back and ahead can make you a little dizzy.

People say an artist should know when to stop. Not many people care to see a vital image turn into a shadowy version of itself. But the artist has his own reasons for stopping or going on. Pride is a good reason. It may not be enough to make a performance, but there is a kind of tragic poetry in the faltering effort. No doubt Miss Graham rises to the occasion of her own effort. To rise from the floor at the end of many seasons is an event in itself. To fall to the floor is more dangerous, and when the fall is unintentional it throws the entire effort into proper perspective. It is no longer a dance one sees but the drama of an artist attempting that which was once possible and becoming a hero of the impossible, if you care to look at it that way. I don't care to look at it any way, but the present has its own authenticity, and the angle of vision multiplies when the present is loaded with the weight of a rich past and the human consideration of a difficult state of mind. Miss Graham could still command the situation if she did nothing more than sit or stand or walk around and look tragic. She does these things, but the power of it is canceled by the embarrassment of muscles being pushed where they no longer wish to go. So that's the way it is.

And as it is I find it more interesting than her company, whose overexpanded acrobatic exertion is further from the truth of the original style than the dry-boned delivery of the creator herself.

In New Jersey last month the leaves were beginning to turn pretty colors, and Steve Paxton brought a group of dancers into the woods surrounding Billy Klüver's house in Berkeley Heights for an "Afternoon (A Forest Concert)." The spectators were led by a guide (her cap said "follow me") from one leafy grove to another where the troupe of five (Paxton, Yvonne Rainer, Barbara Lloyd, Lucinda Childs, Tony Holder) danced and did some natural things like disappearing. I wasn't keen about the dancing because the ground made balancing difficult and the forest was more exciting than human technique. But I liked the unexpected entrances, the nonchalant disappearances, and not knowing or caring too much where to look when something was going on in a specified vicinity and one or two other things were going on in more distant places. The scene I thought best suited to the environment was a sweet transaction between mother, son, sky, and trees when we were led to a clearing where Barbara Lloyd sat with her baby, Benjamin, who played with a leaf, hugged his mother, glanced imperturbably at the spectators, and took a big view of the sky. A little later he had the presence of mind to crawl under a space made by the dancers, who were placing their limbs over and under each other on a wooden plank.

A few weeks later I was driving up the Merritt Parkway, where the colors hung over the road in such breathtaking profusion and variety that the human scheme receded in my mind to a point of mild, if momentary, absurdity. But I was on my way to a human madness in Hartford. Sam Wagstaff is the curator of paintings at the Hartford Atheneum museum, which sponsors an annual ball for Hartford's Class A citizens. For two years Mr. Wagstaff has been introducing these conservative citizens to the most advanced painting and sculpture of the moment, and he had decided that the annual ball this year would have to be more than champagne and flowers. So he invited Dan Basin, young artist from Baltimore now living in New York, to decorate the spacious marble interior of the museum. Basin turned the place into a glittering palace of Pop Art iniquity: blinking lights, road signs, enormous bright poster collages, vertical rows of beer cans, milk cartons, and egg crates hanging in the doorways, and so on. In the main ballroom, which is as white as the Guggenheim, Basin erected several forty-foot shafts of plywood bandaged in open design with white cloth and set up in dramatic diagonals from a central declivity containing the museum's classical white statue and crowded with yellow "caution" street horses.

It was also Basin's idea to have a dancer appear at random during the ball and attract the attention of the happy citizens. Sally Gross went up from New York to perform this incredible task. Nobody had quite visualized the setting for such a performance so that by eleven P.M., when both ballrooms were consumed by the blare from two bands and the bodies of five hundred or more guests, it looked as though it would take more than a dancer to make a dent. Miss Gross's first appearance, in fact, running through the crowd in blue chiffon, went virtually unnoticed. But the second appearance, in white tights and leotard, walking on the rim of the declivity and mounting a yellow street horse, became a center of attraction. This made Basin unhappy, however, for just as Miss Gross mounted the street horse and picked up two red flags, the lights played down on it and the band splashed out "Anchors Aweigh."

The seven remaining appearances were without benefit of spontaneous assistance, and the primary obstacle thereafter to the dancer's professional attitude of creating new situations in movement, with a few props and leotard changes, became the leering manner of champagne-logged escorts who thought that the lady in tights was an imported siren designed to be an entertainment committee of pure body. But Miss Gross turned the impossible into a number of spatial situations, moving into an available space or creating one if it was not available, and developing a simple scheme of movement at each appearance. The social scene in Hartford will never be the same.

October 31, 1963

FLUXUS FUXUS

Fluxus flapdoodle. Fluxus concert, 1964. Donald Duck meets the Flying Tigers. Why should anyone notice the shape of a watch at the moment of looking at the time? Should we formulate the law of the fall of a body toward a center, or the law of the ascension of a vacuum toward a periphery? The exposition became a double Bloody Mary. Some Fluxus experts went to the Carnegie Tavern also. Fluxus moved into the street and on to my typewriter. Polyethelene and people everywhere and some of them have all these voices, Soren Agenoux said (that). The voice of being kind to your fine feathered friends. Put your favorite sounds in a tube and see how they come out at the other end. Be kind to Your Fine Feathered Friends was never so palatable. Take a loaf of Tip-Top bread and try constructing a staircase. What did George Macunias mean by saying that "all other pieces have been performed whether you notice them or not"? I noticed George Macunias enter formally (what is the name of the high round collar you see the men wearing in those old photos, sitting stiffly for posterity) with a French horn but I couldn't determine from the balcony what fell out of the horn when he bowed. Stones or marbles. They rolled. The sound of stones or marbles rolling. It might also be amusing to see the King in his finery walk down the aisle formed by his silent obedient courtiers, turn to prepare to be seated on the throne, and retch. For that to which we are accustomed, prepare to die. What could anybody expect from a French horn in a Fluxus concert at the Carnegie Recital horn, uh, hall. Horns and halls. And the orchestra seated as well known, leader, conductor, immaculate in tails, Kuniharu Akiyama, famed possibly for his interpretations of contemporary music. Silence, order in the court. Arms uplifted. The signal. The single sound. Curtain. The sound of one sound sounding. Another an historic occasion. No, it is not like the baby crying I hear now outside my window. It is exactly like a sound made in the Carnegie Recital Hall made at approximately 10 P.M. Historical as a pumpkin pie. What do my expectations have to do with rolling marbles?

Consider Nam June Paik, Korean expatriot, active in Europe. I knew about his violin piece. I knew he stood behind a table holding a violin in two hands and raised it so slowly overhead and at the zenith brought it down to crash and be destroyed by impact with table. That was the form I expected. But Paik might have surprised himself as well as me. The audience was already giddy from making their own music (laughter) apart from what they might have thought to be the absence of it where they had any reason to expect it from a historical setting of elegant high purpose. Already they had witnessed the wind music of five musicians watching the air from the wings blow gently some sheets of paper off their music stands. And George Brecht placing a vase of flowers (later at the Carnegie Tavern) on the grand piano. And Alison Knowles explaining her Child Art Piece which had been done in Paris and Düsseldorf but which was canceled here to conform to the tenets of the Society for the Prevention of Cruelty to Children and replaced by Version 2: Exit in a New Suit. And Philip Corner at the piano submitting the image of himself, precise placements of hands, no sounds. And a piece for three, four-stringed instruments by Congo, chimpanzee from London. So that if Paik did not want to surprise himself he might have done his work of taut concentration at the outset. A stringed instrument can cost a fortune. Everybody knows that. How much can it cost to change your mind? Paik changed his mind when his arms and violin were extended parallel to the floor. At the moment he stepped aside, spoke briefly, possibly in a white fury, and if so smashed the violin out of a present need, more present than the fulfillment of a planned action. Pure Fluxus. Did LaMonte Young know he was going to burn a violin in a concert at Ninety-first Street several years ago? Modes of destruction and positive statement. What about the excellent fad of college boys which began in Derby, England, and moved on to California where the boys organized a Piano Reduction Study Group to reduce the piano in the shortest possible time to such a state that it may be passed through an aperture of twenty cm. in diameter? The record time was 10 minutes 44.4 seconds. What is to be said about this or about the gradual erosion of a piano left to nature's design in a junkyard? One could observe and record the phenomenon in either case. Is Child Art on the stage any different

from Child Art in the home? Of course it is, and Fluxus fux
any notion of value attached to staying home or going to the
theatre. Fluxus composers are contemporary Pataphysicians.
Pataphysics is the science of particulars, the examination of
laws which govern exceptions. The world is composed of exceptions, and it seems a shame to the Pataphysician to reduce
the universe to unexceptional exceptions by discovering laws of
the correlation of exceptions. All things being exceptions it follows that each thing is a law unto itself, thus how could there
be any competition for value among things which have no
meaning beyond their own particular design? There can, therefore, only be indifference to value and not to the performance
of a particular duty. Value resides in the performance. That is
the elegant high purpose of it. Not indifference, but engagement. Fluxus composers are not pro-art or anti-art. How could
they be for or against anything when the thing to do on the program is to eat the hot dogs distributed by the conductor who
caught them as they flew down to the stage on a rope from the
balcony? The action was also clear in Aye's *Rainbow Piece for
Wind Orchestra* in which the conductor stabbed the bubbles
made by instruments and a toy store bubble maker with his
baton. Nor do I care about Fluxus one way or another. Going
to Fluxus was another engagement. It was a delightful occasion.
Next time I might stay home, or contemplate a hot dog at
Coney Island. Meanwhile, I salute you and fux Fluxus from the
forty-two keys of my typewriter.

July 2, 1964

LaMONTE YOUNG

"Welcome to this presentation of Dream Music" was the first
sentence of LaMonte Young's sheet of program notes for three
concerts at the Pocket Theatre on October 30 and 31, and No-

vember 1, 1964. That this music should begin and end at all is merely a limitation of the human condition, for Young's idea is that such music might persist eternally. As a composer he has always been involved with things that go on a long time, and he says that his longest performed piece was one of the Dreams from *Four Dreams of China*. This piece began at George Segal's farm nearly two years ago, and since silences were included in the composition and the last silence could continue for an indefinite period of time, the Dream is still going on and presumably it will endure forever. One of Young's exquisite ideas for eliminating mortal anxiety is the erection of Dream Houses in which performances of this type would be going on continuously in various rooms. One could visit or reside as a recluse in this "living musical organism."

Sitting cross-legged in a symmetrical formation in the center of the small Pocket Theatre stage, lighted very dimly, before a large gong with a black painted bull's eye (made by Robert Morris), the four performers could have been holy people at meditation in a shrine of no particular religion. The setting seems more Oriental than Western, and the music itself is closer to the Orient than to any Western modes of composition, unless you think of a composer like Morton Feldman, whose music is also notable for its drifting static quality, but who prefers the muted tone, often nearly inaudible, to anything remotely approaching the high-powered amplification typical of Young's music.

Speaking of Feldman I am reminded of what Cage said about him, that the flavor of his music struck him as erotic, that the inclination is toward tenderness, with a sensuousness of sound or an atmosphere of devotion. I wouldn't ascribe tenderness to the shrill abrasion of Young's music, but I find it even more erotic in its sensuous harmonies amplified to penetrating vibrations. Not only does it pierce your vitals, it also induces rest and sleep. A hypnotic state can be caused by pneumatic drills or dripping Chinese torture water so long as the sound persists in regular intervals, and Young intensifies the persistence by having the "intervals tuned exactly according to frequency ratios." Young's concept is harmonic in terms of concomitant or simultaneous frequencies (and by amplification he makes the overtone series of a fundamental pitch audible up to the number of twenty-one); but his work is not rhythmic or melodic in any historical sense. Indian music, upon which he must have modeled his "drone" (a pitch which is held constantly), remains rhythmic in that certain elements of the ensemble maintain a beat which is not fast enough to turn into a pitch. Moreover, to continue the comparison, most classical Indian music assumes a dramatic structure by beginning slowly and building up to a pyrotechnical tour de force.

The drone in Young's *Tortoise* consists of two voices (his own and Marian Zazeela's) and two stringed instruments (played by Tony Conrad and John Cale), one of them a viola converted into a three-string drone. (The bridge has been redesigned so that the three strings are more or less parallel and can easily be played simultaneously.) There is a contact microphone on each instrument and an ordinary microphone for each singer. The gong has two contact mikes, for *Gong Contests,* Miss Zazeela bow the disk gently for a long time standing on either side of it.

Both *Tortoise* and *Gong Contests* are related in strange or obvious ways to Young's other compositions, like the twenty-nine pieces of 1960, each one titled *Draw a Straight Line and Follow It,* which were performed by Young and Robert Dunn in one of a series of concerts at Yoko Ono's loft on Chambers Street, and which, if taken literally, as a verbal instruction, might extend eternally. This important series at Yoko Ono's loft (an equivalent of the underground cinema without the publicity) was organized by Young shortly after he arrived in New York from California in 1960, when his appearance (black velvet suit, voluminous black cape) was such that he might have reminded anyone of what Oscar Wilde said about himself: that he devoted his talent to writing and his true genius to living. Possibly he was taken more seriously as a character than a composer. A number of pieces written in 1960 (printed in the "Anthology" published by Young and Jackson Maclow in 1963) were simple instructions, such as "The performer should prepare any composition and then perform it as well as he can" or "This piece is little whirlpools out in the middle of the ocean" or a piece about bringing a bale of hay and a bucket of water onto the stage for the piano to eat and drink. George Brecht's Yam Festival (1963) and George Macunias's Fluxus operations are full of these serious inanities, more Neo-Dada (without the political implications of the original Dada) than anything the critics called Neo-Dada by the new painters of the fifties.

The pieces by Young quoted above are far from trivial, but taken by themselves they hardly reveal Young's intense dedication to a continuum of music as a way of life, and to a system of multidimensional harmonies that may well be, as he says, a major new development in musical history. Young's first appearance in New York as an underground dandy also belied the fact that he arrived here on an Alfred Hertz Memorial Traveling Scholarship in music composition after a spell of graduate work in Berkeley on a Woodrow Wilson Fellowship. Young says that his far-out activities at the university in California were only tolerated because he was a whiz at conventional harmonies, thereby fulfilling his conventional obligation as a conventional student. Last spring Merce Cunningham used Young's *Two Sounds* to accompany a new work, *Winterbranch*. I described the source of the *Two Sounds* as ashtrays pulled gently over mirrors but apparently it was cans scraping slowly on windows. Both sources were enunciated in California in another form, in a concert with the choreographer Ann Halprin, as a piece with Young dragging a gong over a section of cement floor and Terry Riley scraping a a wastebasket against the wall. The noise was so deafening that the audience screamed the National Anthem and any other obscenities they could think of to induce a termination of the proceedings. A three-hour Happening in California, called *Avalanche Number 1,* included *Poem for Tables, Chairs, and Benches* (the constant wail and moan of that furniture as it was pushed across the floor), familiar to New York from the Yoko Ono series and as the accompaniment to a section of Yvonne Rainer's *Three Seascapes*.

Young's present plans include another series of three concerts at the Pocket Theatre, on November 20, 21, 22, 1964, and a project for selling original tapes of his music. Some artists remind us of real or impending disasters. Others couldn't care less about anything outside of a canvas and a pot of paint if that's what they happen to be involved in. Whether Young cares or not, his music is of a transcendental purity, and it certainly suggests a cure if a cure seems necessary, a cure not to resolve conflicts but to simply forget them. Baptism by music. The dissemination of culture by way of original tapes by Young in house, office, and brothel could conceivably raise the culture to an unusual level of sanity.

November 19, 1964

NEW LONDON REVIVALS: PART I

On August 15 and 16, 1965, I was in New London (Connecticut) for the American Dance Festival, the seventeenth season, for a program by José Limón in memory of Doris Humphrey and a program by Martha Graham more formally announced as a Louis Horst Memorial Program. Limón revived the *Lament for Ignacio Sanchez Mejias,* choreographed for him by Miss Humphrey in 1946, and premiered *A Choreographic Offering,* set to Bach's *A Musical Offering,* containing motifs from fourteen of Miss Humphrey's dances dating from 1928. Miss Graham revived three works with scores by the late Louis Horst, her mentor and musical director for many years.

At the Sunday matinee and evening performances, Mr. Limón and Miss Graham made a white jacket–white gown appearance, embracing each other, addressing the audience informally, as the King and Queen. Their dedicated Establishment flourishes at Juilliard in the winter and at New London in the summer, perpetuating the ideals of a tradition now defunct by reason of age and imitation, but still glorious for those who glory in it and for those like me who, though essentially sympathetic to the contemporary scene, find it possible to be aroused by a museum masterpiece and by the aura of accomplishment not so long gone. After many seasons of dead stuff at New London, excepting Cunningham and a few isolated cases, these two programs were a pleasure. Occasionally in the annals of art, history is focused by a revival or a retrospective which reveals the greatness of a former time now beclouded by weary repetition, by the advance of new methods, by the farce of legend in distorting simple original facts.

The "great" time of the early modern dance was in the decade of the thirties. The important revival at New London was *Primitive Mysteries* (1931), one of Graham's earliest works for large group, also one of the first major dances in a staunch Americana tradition: Indians, Puritans, Provincials, Pioneers, and all that. A writer in 1934 said: "But the subject matter of the dance now is not a story; it is a method to find a rhythm that says America." Martha Graham's "primitive" series of the early thirties was inspired by a visit she made to the Southwest in 1930. *Primitive Mysteries* is a ritual dance derived in spirit from the Spanish-Indian religious attitude of the American Southwest.

The Indians of the Southwest may be on American soil and Miss Graham undoubtedly employed gestures (e.g., her famous cupped hand) that she found on religious objects there, but the dance is more like a distillation of all mysteries than a "rhythm that says America." What says America to me is its spare formality of design, a blessed preoccupation of those early American modern dancers coming after a long Denishawn period of sprawling international interests and fortuitous techniques of composition. Another American thing about it is the stark Puritan posture of a people still hearing the Calvinist exhortations of a Jonathan Edwards. The choice of American subject matter was not simply a decision to make dance in America an indigenous affair. The choice was rooted as much in the background of each dancer as in any artistic considerations. Martha Graham, the biography goes, was the daughter of an upright Presbyterian, a specialist in nervous diseases, who boasted a line of some ten generations of New England and New York Dutch ancestry.

Primitive Mysteries is not like the later dances of conflict and heroic resolution. It is a pure exposition of compassion and adoration on a single plane. Its three sections—"Hymn to the Virgin," "Crucifixus," "Hosanna"—each enclosed by a processional entrance and exit (a broken walk in strict linear formations), are distinct in their motifs, which express three aspects of religion (statement of worship, anguish of the Passion, celebration). Yet there is no drama of opposing forces, the three sections are three aspects of the same thing, like the Holy Trinity, thus the dance moves as a kind of frieze of images depicting a single emotion in various attitudes. The stiff archaic style of the work is never static. The twelve attendants of the Virgin shift constantly from one linear or circular formation to another, moving in two or three distinct groups, or in one mass, always a choral declamation, apart from, yet in direct relation to, the Virgin, who is less mobile, appropriately, than her twelve apostles. The Virgin is the focal figure of inner concentration (beautifully rendered in this revival by Yuriko), much like the fixed frontal severity of Virgins in thirteenth- or fourteenth-century Italian paintings.

To say that the dance is at once stiff and mobile is still, I presume, not conveying the essential visual impact of the work. The rigorous simplicity of design is projected by gesture as well as by formation. Well known, for instance, from Barbara Morgan's book of photographs, is the moment in "Crucifixus" when the group in unison presses the heel of the right hand to forehead, fingers spread above like a crown of thorns, left arm at the side in slight but rigid akimbo. Typical also is another passage from "Crucifixus" when each member of the group takes off, one by one, to encircle the Virgin, with incredible leaps, chin pushed forward, the body doubled over an extended leg, which reaches in the leap, stops, reaches again, until the pace accelerates in a near agony of difficult locomotion. In the "Hosanna," the celebration, a change of position illustrates the tension of design by contrast as well as the expressive power of a simply stylized gesture. The arms are first held rigidly in front, hands clasped, pulling down to the floor. Then as the weight shifts slightly back and off center to one side, the arms move outward to hold in the "cross," a gesture echoing the cross motif of the Virgin in her Passion, but in its awkward asymmetry also suggesting a shout, the shout of the Hosanna.

Primitive Mysteries was last revived in 1947. At that time a critic noted the absence of the "full-blooded vigor of the concert group of the mid-thirties seen in the rousing concert dances that marked the end of a period." Gone, in other words, were the big gutty women of the early days. Referring to the recent performance in New London, an old company member said she missed the hard percussive thrust in the movement. Not having seen it before I didn't miss anything. The present dancers are lithe young girls, typical of a new era remote from the blood and guts of the pioneers. Unquestionably the performance is more delicate and lyrical. Yet I found all the sharp clarity that seemed necessary in a work that clearly requires it. I think they did full justice to Graham's angles and accents and famous pelvic contractions. At no point did I notice a lapse into vanity or any other vice to which this once Spartan technique has so notoriously succumbed. The revival at New London brings back the original idea with such force that it seems possible to forget momentarily, if forgetting is desirable, the strange metamorphosis of a style as it has advanced through various stages of decay.

August 27, 1964

NEW LONDON REVIVALS: PART II

Last column I talked mostly about Martha Graham's *Primitive Mysteries,* one of the revivals at the American Dance Festival in New London. It would have been interesting to see an early work by Doris Humphrey on the same program to note certain striking similarities in the ideas of these two artists who, along with Charles Weidman, emerged from Denishawn in the late twenties to create new forms and techniques, laying the foundation for all future developments. The American idea was basic to the early efforts of the three pioneers. Like Miss Graham, Doris Humphrey's heritage is the lock and stock of the proud immigrants who cleared the land. Her grandfathers were Congregational clergymen, one of them a descendent of Elder Brewster, and her father's stepmother was a daughter of Ralph Waldo Emerson.

Parallel to *Primitive Mysteries* was Humphrey's *Shakers,*

made in the same year, 1931. *Shakers* was derived from the religious attitude of the New England Shaker sect, their belief in celibacy and of literally shaking off their sins. The counterpart in *Shakers* to the Virgin in *Primitive Mysteries* was the matriarchal leader, the central figure of invocation and exhortation. The design of the dance adhered to the design of the Shaker ritual, the men and women divided into separate groups on either side of a rectangular floor plan. Its strict linear and circular patterns followed from the plan, and are close, in essence, to the square formality of design in Graham's dance. Although Humphrey's technique differed in important respects from the technique of Graham (something I can't elaborate here), there was also the similarity of making vivid contrasts of design in gesture (as in *Shakers:* a vertical kneeling position, in profile to the audience, with the hands clasped in prayer close to the chest, followed by a strong diagonal as the arms extend straight downward and the torso leans back in one piece), a technique of composition developed most consciously by Humphrey as one of her theories of theatrical effectiveness.

Unlike the Graham work, *Shakers* progresses dynamically from a quiet beginning through an accumulation of energy to a high pitch of ecstasy, in keeping with the Shaker idea of shaking off sin. The more energetic sections of *Shakers* are remote from the contained intensity of *Primitive Mysteries*. But if one were to superimpose an image from other sections of *Shakers* onto the Graham work, or vice versa, one might see quickly the historical affinity of the two dances. An obvious example is a section in each dance in which the central figure acts in the passageway created by two lines of kneeling penitents. Comparing these works I am also reminded of other parallels, not only in the earlier forms, but in later developments, such as in the work of the now famous protégé of Humphrey, José Limón, whose repertory represents a culmination of the early era. From a twenty-three-year distance, a passage in Limón's *The Traitor* (1954) is curiously like the two just mentioned from the Graham and Humphrey works. In the "Last Supper" scene the Christ figure leans over the symbolic cloth to bless the disciples, who form the same parallel lines, divided on either side of the cloth, extending downstage to upstage, as the audience views it. The big difference is the relative mobility of Limón's passage, characteristic of his style, in which the percussive accents of his predecessors were smoothed out in fluid articulations. Limón's Baroque extension of the Humphrey-Weidman technique was beautifully exemplified in his *A Choreographic Offering,* set to Bach, a premiere at the Festival, in memory of Humphrey. This gigantic dance of solos, duets, and ensembles for twenty-eight dancers contained motifs from fourteen of Miss Humphrey's works, but the piece was all Limón in its massive opulence and orchestration of both movement and groups of dancers, reminiscent of his *Missa Brevis,* but without the Gothic aspiration of eternity, unity, brotherhood, etc., a dance of pure movement and design close to the Baroque music that he admires the most. It is not so farfetched to make an analogy of Limón and his predecessors to the transition in painting from High Renaissance to Baroque. With Limón the classical symmetries and four-square arrangements of the earlier works for large group (a generalization marked by exceptions) have dissolved in a sensual flow of movement whereby the architecture is constantly leaning and shifting, one image melting into another so that the eye is never permitted to settle on a single noteworthy picture.

Limón's new work is a grand symphonic dance in a tradition of plotless ballets dating from Fokine's *Les Sylphides,* the comparatively crude music visualizations of Denishawn and Massine, and, more to the point in Limón's ancestry, a work like Doris Humphrey's, *Passacaglia and Fugue in C Minor.* On the same program at New London was a revival of *The Lament for Ignacio Sanchez Mejias,* choreographed for Limón by Humphrey in 1946, a dance typical of the more prominent interest of early choreographers in literary content. The *Lament* may be a schmaltzy dance from a contemporary point of view, overwrought with passion of life and death, but there are three solos for the bullfighter in this dance that remain exquisite examples of choreography by a woman who put her principles of choreography above everything on her scale of artistic values, and whose work was a constant test of these principles. Here Humphrey combined her craft at its best with an inspiration from the Garcia Lorca poem and a style especially suited to Limón's great weight and refined Spanish arrogance and Mexican-Indian brutality. The death solo, which begins just as the doomed bullfighter pitches prone at the feet of the Woman of Destiny (Letitia Ide) and the Woman of Compassion (Patricia Hammack), rushes downstage at the edge of the pit to bellow the Lorca line "I did not want to see it" ("the blood of Ignacio over the arena")—the death solo is one of the most exciting solos, death or otherwise, including the suicide of Giselle, in my personal vision. Ignacio gets up and begins with a hair-raising rhythm, the top of one foot, this foot crossed behind the supporting leg, beating the floor in a desperate syncopation (coordinated with an eruption of drums in the score), arms spread-eagled but dangling as if broken feathers, the beating foot like an externalization of a wild heartbeat, the whole action a kind of embattled limp—trapped animal in a final ritual of proud if hopeless assertion, Limón bequeathed his role to Louis Falco for this revival, and Falco, much lighter (and younger) than Limón, made something very beautiful out of it in his own way. His agility and phrasing and modulations of intensity are extraordinary. Falco is what some people sometimes call a "born dancer." Also, he carried himself like a Spaniard and satisfied my fussy ideal concept of a classical matador. I also liked Patricia Hammack's guttural melodramatic delivery of the Lorca lines. She belted them out as though her life and everybody's literally depended on it.

The *Lament* is one of quite a few dances in the Limón repertory derived from the content of his Mexican heritage. *La Malinche,* for one, choreographed by Limón in 1949, is about the conquering Cortez, the vanquished people, and the woman of the title who betrayed her people as mistress and interpreter to Cortez, but in legend comes back as a spirit to lead the people against their conqueror in expiation of her sins. I mention this dance because it brings me back to parallels again in its similarity to another Graham revival at the Festival, *El Penitente* (1941), based on the fanatical rites of the Penitentes, a religious sect which came to Old and New Mexico from Spain with the Conquistadors. Like *La Malinche, El Penitente* is a trio, and the form of both dances is that of a group of strolling street players who make a processional entrance and then assume their characters to enact a mystery play. The Mary figure in *El Penitente* relates to the woman of Cortez in *La Malinche,* but chiefly as a prime mover, for in her role as sinner La Malinche is like the penitent figure in the Graham work. The characters in each dance represent different things, but the subject matter is the same.

El Penitente was originally created with Merce Cunningham as Christ, Erick Hawkins as the Penitent, Miss Graham as the Mary figure, and I can imagine it was quite a different dance. I didn't get much from this performance with Gene McDonald, David Wood, and Marnie Thomas in the corresponding roles. The Flagellation of the Penitent, for one thing, which initiates the action directly after the entrance, was done with excessive motion, writhing, and no credible intensity. Nor did I feel any agony when the Penitent pulled the Death Cart (a wooden construction in the original production, here a flimsy rope affair) on his hands and knees. I've seen photographs of Erick Hawkins in the part that look much closer to the masochistic fervor which inspired the sect from which the dance is derived at least in spirit. Having such a specific content the dance is more than its formal arrangement of parts and gestures. I would look for the exorcism in some degree that I gathered from a curdling description of the actual rite, written by a firsthand observer, printed in the *Frontier Times* (1941): "It was like being on the rim of Hades listening to the screams of the damned."

Miss Graham's third revival at New London was *Frontier,* a solo choreographed in 1935, another classic of the 'thirties, another example of the space delineations that marked an early period of rigorous formality in design and simple integrity of gesture. *Frontier* is the dance of American Woman in her pleasure of expansion over herself and the great American plains and all that. The focus of the dance is the straight positioning, vertical and horizontal, done on a centrally placed fragment of rail fence, a V-shape of ropes extending from the fence to infinity. The gestures are broad and open. Ethel Winter performed the role with delightful naivete, probably without the demonic flavor Miss Graham must have given it originally, but strong enough to give me the sense of Whitmanesque grandeur and proud stability of pioneering woman.

September 10, 1964

DECEMBER ROMANCE

Flying in on the run, on a downstage diagonal, Aileen Passloff was not entering any ordinary enclosure where mortals engage in temporal affairs. Miss Passloff's solo, *December,* choreographed for her by Remy Charlip, set to Tchaikovsky, is a romantic piece in the tradition of enchantment and doom common to all stories in which a dream of eternal pleasure, being always someplace where one is not, is interrupted by the alarm clock and other agents of earthly corruption, including the knowledge of futility, which turns a flight into a fall before the imminence of certain death if the flight persists through too many alarms of the clock.

In most stories of tragic romance there is one fall from which there is no return and the rest is gloom and final disaster. *December* is not that kind of romance. The disaster in the dance is as fleeting as the brief moments of satisfaction. The form of the dance, its spatio-physical character, rests on a fluid transition from one state of mind, one kind of reaction, to another. Since the reactions are not to any external stimuli (no visible demons or lovers) the changes are self-reflexive and I assume that Mr. Charlip, in choreographing the dance, let one phase suggest the next in a current of shifting dynamics. Miss Passloff makes the transitions with a sense of organic inevitability so that the phrases are linked by a continuity of breath as the body expands toward its goal, indulges the pleasure of attainment, or retreats under the pressure of exposure.

The cycle is set right away as the dancer stops short in her initial flight track, a full open run of high expectation, steps back slowly, a hand at the chest, a puzzle on the face, a question about the folly or wisdom of a sudden wind-blown impulse. Bewilderment is the first reaction to presentiments of danger. After that the blood flows more freely in countering the rash expansions of desire, and the reactions, the counters, become ready anger, panic (the flight in retreat), and even the sweet melancholy of hands pressed lightly to face, or the soft release in a gesture of sleep.

Coming out of some slow stable turns Miss Passloff races toward a white column and would fly up beyond its smooth cylindrical surface if it was a dream and not a dance and yet the dream is contained in the dance and we get the impact of the intention in that momentary effort. The romantic attitude is nowhere so clear as in the fall from that effort, for while the legs take the weight of the body into the floor, the arms remain stretched, the gaze follows the arms, and the torso sinks to one side, still hoping for the impossible. But since the dance must go on, and this is not a dance in which any single emotion is a cause célèbre, relief is then obtained with clenched fists whirling overhead in exclamation of whipping turns, a fury which makes it possible once again to find imagination for wings, this time in the serenity of an aerial swim—arms in breaststroke parting an ethereal substance while the feet touch the floor in leaps designed to give the impression that the floor is not really there.

Not really being there is the aspiration as a spiral of infinite ascent. The fall is from a rarefied atmosphere impossible to breathe for too long. Another kind of fall is from the frustration of not getting there at all. But these are just literary intimations. The dance is the physical action and I liked the dance not for what it seemed to mean, but for its flow of attack, repose, and retreat in clearly etched images in movement which requires a command of a range of qualities from the soft fluid pull and stretch to the jagged thrust of controlled tension, and which Miss Passloff releases with perfect balance and coordination, with a strength and alignment in back and legs supporting both violent and delicate maneuvers.

The physical action conveyed all I wanted to know: a leap, say, with the body doubled over, and then its polar opposite in the torso and head thrown back, held there a moment, the arms angled, bent at elbow and wrist, up over the face, to reinforce the ecstatic arch. Any exaggeration of facial expression conveyed more than I wanted to know. *December* would be absurd certainly in the current mode of the deadpan delivery, the inscrutable face. Accepting the dance on its own terms nobody would expect a raptured arch to be accompanied by an impassive expression. Yet the extravagance of feeling in the movement alone is self-explanatory, and the problem always, perhaps, with romance, is the temptation to take it too seriously, to command responses of pity and terror which exceed the reality of movement making its own primitive appeal to our nerves and muscles, the drama of expansion and contraction in advance of our capacities for sentimental involvement. But since Miss Passloff did essentially make this appeal, doing the most with excellent material, these comments are not of much consequence except possibly to add a general reflection on the delicate nature of the romantic sensibility in performance.

December is a special dance in itself, but it is also noteworthy for its appearance in the midst of a period not essentially in the mood for the kind of romance we might expect to see at any period in a house of ballet. I am talking about it partly because it is not like the dominant drift of advanced work (by, say, the Judson choreographers); because it appeared on a program in startling contrast to a duet by Yvonne Rainer of similar subject matter, as well as on a concert of Miss Passloff's own—which included, as her programs always do, dances that are as deadpan and offbeat as those of the current bias (exemplified by Miss Rainer's duet), of which Miss Passloff is a harbinger, having made all kinds of dances for about thirteen years project the contemporary atmosphere (that atmosphere includes a revival of interest in the ballet); and because the present scene is not static and a dance like *December* illustrates the fat potential of response to anything well done, be it cool or romantic.

August 13, 1964

MARTHA GRAHAM

Martha Graham has been called high priestess of the dance. The term applies as much to the persona she has projected for many years in her works as it does to her popular position as the most famous dancer of the century in America. With the revival of *Cave of the Heart* in the repertory series on Broadway, Graham's role of woman who officiates in sacred rites is clearer to me than it has been, even after seeing *Primitive Mysteries* for the first time the summer of 1964, and thinking then that I never quite knew why she was so famous. *Primitive Mysteries* was premiered in 1931 and was also included in the season just past. *Cave of the Heart* was made in 1946 as part of a Greek trilogy, Graham's first venture into Greek myth. Reading backward and forward a student of her work might see a prophecy of a later interest in Greek material in the mythic treatment of the rites of a North American religious sect defined in *Primitive Mysteries*. In *Mysteries* any sense of place is lost in a rigid formal structure of great beauty. Later dances, in the American tradition, like *Frontier* (1935) were closer to the local color paralleled by Regionalist painters of the thirties. In the early forties Graham continued her excursions into American landscape with *Letter to the World, Salem Shore,* and *Appalachian Spring;* and into Western literature with *Herodiade* and *Deaths and Entrances.* Then with the Greek trilogy of the late forties she plunged into what Margaret Lloyd called a psychomythological cycle, explored later in *Clytemnestra* (1958) and brought up to date in the sixties with *Alcestis* (1960), *Phaedra* (1962), and *Circe* (1963).

At one time Graham said she read something in Plato that led her to the conclusion that mythology was the psychology of another age. She wanted to go back through motor memory to the ancestral moods to find an explanation of what we are today. *Cave of the Heart* is a ritual of hate and destruction derived from an episode in the chaotic lives of Jason and Medea. In the fifteen years separating *Cave* from *Mysteries,* Graham moved from grand architectonic design to interior monologue stashed with symbolic imagery. In *Cave* the space (relations between performers and of performers to stage frame) is not nearly so important as charged emotional gestures, costume, and decor. Placement of action in *Mysteries* has that overwhelming inevitable look we associate with classic paintings by masters of early or high Renaissance design. In *Cave* one senses that an alternative placement at any point of the four characters would be a happy possibility. Decor, however, in Graham's late works, limits the stage space in a crucial way. Decor is home base. Characters leave decor for a rendezvous with themselves or other characters and return to decor like homing pigeons returning with messages to make declarations about the world "out there." Decor for Graham is an extension of mind. In *Cave* the decor is a desolate mind-scape of low gray stumps (by Noguchi). A sort of altar of four stumps, arranged to form a seat or receptacle upstage center, is the statuary asylum of the Chorus (a single woman—Matt Turney) and of Medea in her consultation with the Chorus, or in her brooding quiescence and her moments of triumph. The other stumps, strung out stage right of the stump-altar, are a kind of base of operations for Jason (Robert Cohan) and the Princess (Yuriko). The remaining decor is a free-standing construction of glistening wires spread out horizontally on either side of a vertical wire frame, within which Medea (Helen McGehee in this revival) is first revealed. The lightning wires could be a headdress; they remind me of Medusa's serpent hair, but they might be closer, in Graham's mind, to the "long white robe" that Medea gave to Glauce (Princess) to kill her with. In one version of the myth Medea kills the Princess with a crown and a robe. No sooner does the Princess (victim, virgin) don these items than she is consumed by unquenchable flames. In Graham's dance the robe or hair of wires is used exclusively by Medea and the agent of destruction is a crown.

Medea crowns her victim after some remarkable scenes establishing the purity and naivete of the victim, the love of Jason and the victim for each other, the tortured jealousy of the conniving Medea, and the oracular wisdom of the Chorus, who seems at moments to be Medea's alter ego. Medea has a job to do and the Chorus is her helper. While the Princess does a light joyous childlike dance, Medea languishes hunched over in morbid meditation by the stump-seat next to the Chorus. She is then hidden behind the Chorus and emerges as though "born" more or less through the legs of the Chorus. Meanwhile the Princess has climbed up the leg of her hero Jason to sit straddling one of his shoulders, to be carried around like that, high above the thronging demons (Medea's heart coils) below. Previously, in another elevated image, the adored Princess posed as a flying angel, standing on Jason's thighs, leaning diagonally into space, arms outstretched, braced in a straight line by Jason's hold on her legs. Before that Jason had posed in a stride position spanning two stumps, looking like the figurehead of a ship's prow, while the Princess sat on a stump next to him holding his back foot, possibly his vulnerable heel, although Jason is not credited with such a heel.

The Princess leaves the scene soon after Medea crowns her. Since the crown is deadly she is naturally wracked with convulsions and she goes reeling off stage in her violent seizure to die in the wings. Medea is then left alone. She reproduces the death throes of her victim with her own contorted vibrations, at the same time symbolizing the act of destruction with a red ribbon (serpent or serpent's tongue) that she pulls out of the bodice of her dress and uses to express a horrifying victory —eating it, throwing it up, tying it at the waist, dangling it as her leg serpentines round her body or as she shimmies on her knees in tremolos of vicious satisfaction—everything an expression of guilt and expiation, she and the red ribbon becoming one. Finally the Princess is lugged in, shrouded and dead; Jason backs in from the other wing, very upset; Jason and the Princess end up center stage in a death embrace on the floor; Medea walks over them carrying her frame of wires, finishes with stately success standing on the stump-seat overlooking the demolished couple.

Graham's *Cave of the Heart* is as modern as the myth which inspired her. Artists are always retelling these myths. Even the far-out French writer, Robbe-Grillet, whose novels are ostensibly studies in the surfaces of things, has written a novel with a subplot involving the story of Oedipus. To make a dance out of a long complicated myth Graham had to choose an episode that would be practical for exposition. I think too much emphasis has been put on the most obvious psychological aspect of her choice, namely, the insane jealousy of Medea's character. Medea was a wicked woman but she was also a sorceress of amazing deeds. In the dance Medea is properly both of the world and out of the world. Behind Graham's persona as Medea is a woman of the world outraged by a travesty of honor. According to myth Medea married Jason and gave him seven sons and seven daughters. Jason swore by all the gods of Olympus to keep faith with Medea forever. He had good reason, for Medea had on numerous occasions by her extraordinary powers saved them from perilous obstacles. But after ten prosperous years together Jason broke faith with Medea, claiming that Medea had secured their throne at Corinth by murder, and proposed to divorce her in favor of the daughter of King Creon, the Princess of the dance. As a woman of the world Medea was clearly done in, but as a goddess of the underworld she remained invulnerable and her long career of sorcery was rewarded by the gift of immortality. Jason, on the other hand, although he escaped the holocaust that killed the Princess, King Creon, and other assembled guests, ended up wandering from city to city, killed by an accident.

Graham's "cave" is the mind's region of darkness pursuing dreams of loss and conquest. Sexual symbology is apparent in gesture, costume, decor. Graham's dances have never been Surrealistic in the academic sense of that word. Images are not combined surrealistically. Rather, symbols are presented in a realistic context of narrative development. If Graham had ever taken a serious step in the direction of Surrealism she would have abolished narrative and I presume she couldn't do that because the old stories mean too much to her. *Legend of Judith* (from the Apocrypha) is a more complex narrative than *Cave of the Heart* because Graham projects the story of Judith and Holofernes by way of interesting flashbacks. As Judith, Graham dreams of her youth, personified in the dance by a younger Judith (Linda Hodes), and the two of them alternate appearances or perform together in the drama of seducing, bewitching, and murdering Holofernes. Yet for all its complexity the action remains a literal enactment of a program note. One simply looks for technical prowess and emotional intensity to get involved in a clearly understood narrative. Beyond that I can see no moral lesson in Graham's telling of the old tales. In *Cave of the Heart* Medea got very angry, for good reason apparently, and she got it out of her system by doing away with her rival, by making Jason unhappy and possibly impotent, and by arranging her own safe passage to the Elysian fields, where some say that she, rather than Helen, married Achilles. Graham's triumph at the conclusion of *Cave of the Heart* is a simple expression of the power she conceives to possess as a woman. In her life and in her work Graham has done an amazing job of substantiating this position.

November 25, 1965

WHICH WAY THE AVANT-GARDE? *

In an essay called "The Politics of Revolution," an interdisciplinary thinker, Harvey Wheeler, defines a well-known process of cultural upheaval in terms applicable to modes of activity within the larger political framework. All revolutions, he says, are tales of two cities. The society of the future is the "second city" which lives and flourishes inside the Establishment. The second city is sometimes hard to see and even when it becomes visible, the Establishment tries to hide from itself the authenticity of the second city.

For some centuries now, the art world of the West has been involved in cyclic patterns of subversion, overthrow, and replacement of one sort of Establishment after another. Many have pointed out that these patterns have increased their tempo in recent years. The dance world tends to linger behind in its reluctance to accept the inevitability, if not the necessity, of revolution.

The avant-garde choreographers of the sixties number a mere handful and their audience is nothing next to the droves who turn out for everything conservative; but they and their dedicated followers (many of them artists with similar concerns) tenaciously cling to the principle that revolution is not only inevitable but essential. Actually, their revolution, in its originial delirium of a sprawling rebellion, is over. It all happened at Judson Memorial Church from 1962–64. Democratically assembled, the choreographers included painters, sculptors, and composers as well as dancers. Within a positive assertion of old creative values was the negative idea of the annihilation of all preconceived notions about dance. In retrospect, it was a beautiful mess. Within that mess certain hardcore positions were taking shape and certain works were undeniably extraordinary.

After a period of some confusion and dispersion, the movement regained its momentum and is now in the process of enlarging, elaborating, and consolidating the dimension of its early promise. It is no longer so much a rebellion as a serious extension of novel positions. Having undermined some cherished presumptions about dance, the choreographers are internalizing the struggle to maintain and to stretch the scope of their new aesthetic.

If the most revolutionary proposition of the new dance was that any sort of movement, or action, and any kind of body (nondancer as well as dancer) was acceptable as material proper to the medium, it was also true that certain choreographers remained in some dialectical relation to tradition, retaining a technical basis for movement while seeking to transform the outmoded structuring of conventional techniques. One of the most encouraging aspects of recent developments is a reassertion of a concern for such movement—as it is still understood in the context of the dance tradition—in a programmatic effort to define it in truly contemporary terms.

Yvonne Rainer, one of the original and most prolific members of the Judson vanguard, set the pace for this development with her *Trio A* of 1966, a short section of pure dance activity which gradually snowballed into a magnum opus called *The Mind Is a Muscle*. *Trio A* constituted a minor revolution in itself. The idea was to reorganize (or to eliminate for that matter) the traditionally conceived dance phrase with its alternating dynamic of high and low points, or its plotlike structure of a beginning, a middle, and an end. The result was a duration of action characterized by a smooth unaccented continuity, each phrase receiving equal emphasis, each movement projected at an energy level that never seemed to change. This was an all-over dance. It was totally de-focused. Its innumerable discrete parts blended into a continuum rendering a sense of the dance being at rest, static, even as it constantly moved.

Two other charter Judson choreographers, Deborah Hay and Lucinda Childs, have recently attacked the problem of advancing the medium within a sphere that lies somewhere between ordinary action (anybody can do it) and a more dance-based idiom. Their choreography, like Rainer's, encompasses both realms. Deborah Hay used five nondancers in two closely related works, *Group I* and *Group II*. The choreography was simple and blasé, both informally dispersed and schematically patterned, with an overall bland consistency and a deadpan, anonymous performing quality.

A trio of a new work by Lucinda Childs, informally presented this spring, involves some exquisite permutations of about five simple actions which anyone could do, but which require, at the same time, the finesse and mild athletic strength that only a trained person could manage. For all its simplicity, it's an extremely precise and structurally complex piece of work.

Beneath individual differences in these dances are a few common denominators. They are making it clearer than ever that formalist structural concerns were always an issue and that the future of dance rests on these concerns rather than on any new cult of personality or new schools of technique. As a historical example, I would contend that the formal contribution of an incredible composition like *Primitive Mysteries* of 1931 by Martha Graham far transcends the myth of high-priestess-dom that Miss Graham became, or the institutionalizing of her technique that followed in the wake of her success. Both processes obscure the real issues.

Implicit in the work of the three artists discussed above is an attack on this very elemental premise of traditional Western dance: the projection of a star supported by a hierarchal imperialist organization (e.g., the kings and queens of the ballet, the tragic heroes and heroines of the modern dance). While I'm at it, I should mention a few other correlative notions that are also under attack. These are, of course, the trappings of any hierarchal system: the pomp and splendor and glamour and spectacle and seduction and virtuosic accomplishments required by aristocratic expectations.

Every underground movement is a revolt against one authority or another. The dance underground of the sixties is more than this natural child-parent affair. The new choreographers are outrageously invalidating the very nature of authority. The thinking behind the work goes beyond democracy into anarchy. No member outstanding. No body necessarily more beautiful than any other body. No movement necessarily more important or more beautiful than any other movement. It is, at last, seeing beyond our subjective tastes and conditioning, always admittedly operative, to a phenomenological understanding of the world.

The inclusive character of the earlier Judson days remains ultimately significant The attitude was nowhere perhaps so perfectly demonstrated as in a recent dance by Steve Paxton, another charter member, in which about thirty-two any old lovely people in their old clothes from our any old lives walked across the large performing space, occasionally standing still or sitting down. For all his training and credentials (several years in Merce Cunningham's Company), Paxton takes the most extreme liberated positions. He likes people for what they are and believes in their physicality (their shape and way of moving) for what it is. The tyranny of the ballet, by the way, lies not only in its institutional authority (it commands the field in numbers, in financial support, in critical acclaim) but in its insistence on the superhuman; on the claim that only a streamlined body of extraordinary prowess is worth our time and money to look at.

I've just barely touched on the activities of the avant-garde dance in New York. Meredith Monk, for instance, is one of the most interesting younger choreographers around. With her multiple concerns she has been exploring the possibilities of dancy dances, of "found" dances, of environmental dances, of "still" images, and of intermedia work. Also dealing with imagery in an intermedia framework is painter Robert Rauschenberg. I think the question whether some of these things are dance or not is irrelevant to the vitality of a movement which, in any case, has questioned the entire fabric of traditionalist dance—both structurally and philosophically.

August 11, 1968

CRITICS' CRITICS

Prompted by say something about the critic and his or her critics and criticism in general and the modern necessity of reforming this ancient practice of pretending to be top man on a barber's pole. As I see it now, the land looks level enough to be a wide open field and I'm ready to run or walk on it without encountering a boogie man who wants to know if he looks tall enough and black enough to be a subject of one of my columns of lasting insignificance. In this respect I join two of my colleagues, John Wilcock and Jonas Mekas, and bow in passing, however reverentially, to Andrew Sarris, who writes the best prose this side of James Agee. Criticism wears me out—it's like riding a bike up and down the country hills in a race against a phantom judge. I'll take a plot of level territory and stake out a claim to lie down on it and criticize the constellations if that's what I happen to be looking at. I also stake out a claim to be an artist, a writer, if that's what I'm doing when I get to the typewriter and decide that I liked something well enough to say what I think it's all about. I think one of the finest pieces of dance criticism or any criticism for that matter was a column written by Louis Horst the grand old man of "the moderne dance" two or three years before he died, in 1957 or 1958 whenever it was that Paul Taylor presented that extraordinary concert, at the YM-YWHA, in which nothing very significant happened except that it was a concert by Paul Taylor and he stood still a lot or changed positions I'm not sure which, it doesn't matter and I remember two girls in dresses and heels who stood still most of the time too and anyway Louis Horst presented his version of that concert—a blank column in the now defunct *Dance Observer*. I like that blank column because I think it meant that its originator was a bit stupefied by Paul Taylor's concert, prompting him (Horst) to present an honest version of a thing he couldn't see very well. After all he was an old man and he'd weathered many early battles of the first modern dancers who also (like Taylor) had a rough time of it money-wise and all the other wises. Louis Horst's blank column might be taken as a model for the criticism of the future (by future I mean right now of course). One reason I'm writing this piece about criticism is that I just read Clive Barnes on criticism in the *Times*. With all respects to Mr. Barnes and I liked his article on criticism, I don't think of myself as a "parasite," which is the term Mr. Barnes used in referring to one who practices criticism. I was about to say:—one who practices the ART of criticism, which brings me back to what I said about staking out a claim to being an artist. And speaking of artists, why is it that more dancers don't practice the art of writing about their work? There's a long tradition of literacy among painters, composers, etc., and I see practically nothing on dance by dancers in public places. Walter Sorell once made a collection of essays by dancers (*The Dance Has Many Faces*) and Merce Cunningham contributed an essay to an edition of *7 Arts* and of course Louis Horst always made it possible for dancers to contribute their writings to the *Dance Observer* and of course there are innumerable books in the Dance Collection of the New York Public Library, among them the autobiographies, but I mean more in the way of contemporary writings by contemporary dancer-choreographers. For instance, I also write for a magazine called *Art News* and over the years the "editorial associates" (reviewers, in effect) have been the artists as well as the writers who are not artists but who for some reason enjoy practicing the art of criticism. Need I say more? The field is wide open as I thought to mention in the beginning, thinking of how I feel about the difficulty of puffing your way up a steep hill on a bike that isn't motorized. The future is upon us and the Art of Criticism has already come into its own in those public places where the critic is lying down on a soft piece of ground to enjoy a bit of blue and yellow scenery. . . . To be continued.

September 16, 1965

ROBERT WHITMAN

Robert Whitman presented a beautiful Happening or theatre thing rather he would prefer maybe (to call it) in East Hampton August 27 and 28. The location was fantastic although I couldn't see it too well. It was a NIGHT TIME event. The location was fantastic. Whitman lit the place up for tripping the lights. I thought I was in a metaphorical paradise. I was. I couldn't find my seat, which was in a field. The field was full of grass and other weeds and there was also a swamp and nobody stepped on it (except the performers). But first of all (and last) I walked through an alley of paper bags glowing candles. They made a curving country path leading from the road where two guides (policemen) led the performing spectators with their flashlights, down to three enormous plexiglass sheets sprayed with copper to make them into mirrors and situated so as to form a kind of room (enclosure). I found myself in the mirrors. I thought I was a clown at a country fair, or an amusement park. I was. Distortions are a riot if it doesn't bother you. From there I watched a number of other distortions, although I didn't get it at first. This is what happened: a young dancer named Deborah Hay stood or danced, in the room between the mirrors; actually she imitated (she told me) the kinds of distortions these mirrors make—by shifting her weight slowly from foot to foot and making other subtle gestures with her head, hands, shoulders, etc., and at some moment she was reflected in herself by a young man who stood directly opposite her (body) and did or seemed to be trying to do exactly what she was doing. Meanwhile a number of children (and other people) were entering the boat tent, for real I mean the swamp-field, for the journey through this outer space Antarctica (later) and as they passed by Deborah between the three mirrors, we spectators by now enjoying ourselves on lovely blue pillows, sailing along as it were, I noticed these children—who were entering—reflected (like Deborah) on another big sheet or screen located directly in front of us. Whitman somehow connected (transmitted) these images from one place to another. It reminded me of closed-circuit television where you look at yourself in store windows. It was great. Okay. Next. By this time I was so comfortable I didn't feel like moving but a gentlemanly neighbor suggested we pick our bodies up off our pillows and take a stroll to our right where events themselves in this boat of a Happening theatre seemed to be moving. The water became more apparent. I saw myself reflected in it. After all it was a swamp. As we moved along I saw what I had already seen which is to say another large screen (in the trees) upon which (the screen) a naked lady was robing and disrobing. The other performers (spectators), or most of them, didn't move along with me and my neighbor. They must have liked the screen lady. The sky was also voluptuous. It was night time. After the Happening I mentioned to a friend that I thought the sky was El Greco (Toledo) that weekend and we agreed. But as for the Happening itself: there were literally two more screens in the trees, moving always to the right as it were. On one of them I heard some sound, which was coming from a noise box situated someplace in the swamp. On the screen itself Whitman made a journey to Antarctica (mentioned earlier) utilizing icebergs, boats, penguins, and other paraphernalia that I'm having difficulty re-

membering since so much was going on all at once, including
the crickets in the thickets. The noise box was transmitting a
man's voice talking about what we were fortunate enough to be
looking at on the screen. I liked the connection. It was almost
osmotic. On the fourth and last (to the right) screen another
film appeared but I couldn't make it out so I thought about it.
A few children standing nearby, close to the water swamp,
mentioned that this screen looked like a whale or a cloud or a
balloon and I instantly (later) remembered Moby Dick, which to
my surprise was not an original thought because one of the performers (Julie) told me it looked closer to a whale of a Moby
pillow. Wow. Bemeantimes I was standing as far to the right as
was possible (without keeling over) when along came about six
penguins or girls in plastic bags sort of waddling by the grass.
Then they disappeared. Now I recall seeing (earlier) a number
of phosphorescent figures at a great distance from our blue pillows who also retreated into the forest. June bugs. Lightning
flies. The night was still clear and while I was noting various
other phenomena in my trusty notebook I spied a tent (taber-
nacle) deep in the forest. I was beginning to think I should go
there (the next stop on the right see) when a confident performer notified me that the lit-up tent was actually a supply
place for the theatre event and I could go there if I wanted re-
freshments. I didn't. One of the last things I saw in this "metaphor" was another young dancer by name Tony Holder paddling about very relaxed in something in the reflected
water—towing behind him an incredible white sculpture construction. I didn't mention all the colors in this event but I'm
sure you can see for yourself. White stands for Moby. Soon I
wandered back over my path to the left thinking a great deal
about how nice it was to be there. The crickets were sounding
off. So was a finale noise box interpreting the sounds of the
swamp. Simone (Whitman) told me it was more truly the sound
of paper crackling through the trees in the wind. At that point I
couldn't have cared less.

P.S. Norman Brown is a genius. This revue could be tran-
scribed as a parody of Brown. Synaptically speaking. If you
saw something I didn't see, sorry. Oh, one more thing: when
Tony (Holder) was in his rowboat someone behind us tossed up

firecrackers (maybe flashlights) which landed all around Tony especially for him to fish for. The noise was *Fantastic*. I guess Whitman is a genius too.

September 8, 1966

TAKE ME DISAPPEARING

Someone told me I like nonart. It sounds good but I don't know what it is. I'd probably like it. I'd have to see it first. If we prefixed all our indications of things with "non" we'd always be looking elsewhere for these things. The confusion would be terrific. Probably the world is too sure about its things. I like things that are certain about not being very sure about what they are. "I am for an art that grows up not knowing it is art at all" (Oldenburg). When things get very certain about themselves they tend to tell you to look out, stand back, make way, shut up, and put down your money. When it's settled it's finished. "The beautiful is what your servant instinctively thinks is frightful." This is your local reporter always "looking elsewhere" —for the nonthing of the thing—for whatever isn't settled, labeled, canned, caulked, cherished, claimed, and consumed. "Take me disappearing through the smoke rings of my mind."

Going back a pace—at the School of Visual Arts: two pieces happily vague about themselves from any view of mediumistic or other types of certainty. *Group I,* Deborah Hay's formal austere piece. Four elements. One a kind of introduction, the other three occurring simultaneously. The introduction is a movie and it sets the tone, the pace, the spatial idea. About twenty people in the movie make a stylized crowd scene. The men are in dark business attire, the women in dark dresses, heels, etc. They define the architecture of the room, specifically a corner. First they walk one by one into this corner, stand in rows facing the camera till they're all assembled, then walk toward us in shuffling baby steps. Shot of the empty corner. They walk back in en masse. Baby steps back out. Empty corner, etc. and two other variations. The next three parts occur together as I said, and continuously until the end. A tape recording of vague incipient vocal sounds. Eight people forming a kind of static physicomusical chorus. Physically they assume the shape of an angle, and, as in the movie, they punctuate a real corner, standing against the walls converging on the corner of a platform-balcony on an eye-level with about the middle of the steep bank of seats in that space. Each holds a ten-foot pole painted white. They hold the poles vertically in front of them. At irregular intervals, on cue from an invisible conductor, they shift the poles so that the end that was bottommost becomes topmost and so on. Being close together, on each shift, there's a great clatter and jumble of poles until they become upright. The third element is another environmental chorus of five who make simple geometric patterns on the little stage area, in between dispersions out the doors and into the audience. They also perform minimal choreographic gestures—swaying, knee-bending, flicking hands in air in unison, etc. In all: compelling boredom in elegant nonobjectivity with inexorable insistence on the definition of a space. People framing a space, or space framing people.

Steve Paxton: a strange collection of excerpts from pieces. A pornographic movie, an obfuscation of the movie by a girl who poses against the screen with a sheet (like in bed), an incident with a chicken, a sequence of several girls changing clothes as though abstracted from a speed relay, and a final section that I liked a lot for its pedestrian nonchalance. Six people on the stage area casually at their own pace go through five events: speak a line about their lives, eat something set on a table, drink something set likewise, change sweaters or jackets, perform lip service choreography—swinging the arms, bending a knee and raising an arm, lying down and getting up. Nothing to it. It looked like part of the fixtures.

December 14, 1967

Jill and friends Sheindi and Ann and their children.
Photograph by Les Levine.

DANCING IS A DOG

Remarks occasioned by a program at the New School called "Avant-Garde Forms and Sources":

Funny how you see a thing when it isn't there and when it's there you don't see it anymore. I don't clean my house but I polish my boots. Much of theatre occurs on the stage and much of it occurs in the heads of the audience. Dancing is a dwarf lady, Yvonne said once. Or dancing is a dog. Steve Paxton had a friendly dog on stage with him and they had this nice relationship. Somebody asked Steve how much of the dog's action was on cue and he said it wasn't that kind of relationship. Steve has a lot of dancing credentials. But he doesn't see it skillwise any more. His body isn't up for sale. (Economically, things get tougher.) He has a sort of casual friendly attitude about the business. Clasp your hands and there's the steeple, open the doors and see all the people. If the world's a stage nobody should mind showing off. Theatres are special gaping places, like monkey houses. At the Bronx Zoo in the ape section a wise joker played a neat switch with a mirror and a sign under it that says "you are looking at the most dangerous animal in the world." Well who did we come here to look at anyway? So sometimes an audience gets to look at itself. The Pied Piper hands out a bunch of cards with silly word cues on them. They function like a mirror. Certainly the stage is invisible. Once I remember Steve did a dance in which he snapped pictures of the audience. Another guessing game about who's who in anybody's arena. Walk out of the house and you're on, baby. The cards had name cues on them. Call out a name, a body responds and reads a line on the card. "Margy" and "Leon" stole the show for a while. Margy kept standing up on her seat to acknowledge herself. Finally she and Leon jumped into the aisle and hugged each other. Dancing is also disregarding instructions. Thou shalt break the rules to play the game with maximum satisfaction. Like even the low wit of mixing sexes. Some girl said she was David, another insisted she was George, and a guy said yeah he was Liz. Everyone was thrilled. Audiences are good to themselves.

Gus Solomons, Jr., also gave them a whack at it, but he didn't hand it over. Audience participation they call it. I think that's a slimy expression but maybe it says something about the state of the nation. Gus alternated speaking into a mike and dancing a few set movement sequences. At the mike he encouraged people to "make noise or ask questions during the piece" because "if you make noise while I'm moving it will affect your impression" and "one way to understand is to participate" and "one way to understand is to ask questions." So there were noises and questions. Curiosity about the performer. Where is your abdomen? Why does he want to know where your abdomen is? Do you like what you're doing? Why don't you answer the questions? Gus concluded by asking, "Frankly, are there any answers?" An academic question. The form of the piece is partly a question. Answers are fatal to the entertainment of questions.

Dancing is questionable. Dancing is sometimes not being there. Can you know what a thing is without knowing what it isn't? The form of Kenneth King's piece was his absence. He set it up as a hoax: a phony letter about being in Hong Kong and a brief appearance before the concert began (walking in front of the curtain) in an outfit only people who know him would recognize him in. Absent with true regrets was Yvonne Rainer. Dancing is information about an illness enforcing absence. A tape recording of a technical letter from doctor to doctor on the nature of a frightful intestinal condition. We wish a speedy recovery. Probably it's a poor joke to suggest that dancing might be a "blind loop syndrome involving a defunctionalized colon." Yvonne was represented on the program by what she does best, in this case a section called "Mat" from *The Mind Is a Muscle* performed by William Davis and Becky Arnold. Mildly gymnastic and stuntlike, changes of position without stopping, no confrontation with the audience, an uninflected dynamic, a continuum of movement with no apparent beginning or ending, very smooth and relaxed, as much not there as there—it's hard to imagine a dancing dance less like dancing than this sort of dance. It's impressive to be so unimpressed.

November 2, 1967

SHIP AHOY!

Board the "J. F. Kennedy" ferryboat noon Saturday for the avant-garde festival. First thing there's Charlotte Moorman all smiles in a maroon velvet gown. She's been up all night I guess. And there's Lil Picard who also looks chipper. She's ensconced in an improvised booth of sheets between two benches. She's got sheets on too, and a string of lollipops around her neck. Her equipment includes a lollipop peace painting and some cans of Big Apple peas. Not many people around yet. Next to Lil there's a combo setup. In a corner a light box and tape recorders and two huge plastic bags full of paper and stuff. Music later from the same corner: thunder by Stockhausen.

Ambling outside to look at the whippy bay and Our Lady from France I see on a clothesline two stiff pillowcases dyed blue and painted clouds. And somebody rigging up a blue canopy. Two bunches of white balloons fly away to the sky. A tug tows a barge carrying rusty old scrap metal. On the long bench running the length of the boat on the outside deck, three men and a girl in black tights, black shirts, black heads, and orange faces snake along a fat rope. They sport miner's lamps and hold batteries that buzz a bit. Inside, a jazz combo is very popular. The crowd thickens. Fred McDarrah says the real show is the people. Maybe so.

Anyhow I see some peacock feathers and painted feet and a guy with a black kitten in a little basket and some cheerleaders in green sweaters and yellow socks. Plenty of straight heads on the bottom decks who don't know or care about what's going on upstairs.

Outside again, approaching the Manhattan dock. Rainbow streamers flying off a top railing. Bubbles round my shoulder. A big crowd is waiting to board. David says, "How will they get all these people on. We're going to sink." Enter Carolee Schneemann. She says she made a cave environment the night before on the starboard New York side with three bales of pink foam rubber and the people devoured it destroyed it. Pretty soon I see Carolee working the foam rubber again. She's hanging it up on the starboard New York side. In a far corner there's a trio handing a mike around reading a trialogue.

I passed by Lil for the umteenth time, Uh oh. A mob is running. They're after the lady with the cello. They make a big crush around her. The TV cameras move in. I stand up on a bench. There's Charlotte in the middle and next to her Kosugi and Nam June Paik raising something electronic passing hands over a little instrument connected to the cello. Next time I look Nam June has a red pail on his head. I wander away. Hot dog and chocolate milk and back to the skyline. Those bubbles smack into an orange boat. Department of Marine and Aviation. Enter Jackson Maclow. He heads for a tape recorder by the windows. Someone propels me toward the outside deck saying "this is the only way to enjoy Jackson, through a sound-proof glass." Oh what a beautiful day.

October 5, 1967

A LIKELY STORY

Wednesday, November 1, 7 P.M., Fifty-third and Broadway, the Harkness Ballet. I'll get some coffee for a bracer. I won't look at the audience this time. I'd like to be in Picadilly Circus. Last night I was outside the Metropolitan Museum with thirty other people with my head in the hole of a plastic "dress." There was a hole for every head. Some places you go the supply equals the demand. What's the trans(attr) action at the ballet? It's way over my head. I'll be a crude customer. The *Times* will say something respectable. What I really come for is expecting in my lifetime to see one of them stop dead in his elegant tracks and scream bloody murder. No luck tonight I guess.

What to expect from Norman Walker, John Butler, Brian Macdonald? Here comes Walker's *Night Song*. I'll get my jollies somehow. Can't see the girls for the boys, who are topless.

Sleek young chests to look at, and none of them hairy. Maybe they shave. One is a yellow giant, a regular Samson. Now they stop perambulating and languidly pose in a pretty line. Museum gods. They'll show their stuff in the air soon. Put a twitch in my legs. I come for that too. There they go. That one should be filmed in slow motion. He takes off and spins twice or thrice and one leg looks detached from his body, whipping around at double the speed of the rest of him. A born highlight. So it goes.

Next: *Sebastian* by John Butler. Read the program note. A Prince loves a Courtesan. The Prince has two wicked sisters. They'll kill the Courtesan by making a wax image of her and piercing it with arrows. Sebastian the slave also loves the Courtesan. He'll sacrifice himself by substituting himself for the wax figure and taking the arrows. Guess who lives happily ever after. A likely story John. Wonder if there's any graffiti in the ladies room. I bet Butler would like to go fly a kite someplace.

Now here's the real McCoy. A classical trio, *Zealous Variations* by Brian Macdonald. I think it's quite sexy and inventive. Little black jackets with a ring of gold braid around the shoulder. Bare-assed in white tights. The girl is a hothouse plant. The boys do amazing things, first one, then the other. After you Alphonse. They're good. And cavalier too. So polite with the lady. Wait till I get you home dolly. Oh to be in England. I can't believe it. Another *Firebird* (Macdonald). Argh, they'll pay for this. I'll submit a petition for Ray Johnson to give the world its next *Firebird*.

November 9, 1967

CANCELED

Fun City is picking up. I must congratulate Elaine Sturtevant on her revival of Satie's *Relâche*. It was a total success. A cancelation can't go wrong. Things are always going wrong. Absence is perfection. "Thou ceaseth to be something thou hadst done better never to become." Life is a rain check to oblivion. If we could earn a living on cancelations we might forget ourselves when we leave the house and go straight to the sandbox. "Relâche" does mean "suspension of performance." I refused to look it up in the dictionary before going to the theatre. Someone told me there would be a performance. Someone else said there wouldn't. Rumors of Elaine and Bob Rauschenberg appearing naked. Rumors of omission. A friend said he wouldn't miss what Elaine does because she comes to his things. "But you'd better look it up in the dictionary before we go, Jill." In *The Banquet Years* Shattuck says that *Relâche* was scheduled on a Thursday in November, 1924, and the people found the theatre tight shut. A week later there was a performance. Both evenings were scandalous.

There was no scandal Monday night, November 20, at the School of Visual Arts. Westchester might find it disgraceful, but not the people I know, for whom scandal is a way of life. Well—a few of us in the lounge were mildly enjoying the joke and the good company. Niceties all around: "That's what you get for having a smattering of French." Or, "How long shall we stay to experience the cancelation?" We exit and appreciate the fine lettered poster pasted on the door: "Sturtevant—Relâche." Two people get out of a taxi and approach the door. It's Marcel Duchamp and his wife. We have a few words. Yes there's no performance. Yes "Relâche" means cancelation. Yes he appeared nude in the original production. They've kept the taxi waiting. I watch his diminutive figure retreat in the night. Beautiful. Wouldn't have missed it for anything. From Paris to New York and forty-three years in between. Nothing is deleted. That which is deleted has always existed. Whatever is is constantly in deletion. Existence and deletion the same thing.

Cancelation art: demonstration of the void in the thing and the thing in the void. Also a demonstration of subjective continuity. Monuments in the mind. Easy come easy go. In Chicago a home for the elderly is being built on the site of the landmark of the garage where the St. Valentine's Day gangland massacre took place in 1929. Last Thursday, November 16, James Byars, itinerant artist of the world, paper expert, commuter to Japan, laid out a 500-foot paper man on Fifty-third

Street between Fifth and Sixth Avenues. Fifty St. Thomas Choir School boys stretched out flat along the edges of the man to hold him down. The head was at the Modern Museum, the crotch at the Craft Museum, the feet at the CBS Building. Flusher trucks from the Garbage Department moved in with 20,000 gallons of water. They slid and skid, confounded by a sheet of paper. It took 100 hours to make and 10 minutes to destroy. The exhibit ended at noon exactly. The Donnell Library was playing a movie: *No Reason to Stay*. The half-mile of paper was furnished by Gilreth International Company which makes this dissolvable paper—a recent biochemical discovery. Spy paper. It's a sterile edible material. Spies can now eat their information. A fat man in a gray flannel suit protested the papershow by tearing up his *New York Times*. "This paper has undone me."—"Shut your mouth dame or with this paper shall I stop it" (Shakespeare).

November 30, 1967

ON A WHITE CAMEL,
INVESTIGATING EVERYTHING

"This is my year you know, the year of the gorilla in the Chinese zodiac." That's James Lee Byars, standing there in a big white woolly coat. I checked his pants. Blue corduroy. January 1, 1968, noon, I approach the CBS plaza on Fifty-third Street. There's Byars in a more familiar outfit: black felt derby hat (rim down), large blue shades, black leather suit, black silk shirt, black bow tie. A CBS reporter called him a hippie artist. He's just a conscientious maverick, enchanted by projects for disarming any bystander. He's standing in the middle of the street in the middle of a small clump of people surrounding a little roped-off area where a man is pumping helium into a tan heavy-duty weather balloon. It's capable of being inflated to ten feet in diameter.

Byars holds a spool with a mile of gold thread wrapped around it. The balloon will take off carrying first some yards of white cotton string (a tether to carry the balloon above the heights of the buildings), then the gold thread. It goes up at only 100 feet a minute. It's been calculated to rise at 1,000 feet a minute. Rising, hovering, rising again, buffeted north and south by strong winds, it gets stuck on a building someplace dead ahead, probably around Park Avenue. The second balloon explodes on the street. "Accepting variables." The next two are red and capable of being inflated to four or five feet in diameter. They rise beautifully at the calculated speed, clearing the buildings, veering off to the northeast, but carrying only part of the mile of gold thread. The thread breaks and decorates trees on the street. A couple of scavengers make off with it. It was purchased by the Craft Museum at $100. "Accepting the notion of celebration." The street was closed for the event, classified by the city police as a "street fair." The helium man launching the balloons is an expert from the New York weather bureau at Kennedy Airport. The balloons were passed by the Federal Aviation Bureau as "aircraft." Eight hours before the release of the balloons the Craft Museum had to notify the bureau about the launching and the anticipated heights (i.e., at 12:05 P.M. the first balloon would be at 5,000 feet) so that all pilots could be warned that a mile of gold thread at the end of a balloon would be flying in the area. The permit to launch the balloons was obtained only because there are no rules about sending up something that weighs less than six pounds.

Byars said he enjoyed watching the sky and speculating on the gold thread falling down anyplace at someone's door. He also says it may be on some air wave and moving to England. "It may be there when I get there." He's going to be the "extraordinary student at Oxford in philosophy for a week." He'll advise them to take him on when he arrives. Thus finishing up his formal education, having completed elementary school at the Edgar Allan Poe School in Detroit.

But right now in his white fur coat he's off to Chinatown to confer with a seamstress about a piece of pink silk, 12 by 100 feet. This "dress" will have a number of holes in it. Byars will have his head in a hole at one end of the silk, Dick Bellamy at the other end. Byars is going to be Bellamy's "consciousness ornament" for about 100 hours, echoing everything he does. He'll try seducing other people into the holes to be additional ornaments. "What is a dress?" "How do you negotiate a door in a 100 foot dress?" "How do you sit down?" "What does plural clothing mean?" "Why shouldn't a man and a woman wear the same dress?" "What is a group?" "It's a pleasure to see pink in midwinter." "Pink is such an abused color in the U.S." "I looked all day for a pink pencil." "Imagine the pleasure of just suddenly seeing 100 feet of pink." "I want to take this dress to Oxford and get the dons into it." "Supposing a million four-hole dresses 16 feet in diameter, white and cool appearing (phosphorescent algae), were available on every walking street corner on a summer day for free, popping out of boxes. People might throw off their hot stuff in the gutter and jump under these dresses. We could dress up the whole city in an hour."

Last month Byars dressed up an Ailanthus tree (tree of heaven: symbol of the unkillable infants of the extremely poor) on Eighty-fourth Street and Madison Avenue. As a tribute to this tree he wrapped all its circumferences in thousands of little pieces of red paper (hand-painted vermilion) and red string. Then he unwrapped it and the operation took a whole day.

"The best dances are by the people in the streets." One day he saw a waitress in a donut shop who had fantastic coordination and attitudes of surrender to a lowly duty. He asked her if she'd had any dance or drama training. No she hadn't. "Do you have any philosophical presuppositions that influence your daily patterns of attention-giving in submitting to your task?" No, she said, she was a part-timer. Byars asked the Jewish Pantomime Theatre if they'd send 100 white-dressed mimes to come and admire her. They thought it was out of sight. "So I flew to San Francisco and wrote on white paper 100 feet by 6 inches. 'One hundred white-dressed mimes came at once to see you,' sent it to a friend in New York and asked her to deliver it to the donut girl, which she did."

Simultaneously generous, offering himself, and demanding, probing, and pressing people for things. Underway now: a consciousness sample—ask one million people to put one minute of attention on a piece of paper and send it to the Museum (Goldovsky-Bellamy) at 1078 Madison. Next, after Oxford perhaps, a walking tour around the world to pay tribute to things like Abebe of Ethiopia, the world's Olympic champion long-distance runner, and to the insect hospital in Amedabad, India. Also to white camels, wherever they are, and to the Golden Temple of Pattan in Nepal.

"My mission is to investigate everything."

"I think of myself as a kind of cosmological cavalier."

"I'm interested in the interconnectedness of imaginative affairs."

"I'm interested in numerical manifestations. My favorite number is zero."

"I don't think we can persuade accident in our direction. Had I made some appeal to the unknown in trying to get the gold thread up I might have been too disappointed to try to get the next balloon up."

"By the way, would you ask *The Village Voice* if they'd like the remaining gold thread to inset a piece in every copy of this issue?"

January 11, 1968

WHERE'S KENNETH?

"Now what is he doing, or where is he now?" I ask myself, and determine to ask the artist if he can tell me what he is doing or where he is, as if it shouldn't be plain enough he's doing and is whatever there is there to see. This is always true of course. There is nothing more than what there is just there to see. Yet with some perverse persistence I ask questions about the creation of a figure who must remain a mystery to be effective as a cover agent for whatever he's designed to cover, which is probably none of my business.

Kenneth King's mystery man: white doctor's coat, white pants, black boots, white gloves, black gauzy looking hood, rubber snake and lizard around the neck, accessory rubber spider attached to a white pail. His latest appearance, at Judson Church, January 4, 1968, seated immobile for a long long time in a spotlight in a religious atmosphere of incense.

"This was Pablo," King says.

"Who is Pablo?" He's one of King's men and his whole name is Pablo. "Where were you during the performance?" He was out, he said. "But you just told me you told that girl she'd better leave the space." Well that's true, he was there in the wings, but then he left. An interesting development: this girl, a friend of King's, apparently decided impromptu to incorporate herself in the piece by stepping over a string separating audience from playing area and approaching the mystery man in the spotlight. I thought correctly at first she had no business being there, but she stayed such a long time and with such quiet conviction that I assumed she was intended and accepted her that way, which throws some question on the relevance of intention. Whose intention? As it turned out she expressed a collective curiosity about an impenetrable object of attention. Much of the time she appeared to be checking out the figure against the program she held in her hand.

Was this Pablo, or Kenneth, or Sergei? And who was she? "Was this Sergei?" I asked Kenneth. No, he said, he already said it was Pablo. Oh of course. "Who was Sergei?" The program said this was "A Show" to be performed by Sergei Alexandrovitch, a young Russian dancer discovered by Zora Zash, director of Global Art Shows International. "Who is Zora Zash?" He's not sure if Zora is a man or a woman. He or she was or is in Hong Kong and wrote that letter delivered at the New School (at a performance of avant-garde dancing there) about Sergei not being able to perform there that evening. I think Pablo delivered the letter.

"Was it you or Sergei who couldn't perform that evening?" It was Sergei. "Where were you the evening of January 4?" He was out, as he said. Ah yes of course. Sergei did all the dancing. That was the second part of the program. In semidarkness a tall thin man in tails and sneakers danced all around the sanctuary space, stopping at times, disappearing at times, to the accompaniment of many records, mostly Bob Dylan. Stiff torso, looser extremities. Skitter-running. Improvised inertia. Appealingly whimsical. Le Petit Prince.

"Where are you now?"—"Do you answer your telephone?"—"Are you en route someplace?"—"Do you remain yourself under varying aspects or conditions?"—Feats of devious navigation. "Now look, Kenneth," I said, "that was you, not Sergei, dancing around there in the sanctuary. I know what you look like." No, he said, it was Sergei. "He does look quite a bit like me."

I call him on the phone for final verification. "Where is Sergei now?" He's in Leningrad, resting. He's just a dancer. He carries airline bags and eats cottage cheese. He's tall, thin, nice, hardly ever talks. He calls on a blue plastic phone. "Yours or his?"—"Excuse me, I'm eating a baloney sandwich." Probably Kenneth is in Hong Kong and I've been talking to Pablo all this time. When Sergei comes to town I'll ask him where Kenneth is.

January 18, 1968

PHOTOPLAY

"What is a photograph? A photograph is a sight. A sight is always a sight of something" (Stein). That may say more than a lot of academic interrogation into the use of film (and other photoplay) by choreographers and theatre people these few years. I'm prompted by a recent concert where the dancing was no place but the films were interesting enough, in fact the films fairly eclipsed the dancing. Possibly the concert was more about films than dancing. I doubt the choreographer thought so. Certainly the films wouldn't have stood alone. Nor would the dancing. They kind of leaned on each other. But this isn't generally the case. Leaning implies a deficiency. I suppose the problem in artistic collaboration is to get the leaning properties looking so essential to each other that nobody would guess they needed each other in the first place. Then, it isn't always a matter of need—what a thing needs to complete itself, but a matter of addition—what can be added to strengthen or emphasize or advertise or illustrate a concept. What's added may finally appear a necessity (a need-lean), but the object in any case is to make it function somehow. Don't just stand there, do something, etc. Film is a new useful tool. At its worst it looks like a piece of improbable decor. At its best it's a "sight of something" we conclude we can't do without.

A classical integration of film with stage action was achieved by Robert Whitman in his theatre piece, *Prune Flat.* Interlocking references back and forth from screen to stage. Live figures absorbed by screen images which threw the figures back again, then reabsorbed them until the real and illusory became magically confused. No single camouflaging device. The cumulative deception exceeded any transient "effect." Most striking perhaps: a sequence of grafting a film of a girl onto her body, attempting a synchronization of film and live action. What was really real? It didn't matter.

In 1963 Beverly Schmidt camouflaged herself as she appeared in a red gown against a lush screen image of red flowers. That was the first film-stage piece by a choreographer that I can recall. Everyone was excited about it at the time. The gown-and-flower image was a brief interjection in a tract consisting largely of Miss Schmidt dancing in an ambience of her own image projected behind her much bigger than life and fractured in such ways that attention was directed to parts of the body not ordinarily singled out in the live performer. There was also a film of herself (the total figure) dancing a piece she simultaneously danced on stage. Here was the extension of the performer by enlargement and by double and multiple exposure that has since appealed to choreographers in their acquisition of a new toy to stretch their scope.

I have an old children's book called *Queen Zixi of Ix.* It's all about a magic cloak. The wearer is granted a single wish. When the Lord High Counsellor, Tellydeb, puts it on he wishes to reach an apple in a fruit orchard at least forty feet away and he immediately acquires an elongated arm. The wish is father to the need, or some such truism. That in turn reminds me of Trisha Brown's delightful protraction of herself in *A String* (1966). Like Schmidt, she projected a film of herself dancing the piece she danced in the flesh (both occurring simultaneously). But Brown carried herself on her back so to speak. The duplication issued from a projector strapped to her body. The images varied greatly in size and clarity according to the surface they happened to meet. I'd say the artist put herself in flight. How to succeed in orbit without really trying.

When the audience is viewing rectangles of light speeding in all directions all over the place they're in, the effect is "environmental." The audience is encompassed. Although Judith Dunn's mobile decor in *Last Point* (1964)—films of herself and her dancers at the beach, in the studio, and at various Manhattan sites, thrown by three projectors onto a cluster of seven narrow right-angle screens of two panels each, arranged in depth like a setup of tenpins—was frontally situated, I thought the arrangement somewhat environmental because the images were so diffused, fragmented as they were by the gaps between the screens, and further complicated by shifts of speed, color, and superposition. Also they were a kind of environment for the dancers moving around, between, and behind them.

More of an environment proper was created by Elaine Summers in *Fantastic Gardens* (1964) with a section called "Films All Around the Hall"—meaning just that. Any conventionally focused attention was utterly discouraged in a multiplicity of sights spatially diffused. This was Merce Cunningham's original plan for *Variations V* (1965): TV cameras to pick up the dancers and send the images, distorted by Nam June Paik, onto huge screens situated around the audience. As it was, Stan VanDerBeek provided films combining Paik's stuff with shots of Cunningham and his company, shown on a screen behind the dancers. In the version I saw at Philharmonic Hall the outsized screen dwarfed the dancers. Later the screen was proportionally reduced, integrating films with sound and live action. Environmental or not, the films here clearly served as an additive element, in keeping with a Cage-Cunningham philosophy of inclusiveness—a multiplicity of events of equal value simultaneously produced.

Okay. Addition—for other purposes: In her latest and possibly final version of *The Mind Is a Muscle* Yvonne Rainer includes a long close-up film sequence of a basketball endlessly rolling into a corner or against walls or into the feet of a sneakered "player" seen from the knees down. Placed downstage center the screen serves the obvious function of obstructing a total view of the dancing going on behind it. Like the film "player" the live players are often amputated. But I see the film chiefly as illustration of an aesthetic position. Surface-wise: Rainer has referred to "the rules and boundaries of my artistic game." The game here, on film and on stage, might be explained by another quote—". . . inconsequential ebb and flow producing an effect of nothing happening." I'd add that our associations with ball and sneakers are loaded with anticipations of goals to be accomplished. The ball here is its own object. The dance also, by the way, includes a slide of antelope in a landscape, relating to the "herd" action of the dancers enacted while the slide is shown.

A classically illustrative use of photo material was Robert Morris's projection of ten slides from a series of Muybridge photos of sequential action in his great dance, *Waterman Switch* (1965). Views of a nude man, front and back, lifting and putting down a rock. Nudes and rocks were two continuously revealed motifs of the piece. The slide sequence (projected very fast, tending to blur into a film strip) was a stunning interjection and commentary by emphasis on the facts of the dance. At the end of the sequence the nude Morris appeared for an instant against the white rectangle of a "blank," moving across it holding a rock aloft—illustrating the slides which illustrated him.

I thought Deborah Hay's film in her recent *Group I* of a large group of people walking in and out of a corner was a pointed illustration of the spatial concept of the piece: defining the architecture of a room. It was also a proxy for live action that wasn't practically feasible in the space available at the School of Visual Arts. Possibly Meredith Monk was accomplishing a similar substitution in *16 Millimeter Earrings* (1966) when she rose up in silhouette against a movie of a raging fire. Imaginative projection by illusory film image. How to be someplace you don't seem to be. Robert Whitman's lovely suggestion to his audience in *Night Time Sky* (1965) that they pretend (therefore believe) they were embarking on a journey by watching a movie of departing boats in a harbor right after entering the tent (boat) where the Happening took place.

Finally: "Found" films. Whitman's movie of an operation in another theatre piece. Steve Paxton's pornographic movie in a recent event. Lucinda Childs's excerpt from a Gene Autry cowboy movie in a piece involving the audience watching a "performing" audience watching the movie. And Carolyn Brown's newsreels in *Balloon* (1965) dramatically overwhelming two dancers as the reels played on the surface of an enormous balloon. Diminutive people posed below a puffed up global bag broadcasting its incredible news noise.

The information above is not meant to be complete.

"He's a gentleman, a scholar, and a good judge of bad flickers." The idea is, rather: "Does it hold your attention and do you like to look at it?"

February 1, 1968

TIME TUNNEL

Recently someone I know turned to someone else I know and told them that my original entry into dance was through José Limón, or words to that effect. The tone of the statement was: "Can you believe it?" I can't believe it myself. But at that time I wasn't living in this century at all. I was living in a museum. Education is a museum game. The dance part of it for me ended quite naturally. One day I broke my foot and left the studio feeling greatly relieved of the necessity to go on. In that manner at least. When the foot mended I was happy to possess two good feet in condition for nothing better than getting myself from one place to another as I was accustomed to doing before seized by a zeal for astounding myself with feats of unusual locomotion.

Of course I didn't at that moment emerge from the dance museum I had entered upon delivering myself all innocent to be educated. No, I remained devoted. José was a King. I honored his presumption. I just waited, characteristically, for other accidents to indicate what century I was living in. Actually, I went back even further (I've placed José in the sixteenth and/or seventeenth century) and spent a lot of time in the library translating a book by a French musicologist called *The Court Ballet in France Before Louis XIV*. I was pretty hot to be educated. I'm not going to enumerate the accidents that led me eventually to the time I'm living. I've lost track of it all anyway. At some point travel accelerated and I think I woke up one morning and stepped out the door into the twentieth century. Nothing looked different. My head was just suddenly empty. Naturally one of the first things I did was to privately depose the King. Thereafter I viewed the master's concerts with clinical detachment and even conceived the idea of a thesis expounding the psychology of a man whose face was so often tilted in a position parallel to the sky. It seemed significant. Even off stage: my memory is of looking up at a chin upon a daily greeting.

I began to be very interested in the novel phenomenon of dancers looking me straight in the eye. A reasonable attitude. I didn't like to see them groveling around on the floor either. Up or down seemed excessive. The dead center thing was what I first remember liking about Cunningham. Of course he went up and down. His head too. But with a difference. He didn't have his head in the clouds and he wasn't hanging it between his legs either. I mean you didn't have to feel sorry for him on the one hand, or hope for his redemption from the powers above on the other. Quite considerate. With all this and other things in mind I'd go back to see José and puzzle over his intractable habit of looking so remote. He was certainly sincere. Well, I went through some changes. First I deposed him, as I said. Then I became an academic investigator. Next I denounced him as a stuffed museum piece. Then I saw what seems very good about him, never mind his century. At last I lost interest. And now the other evening I had another attack of curiosity (or responsibility) and went to the Brooklyn Academy of Music to see *Missa Brevis* and a new work, *The Winged.*

Both works are skyborne. *The Winged* is a kind of bird-lore study set forth in a long series of divertissements (solos, duets, group, etc.) to a nice score of "incidental music" by Hank Johnson. The bird action is a lot of surprisingly inventive detail (especially for five girls in an angular predatory sequence) embedded in or welded onto the basic Limón vocabulary. Always the large fluid gliding weighted articulations of a body appearing in group form in swelling opulent, well-crafted symphonic orchestrations.

That applies to *Missa Brevis* though the dancers here move in the upper atmosphere without benefit of metaphor. The tilted heads were all there as I remembered. The group begins in a cluster stage center peering upward, possibly through a hole in the "bombed out church" where the dance takes place. José stands apart looking on his "flock" with paternal benevolence. José is sixty now. He doesn't look so much the King as the father-of-us-all type of thing. I'm still intrigued by his head. Imagine a history of the transition of style and attitude based on carriage. The proud Spaniard. The arrogant Conquistador. The stricken aristocrat. The Mexican-Indian underdog. The imperious matador. Jesus and Judas, Adam, Othello, Agamemnon, the Emperor Jones. He's played those roles. And he'd be delighted I'm sure to be a guest on TV's *Time Tunnel*—be sent back in time for tea and conversation with Bach, El Greco, and Michelangelo. He's a walking history book. The background might actually be more religious than I ever suspected. I thought of that as he lay prostrated in *Missa Brevis* in the form of a cross. He's probably simply a God-fearing man, but not in the American Puritan tradition, rather in another bygone manner of the exalted tragedies of saints and martyrs per Jesum Christum Dominum Nostrum.

February 8, 1968

WELL-HUNG

En route to a concert, I see someone on a curb looks like Meredith Monk: long hair, fur coat to the ankles. I note to my friend she has all this equipment around her shoulders. My friend says, "Everybody's equipped today." An interesting thought. To fit out, as a ship. Or the knowledge and skill necessary for some task. The best equipped person I know is LaMonte Young. Physically, that is. Perreault said it made his body become a "column of sound." Equipment as electrical current. Transmitted energy. Knowledge and skill as a refinement of the apparatus. Crudely speaking there's the apparatus. Another friend was raving about his new vacuum cleaner, especially the long hose attachment. Something about Robert Morris being exquisitely explicit in his pre-Minimal sculpture (and dances). That photo, for instance, of himself naked inside the "I-Box." His dealer said he was well hung. He wasn't undressing in public exactly. You had to open the door of the box to see for yourself. Hanging a show. Hanging equipment. Some dealers hang a good show. What is anybody showing—or transmitting? A column of sound. A monument energized. A body fathomed. Young used to talk about getting "inside a sound." Equipment. A lady's bag. A guy in a movie scrabbling in a bag, licking his lips looking for the lady's keys. The keys to the kingdom. The lady keeps her privates in her bag. Pandora's Box. Alex Hay is making new replicas of brown paper bags big enough to get into. Young's inspiration for durational sound predated Cage by about fifteen years. As a child he was impressed by the steady hum of telephone poles bewitched by their wires. A pole with the sound of its own wires. A body as a column of its own energy.

The dancing body. Pure equipment. Merle Marsicano's equipment is the body as an instrument of seduction. On the same program (Judson, February 19–21, 1968) Eugene Lion adorned his wife (Jo Lechay) with regal presumptions. Seduction become supercilious. Overkill. Equipped to kill. Or equipped for locomotion. Vehicular extensions. On the same program: Sally Gross in lateral traversal conveyed by jump shoes (foot springs); by three mats indicating bases for stopping and going on; by a jump rope with kids' pyrotechnics. Equipped for action. For display. James Waring's bodies as columns of costumes. The costume is the "thing." The envelope is a gorgeous costume. The Plumed Serpent. Dressed to kill.

Considering an inversion, there was Jack Moore's *Autopsy*. The equipment dismantled. The dance was hopeless. The idea was interior and domestic. Exploration of the body to see what caused its death. It seemed to be a love problem. ("I have no solutions, I'm part of the problem.") The problem wasn't love or death or dissection but a dead metaphor (constipated "modern dance") expressing the subject. The death was endemic to the dance. See *The Green Table* for death as a subject commuted to life by love. The loving craft. Equipment as the knowledge and skill necessary for a task. To fit out, as a ship. The ship as a body of love. Kurt Jooss said *The Green Table* was a disaster because it was the only dance he made that he was known by. One was enough.

February 29, 1968

THE HOLY HURRICANE

I've been thinking about messes and conclusions lately. Who believes that he is a poached egg is to be condemned solely on the ground that he is in a minority. I saw a beautiful demented girl on a bus about to be molested by a lousy lech. Where angels fear to tread. Who knows what happened at the end of the line. Levine says he just made the first electro-energy environment. That's the world isn't it? What can we salvage in the way of property from such an environment? The world is in a mess because of its clean boundaries. A truly messy world is a consummation devoutly to be wished. When the beans are spilled somebody loses a secret. When the dam breaks a private pond becomes a public ocean. An Australian girl thought the ocean was the sky lying on the ground. The windows become glass rectangles in their stack against the cellar wall. The rectangles are the windows of the mind. I am a wall, or a lamp, or a post, or a book, or a poached egg. The fucker on the bus thought that girl was a girl. She was too crazy to be so simpleminded. Lunacy is a perception of disintegrating boundaries. The solution to the problem of identity is, get lost (Brown). That's one way of looking at the conclusion of Joffrey's *Astarte*. I imagine Joffrey's idea was a theatrically effective finale and that it is. But I like to think of his hero being evacuated into a night of no return. If you haven't heard, he walks out through an opening made in the sheet-drop screen (upon which we've just witnessed a virtuosic mess of filmage), through two huge doors and onto Fifty-sixth Street.

I'll mention two other conclusions I've seen recently before saying what I really want to say here about a positive mess. Artists periodically are seized by eschatological reflections. A kind of artistic theology. Arpino concludes *The Clowns* with a doomsday message. Excepting the hero clown, who lives to tell the tale for some reason, they are all engulfed in a mountainous pillow of inflated plastic. On the lighter side, Aldo Tambellini (in a theatre piece on an Intermedia program in Brooklyn) got his audience playfully involved in their demise by releasing a great black balloon from the stage (the whole place meantime supercharged with an electronic racket and a barrage of visual data—superimposed slides, films of light abstractions) to be tossed, pushed by any crowd it blimps into until it bursts, which is the end of the piece. I deduced the doomsday bit from the Black Power pitch: two hysterical monologues by a Negro on tape getting after whitey. I didn't know that Tambellini's "black" art was thus associated. I think Tambellini is Italian. The piece was called *Black Zero* by the way. Well, there are these various theatrical representations of a foregone conclusion. My own conclusion is Mulatto Power backed up by the poached egg principle and worldwide metaphorical confusion. A truly messy world.

I wish to pay belated tribute to some artists who've consistently strained artistic credibility (whatever that is) in dumping their mud pies on the last clean shirt. The first funky thing I saw in New York was Robert Whitman's early Happening at the old Reuben Gallery: *E. G. Opera.* I was ecstatically horrified. I was converted. A few memories at random now: the great mess of old tires that Allan Kaprow threw into Martha Jackson's backyard; Young's burning violin (bonfire of instruments); Rainer's brilliant hemorrhage of screaming in *Three Seascapes* (a choreographer was born); Marty Greenbaum's books and books—children's notebooks, crammed with mementos of the day, the clippings and scrawlings, bulged out from wax drippings, gouged out with cigarette burns; Al Hansen's toilet paper and newspaper and spray-paint word jumbles and hopeless disorganization; and three people I sometimes fantasize into a collaborative festival: Ann Halprin, Carolee Schneemann, Joseph Schlichter. Three elderly flower children. The insurrection of the flesh. The descent of the spirit into the body. In the beginning was the body. A covenant of bodies. A theatre of gang bang. Of violence. Of excrement (paper, paint, paste, excelsior, it's all the same). A world united by its garbage.

And there was Carolee after the Intermedia concert at a party gleefully naked with two of her comrades-in-arms. O Christ, she said, Jill is going to write about this. And so I have. And now I'm going to write about the latest reason for rejoicing in the possibility of getting lost and drowning in a public ocean and turning into a poached egg. The Orgy-Mystery theatre of the Austrian, Hermann Nitsch. To twist Phaedo's last words on Socrates: Of all the theatre of my time which I have known this is the bloodiest, the cruelest, and the best. Carolee's *Meat Joy* was a sweet daydream next to this nightmare of savagery. A blood bath. A bloody brutal sacrifice. "There is no way to avoid murder, except by ritual murder." The animals and parts thereof are presented as dead before the ritual begins. The altar is a clean floor of white paper, of two tables likewise covered. The priest wears black pants and a clean white shirt. The carcass of a lamb is suspended from the ceiling on a hook. Another carcass is pinned in cruciform against the wall.

Clumps of brains, entrails neatly spread on the tables. A mass of liver on the floor. The Austrian takes his time. He has cans and bottles of the liquid which will drench everything in a common bath. He begins just mildly saturating each clump of gut, staining the white it sits on. I'm losing my taste or patience for a verbal transcription. The oblations are the blood; the man, the bull; the virgin, the paschal lamb. One is to the other as milkweed to milkweed. Yes there is a chorus. The ancient ancestral voice of the dithyramb. A beautiful terrifying noise. All at once of shrill whistles and screams and pots-and-pans of kitchen brass shattering cymbals. Yes the place becomes a holy mess. A holy hurricane of blood. A riot of red. A holocaust of bodies. This is a catechism and a cataclysm. The baptism by fire. The remembrance of things past. The resurrection and the life. "Drink of it, all of you, for this is my blood of the covenant, which is poured out for the many for the forgiveness of sins." This is the eye of insanity of the dissolution of boundary. A consummation devoutly to be wished. Inferno Purgatorio Paradiso.

March 21, 1968

OVER HIS DEAD BODY

I was privileged to be present Friday night, March 21, at Judson Church, at the most unusual manifestation of a performer-audience situation I have witnessed in a decade of attending a theatre in which the performer-audience relationship has been pushed in every conceivable direction. Unusual is a mild word for it. It was a kind of psychological trauma involving two principals and the rest of us in a spontaneous drama expressing the agony and the comedy of the condition called human. The occasion was the Destruction in Art Symposium preceded by Destruction events in Judson's backyard.

The atmosphere in the yard was a bit like a bazaar—the spectators milling around passing from one setup to another: an excerpt from Hermann Nitsch's Orgy-Mystery theatre; Lil Picard with plastic bags full of feathers set to flaming on a charcoal burner; Steve Rose standing by a frying pan on a hot plate cooking an orange and a banana; Bici Hendricks handing out ice picks to anyone wishing to hack at a large vertical hunk of ice surrounded by raw eggs; and preparations for Ralph Ortiz's chicken-killing event was the first presentiment of a rumble nobody expected. The two live chickens were strung up from trees several yards apart. John Wilcock calmly cut the chickens down and, assisted by Michael Kirby, made off with them to an adjoining yard to release them over a high fence. Ortiz later said he was delighted the chickens were rescued. He accepted the frustration of his plans as a worthwhile event in itself and reprogrammed himself by subsequently attacking the two trees (he climbed one, Jon Hendricks the other), sawing a limb off each one after a preparation (pouring) of the cow's blood originally to have been part of the chicken scene. The attitude Ortiz assumed about the interference in his thing became relevant to the amazing drama that ensued inside at a scheduled panel of the artists involved. A soapbox orator from the yard, whose hysterical blather was punctuated with a few brilliant remarks, threatened to dominate proceedings in the lecture room. Hendricks, Ortiz, and Hansen accepted him without relinquishing their own purpose and somehow finally integrated him in the total situation.

Hendricks announced a performance by Charlotte Moorman of Nam June Paik's *One for Violin,* a piece dating from 1961. I knew the piece from Paik's performance of it in 1964 at a Fluxus concert. In a rather disorderly atmosphere Miss Moorman assumed the appropriate concentration and a courteous hush fell over the room. The piece entails the destruction of a violin after a long preliminary passage in which the performer raises the instrument in slow motion from a position at right angles to the waist to a position over the head in readiness to smash the thing on impact with the table. Miss Moorman got maybe one minute into the act when a man from the back tried to stop her. She dispatched him with a push and resumed the performance. And her more determined spectator approached the table and the war was on. Charlotte was angry. She demanded to know who he was (translated: who the hell do you think you are?). He said he didn't want her to break the violin. "By breaking a violin," he said, "you're doing the same thing as killing people." And something about giving it to a poor kid who could use it. Attempting to go on with the piece she said, "this is not a vaudeville routine" and "this is not an audience-participation piece." But he persisted and I think Charlotte slapped his face and suddenly there was a tragedy in the making and shock waves in the air and terrific agitation all around. Someone suggested he give her his coat in exchange for the violin. He removed his coat but she wouldn't have any of it. I was inspired by this suggestion and found myself hollering in the din: GIVE IT TO HIM. Charlotte accused her intruder of being as bad as the New York police. He announced that "we are sitting down and refusing to allow this violin to be broken." He forthwith stretched himself out on his back on the table in front of her. As Ortiz said later—she had to over his dead body. It happened very fast and there are probably as many versions of the climax as the number of people who were there. As I saw it, Charlotte's tormenter sat up and was sitting on the edge of the table and at some moment turned to face her at which point with malice aforethought she bashed him on the head with the violin and the blood was spilled. My description can't do justice to this extraordinary situation. The ramifications are extensive. It wasn't so much a question who was right or wrong (I thought, if pressed, both were right and both wrong), but what might have been done to avert the inevitable. That seems the ultimate political question so brilliantly posed by this little war right in the ranks of those so violently opposed to the war at the top.

The victim introduced himself as Saul Gottlieb. Charlotte was contrite and ministered to his wound. She explained the point of the piece is to show that we think nothing of killing people in Vietnam and we place a higher value on a violin. She said she didn't mean to hit him but he was in her performance area. Speaking of the therapeutic value of such actions Ortiz said Charlotte was trying to displace her hostility onto an inanimate object and Gottlieb wouldn't let her do that. Our soapbox man said that if "we the people want to come into the govern-ment" (represented here as artists) "we should be able to." He also told Gottlieb he was sick because he stood there and let her hit him with his back turned. Gottlieb said that Charlotte was determined to break the violin regardless of what happened and was unable to de-program herself. The adjustment Ortiz made in his chicken event became instructive. What were Charlotte's alternatives in the face of being robbed of her artist thing? Blowing her cool she was left with a literal destruction. The irony of a symbol converted into a reality. Yet why didn't Gottlieb honor her appeal for attention? "I request the honor of your presence at . . ." etc. At what? At the daily level, let's say, how we take turns in a conversation piece. Many more things were said at the Judson gathering. The last thing I saw was a touching demonstration by Steve Rose of a simple ex-change based on respect. He requested the indulgence of his au-dience in a piece he wished to perform. He said it would begin when he finished talking and it would end when he sat down. He stood as he was and looked round slowly at the people there gathered with some slight perplexity I thought. And that was the piece. And the audience expressed their appreciation at a point well taken.

March 28, 1968

PAXTON'S PEOPLE

"Like the famous tree which is uncertain if it will be heard should it fall in a forest without people there is a way of look-ing at things which renders them performance." That's the first line of Steve Paxton's taped lecture accompanying a piece for man, chair, and dog presented in the gymnasium of St. Peter's Episcopal Church, March 22 and 24, 1968. I asked Paxton what he meant by the line and he wasn't sure but we agreed it was poetic. I've been twisting it around looking for a key to open it. "Like the famous people who were uncertain if they would be heard should they fall in a forest without trees . . ." etc. In 1963 Paxton did a concert called *Afternoon* in the forest surrounding Billy Klüver's house in New Jersey. There were six performers in the piece, or more correctly eleven since five trees were singled out to wear costumes. More correctly beyond (or within) that an indeterminate number of people, the audience, "whose shape and figure moving from place to place determined much of the timing, the forms, the ideas behind the dance." And of course the trees, all the infamous trees without costumes. Not to mention the sky, the ground, the leaves, the shrubbery. When and where does a performance take place and who are the protagonists? "I think theatre is like everything else. Any time you want theatre you just turn it on in your head."

One day I was rounding a corner with Paxton and Robert Rauschenberg. Paxton spied a truck rumbling off a bridge. He took off flying to examine I guess what he considered to be its unusual shape. I turned to Rauschenberg and said I thought it was unfashionable to get so excited about things in the street. (An affectionate joke.) Paxton brings the street into his theatre. Or puts the theatre back on the street. "Like the famous person who is uncertain if he will be heard should he fall in a forest without other people who were uncertain if people . . ." Change that to "Like the ordinary people who were uncertain if they would be seen if Paxton didn't put them in one of his dances" and you have a more or less inaccurate idea of what transpired at the concert at St. Peter's. I mentioned the man-chair-dog dance. This is a dance for dog mostly. Paxton accommodates himself to a sweet black-haired dog. Laika may not be an ordinary dog. But this is an ordinary dog dance. No tricks I mean. It's like well here's a dog and he'll do his dog thing which is just being a dog, under any street or living room conditions, and we could take it or leave it from there, the dog quality of this particular dog. Now for Paxton's people, who appear under similar conditions. *English,* a revival (1963), is not the best example of this tender attitude toward the special thingness of things (not, however, invested with anything special, that is "with problems or relationships or fantastic techniques" or the like). For all its ordinary aspects it's a rather stiff formal piece and I guess I'm partial to the recent more casual explorations of the familiar. *English,* for nine performers in black tights and leotards, combines movement derived from photo sources (photo scores, mostly of baseball action, interpreted by several dancers) and the pedestrian forms of walking, standing still, and pantomiming routine activities.

The Atlantic is a talk piece. Four people choose spots to sit close to the audience and speak in offhand conversational style, a kind of bland domestic intimacy, about (1) the colors of any situation (Simone Whitman); (2) a personal story (Tom Gormley); (3) important movement experiences (Paxton, Deborah Hay). The voices are heard simultaneously, with pauses by one or two or more for relocation; so you hear snatches of one or the other or combined snatches or an unintelligible garble depending on your place or point of view and all that.

Returning to *English* a moment—I think when this dance was done originally the performing bodies were as a whole more like Paxton's, like the "trained" ideal type body. Maybe not, but I don't recall being impressed as now by the incredible assortment of bodies, the any old bodies of our any old lives. And here they all were in this concert in the last dance, thirty-two any old wonderful people in *Satisfyin' Lover* walking one after the other across the gymnasium in their any old clothes. The fat, the skinny, the medium, the slouched and slumped, the straight and tall, the bowlegged and knock-kneed, the awkward, the elegant, the coarse, the delicate, the pregnant, the virginal, the you name it, by implication every postural possibility in the postural spectrum, that's you and me in all our ordinary everyday who cares postural splendor. Like the famous ordinary people who are certain they will see and be seen whether they fall down or keep walking in a forest with or without other famous ordinary people there is a way of looking at things which renders them performance. Let us now praise famous ordinary people.

April 14, 1968

HAY'S GROUPS

Deborah Hay's concerts at the Anderson Theatre, April 4 and 5, 1968, leave me searching for superlatives. I'm tempted with platitudes like "breakthrough" and "come a long way" which may not be so impossible for a starter. The three works here presented are one person's victorious fruits of a personal quest within the larger collective enterprise known originally as the Judson Dance Theatre. I bring up Judson here because I left Hay's concert feeling the same kind of excitement I used to feel when some one thing or another in the Judson scene shot through the general effort with glittering clarity, always affirming that indeed there was cause for excitement—not in any one thing but in a total dance revolution. Hay's work must be seen in the context of that revolution. I say "must" advisedly. A direct naive appreciation of things uninformed by a historical frame of reference is always a possibility. The entry has to be made someplace in any case. I'm inclined to the view that the broader the frame of reference the richer the possibilities of involvement. Passing from naivete to sophistication in any medium, our perceptions become charged with the complications of historical issues. The new dance movement has its own complicated history, which in turn evolved from other complicated histories (ballet, modern dance, Happenings, etc.). To define the movement as revolutionary is to observe simply that its deviation from precedent forms was much greater than its conformity to those structures.

My academic asides are prompted by the tiresome ignorance of those in influential places who, unable to come on a thing with that direct naive appreciation mentioned above, continue to distort the picture for a wider public in refusing to educate themselves to a splendid phoenix that has risen from the ashes they keep poking around in, perpetuating the myth that anything livelier than dancing money from the Ford Foundation is happening there. Money is traditionally poured into an ash heap. But that's beside the point here. A wider public may also be a pointless issue. Having said what's on my mind I could as easily cancel the thought. The artists will continue to do what's essential. Yet I see prospects of more making things merrier with the kind of informed and sympathetic exposure that would draw potential talent into this orbit of activity. I used to say it a lot—that such talent is continually snared and waylaid by the deathly institutions of the dance world power structure. And again, I cancel the thought. It takes just two to knock heads together to keep this medium alive. Fortunately there are more than two, and currently a surge of action is both reinforcing and expanding the various positions of the movement, all testifying that the phoenix keeps rising even if in the shadow of the monumental ash heaps of those incredible institutions.

What's especially gratifying to me about Deborah Hay's concerts at the Anderson Theatre is that this choreographer intelligently grasped the possibilities she set forth herself in a piece given earlier this year (*Group I* at the School of Visual Arts) to present a concert of unified conceptual energy. *Group I* was repeated here, although on a proscenium stage it looked quite different. Within a frame the two complementary groups —the eight static standing figures lined up elevated on a white table each holding a ten-foot white pole, and the five mobile figures below them—project a greater visual sculpturely impact, especially in its heightened verticality. The bare minimal choreography and the horizontal uninflected energy-dynamic of the piece (called boredom in common parlance) are thrown therefore into greater relief. I described the piece in December. Briefly: in a preliminary movie some twenty people walk in and out of the corner of a room. There are several variations on getting into the corner (one at a time or en masse) and on moving out of it (always in shuffling baby steps, but facing in different directions). An equal emphasis on getting there, on being there as a mass, on moving out of there. A subtle pedestrian stylization of a crowd scene. The live action of the five mobile performers may also be viewed this way. Walking casually businesslike on and off stage in no special formation they coagulate in simple linear patterns and go further than the movie in the very plain (anybody can do it) unison choreographic gesturing. I think Hay is working in an area here that lies somewhere between the outright pedestrian action exemplified in

Paxton's recent concert (and earlier Judson work, including the functional manipulation of objects) and the more technical dance-based choreography that Yvonne Rainer is exploring. There are points of agreement in the three areas. It's a difference of degree and/or emphasis. The eight people with the poles, by the way, aside from their visual importance, establish a musical counterpart to the "dancers" as they shift the poles, clattering together on the shift, from upright to upright.

The blasé perfunctory choreographic style of *Group I* assumes greater individual significance in the emphatic accretion of *Group II*. More of the same with unassuming vengeance. In *Group I* all performers wear black business attire. In *Group II* the shirts, pants, and skirts are in colors, some of them bright (not costumes, just the red shirt in your closet). The poles are metal and brightly painted in red, blue, yellow. The format of the piece is similar: the movie followed by two groups of live performers. An apt analogy to this variation may be a Stella black-and-white stripe painting set next to one of his vivid-colored striped works. The color here in both *Groups* is as important as the mood-tone of a Cunningham *Summerspace* as distinct from a Cunningham *Nocturnes*. The analogy ends where the energy level of Hay's *Groups* remain the same. In the movie of *Group II* about twenty people on a concrete outdoor space (a flat "ground") move in and out of the picture in a paired column, walking or running, straight, in circles, diagonals, etc., with a brief cut of chaos. On stage there's the initial impact as I said of color and sculptural arrangement. The musical pole holders are separated in two groups of four each, standing in lines on a slight diagonal bias on white tables, symmetrically disposed right and left stage. The noise they make is a gentle metallic clang each time they dip the poles into a meshed contact on cue from the conductor. The choreography below them is both informally dispersed and schematically patterned. It's a deceptively simple choreography. It looks "right" to me—just the right bland consistency. And I'm impressed by a simplicity which adumbrates the obvious while pushing us into a new realization of the obvious. A feature-less, diversion-less work energized by much more than meets the eye—by a tenacious aggressive concept. The intellectual pleasure of the concept is complemented by the physical pleasure of involvement in revelations of the ordinary. The work is feature-less in one sense but full of peculiarities in another sense—how, for instance, five people doing ostensibly the same simple thing look infinitely different in every aspect of their bodies.

All this is brilliantly clear in the third work, *Ten,* which includes the rock group, the Third Eye. I think it's a smashing piece. The rock people are ranged out upstage behind a low metal bar stretching from wing to wing. Left of center and a yard or so downstage of the bar a pole stretches from floor to flies. Bar and pole are "home base" constants for the ten dancers, all in white shirts and pants, who do nothing more (which is a great deal) than position themselves in contiguous relation to these properties throughout the forty minutes of the piece. They're in three groups: five men, three girls, a man and a girl. Each group alternates leadership in determining the position, or design, to be assumed in relation to bar and pole. When the leader arranges himself the others assess the exact disposal of the body and align themselves next to him in the same shape in accordance with their observations. The variations are interminably beautiful. Yet once you get the idea it's unnecessary to look at it and the length of the piece substantiates the idea that it's beyond entertainment (getting screwed by this "art" thing) in suggesting the total life situation of the illusion of an occasional clear configuration emerging from an equally illusory chaotic tumble (the milling around of the performers in between their positioning). The constant order and confusion of our improvised orderly and confused lives. I could go on with this: the adroit use of the rock (the cool dance, the hot jazz, etc.) but save it, there's more to come. The concert is a major achievement in the short career of a very young artist.

April 11, 1968

PIECES OF GENE

The lavender angels return from one white house to another. Gene Swenson has been banned from the Dada Surrealism show. The constant shape of the cube held in the mind, but which the viewer never literally experiences, is an actuality against which the literal changing perspective views are related (Morris). But I ask you, how much arms can you smuggle in a canoe? Gene is waging a one-man Happening against the art world. Doesn't the night always belong to the day before and early in the morning is a new day again? He went to the UN to give himself up as an international citizen. The state, Trudeau declared, has no business in the bedrooms of the nation. An intruding pig throws the family in an uproar and forces the girl to hide behind the piano.

I'm organizing a demolition team to take care of the ballet studios. If I wanted to stand the glass on its border I should want to spill it shouldn't I? Ortiz said if you don't know when to pause in Destruction Art you don't know what destruction is all about. Marta Minujin is planning a detailed description of the extermination of Penn Station. There's a story about a little Jewish boy at a Seder. Why are we here tonight, someone asks. Because the Jews killed Christ the little boy replies. Don't you know, Leonard, that you're a Jewish boy? Oh no I'm not, he said, I'm a nice New York boy, and besides I didn't do it, I was home all day.

How long will a new day always come again? God is alive but he doesn't want to get involved. Show me something new; I'll begin all over again. For that to which we are accustomed, prepare to die. How long does the day after go on coming? He wanted to know if his uncle was as glad to see him as a leopard runs fast. Rainer told me she's going to quote my review as the statement I've requested for my book. I told her she can't get away with that. There's too much quoting going on today. I'm getting a book of things that kids say. This whole business has been simplified by the children who say all smart things. Cage said he knew when she was going out of her mind because she

Jill with her son Richard.

Jill and her daughter Winnie.

would begin to speak the truth. Alan Watts told me there's no place to go in this country if you're enduring an expansion of consciousness. Gene was thrown out of the UN by the way. A strictly local approach. For how long does the day after go on coming? Consumption be done about it? Can tomorrow and yesterday creep in this petty pace from day to day?

Is the shape of a phrase determined by its time length? Correction: I said last week Rainer's trio could be viewed as a single phrase. From the definition I gave of a phrase the trio should be viewed as no phrase at all, merely a continuum. Just as Trisha Brown (on an Intermedia program in Brooklyn) had her three dancers plastered against her big film screen with forty-eight circular indentations for footholds and handholds. Moving from hole to hole and occasionally resting. Like climbing from mountain ledge to mountain ledge. The mountain shape makes the phrase, which is no phrase, merely a continuum, from ledge to ledge. For how long does a new day still come? When does a phrase keep on coming into a no phrase? Was the shape of the movement determined by the circular holes in a square screen? The holes or the screen or both?

In the dimensions of her paintings (Agnes Martin's) the current Romanticism is given a square deal. I went to a lovely square meal last Friday. Theatre activity by Bob Wilson (alias Byrd Hoffman). Byars told me it was a quincunx. A quincunx is an arrangement of five objects (as trees) in a square or rectangle, one at each corner and one in the middle. There was a huge square room. For performers with identical groups of construction material stand in the corners of a square within the square of the room. The audience sits in four groups on the areas between the corners on the parallel lines of the square. Or they form the points of a diamond if you draw diagonal lines from group to group. In the center a square space is demarcated by tape and cloth or paper. Suspended from the ceiling over the center is a piece of square silver glass. The four performers move back and forth from corner to center erecting a square house (room) of twelve two-by-fours with sheets for walls. Bucky Fuller is talking on tape. "My granddaughter saw hundreds of thousands of airplanes before she ever saw a bird." —"The fundamental changes in our life are all invisible."—

"We're unconscious of our tongue until we bite it."—"Once the environment is altered the altered environment alters our life." The house will have to fall down I think. In place of their house I see my son Richard's early block towers going up and crashing down. His own demolition team. The house'll fall for sure I think. Two performers enter the completed structure with blankets. They stay a long while. The silver square, now invisible, is the instrument of destruction, simply destroying itself. The house remains intact. Splintered glass on the floor of the square we can't see. The performers emerge unscathed. I walk over and look inside. I see the glass and my son's blocks and pieces of Gene on the sidewalk outside the UN.

April 25, 1968

SHEBOYGAN

Monday evening, April 29, 1968, I'm making irregular plans for Tuesday. Pick up photos for a lecture, go to a performance at the New School, etc. Actually I'm schlumping around the house dejected by the plunder of my TV and typewriter and some busted plumbing. Maybe I'll spend Tuesday barricading the windows. Maybe I'll buy myself a present. Maybe I'll stay in bed. Well, I'm creaking about like this when I spy off in a corner in a litter of old mail a postcard I'd forgotten about, read dimly one morning between after-sleep dozes. The card says "On April 30, 1968, in Sheboygan, Wisconsin, the Once Group will begin the trial of Anne Opie Wehrer and unknown accomplices for crimes against humanity." Sheboygan, terrific. A decision formulates with my eyes still on the card. I'll go to Sheboygan. Sounds as remote and romantic as Kalamazoo or Timbuktu. Besides I like trials and I miss Perry Mason and I've been writing about the Once Group for years—without actually saying anything. I was supposed to go to their Festival in

Ann Arbor, their home base, in 1965, but I was insane at the time. Later they came to New York but I was too battered by the new sensations to make a proper verbal transaction with it.

Sheboygan. Somebody should cover the trial. I get on the phone and make a lot of calls, accomplishing nothing. I go to bed. Forget about today until tomorrow. I wake up and begin the phone calls again. Go back to bed. By now it's almost noon and I presume the performance will be around eight that evening. Finally I'm talking to American Airlines and they say I can get a two o'clock flight to Chicago but the air taxi situation to Sheboygan is complicated and they make three possible connections. Okay leave it at that. It's close to one and I'm dressing and talking at the same time and grabbing writing material. I'm thinking I could've planned this a week ago but then I wouldn't have done it so I'm very pleased with myself as I fly out of the house all askew running down the street after a taxi. I tell the driver we have just forty-five minutes to go to Wall Street to pick up plane fare from my benefactor and then to La Guardia. He's an obliging jockey—and we make it in plenty of time.

Arriving Chicago I check out the air taxi business. No they can't put me on the flight to Sheboygan at 3:45 and the next one isn't till 7:15. But I can go on North Central at 3:55 to Manitowoc. Christ where's that? It's thirty miles from Sheboygan they say. Then what? You'll have to see when you get there madam. Fine, I'll take it. Meanwhile I call the *Sheboygan Press* to find out when and where in Sheboygan the performance will take place. The information on the card was certainly sketchy. The *Press* is helpful and they also offer to call the Once Group at the campus to see if someone could pick me up in Manitowoc. Now I'm on North Central and decidedly happy about the whole thing. Haven't been on a decrepit aircraft like this since flying from Havana to Santiago to visit a friend whose husband fought with Castro in the mountains. The cookies are lousy, the hostess is ugly, but the windows are big and when my wing dips I'm up against the glass hanging over the geography all dizzy and delirious. Then there's a shadow of us in the clouds—toy plane lit up in a circular rainbow.

Manitowoc looks like God's little acre. I'm about to ride toward Sheboygan with two people in a Hertz car when a student approaches me, courtesy the connection made by the *Press* with the Once people. He has instructions to take me to the Witt's End Motel. Perfect. The conversation is political. What do I think of Nixon he asks. Nixon would blow us all up I say. He's the head of the student committee supporting Nixon. End of conversation. So here we are at the motel and there's George, Bob, Harry, Joe, Anne, Mary, and Cynthia—somewhat agog as I am at my attention to their activity halfway across the country. George Manupelli, Robert Ashley, Harold Borkin, Joseph Wehrer, Cynthia Liddell. They comprise the core of the Once Group as it stands now. They break open the vodka and orange juice and we swap stories and already I'm writing in my notebook about the violence provoked by a performance they gave at a Midwest conference of theoretical physicists. Their piece, called *Unmarked Interchange,* always occurs as a superposition upon another cultural event. In this case the plan was to stay one step behind in phase so that while the conference people were taking cocktails they'd be arriving and while the others were dining they'd be taking cocktails. The waiters were instructed to serve them when the after-dinner speaker began speaking. Mounting anger at their chatting during the speech resulted in one man pouring his wine on Ashley's hair and breaking the glass over his head, whereupon Ashley and Manupelli became engaged with two guests in a wrestling floor scuffle. Order was restored until after the speech when the guests were watching Once's prepared entertainment of films projected on three screens (three days of television compressed into a half hour) and a little physics professor dumped all their equipment to the floor. The professor was apprehended and prevented from doing more damage but "the films were running on the floor and mucked up with the food and sparks were flashing and we were afraid of being electrocuted." I say it sounded like a beautiful mess, I mean a first-class interesting event in itself, but we agree the danger and the busted equipment were not desirable by-products of the show.

I ask them about the trial. They say it will continue in other locations. This is the first installment. They don't know how it will end or even if it will have any definitive conclusion. The defendant emerges from the bathroom and I regard her with some stereotyped prejudice. It's time for the performance so we drive to the campus, buying more vodka on the way. In the dressing room they mix the booze and juice in three silver pitchers. It's a small theatre. All the action is on stage. The trial begins with an introduction of earlier work: *Orange Dessert*. Mary and Cynthia sit on chairs facing us on either side of the stage. They do as the man says on tape: "Okay let's cross your legs . . . Now I want you to look relaxed . . . No I mean really relaxed . . . Now I want you to come all apart . . . I want you to be like a real slob . . . Okay try uncrossing your legs . . . all apart . . . Your head's too stiff . . . Let's do it like you were drunk . . . Try taking your hands off your lap . . . Come all apart . . . Worse than that . . . Slowly I want you to bring the whole thing back together . . . Hands on lap . . . Legs together . . . Would you light a cigarette please . . . Okay now you've got it lit I want you to put it out like a lady . . . Light another cigarette please . . . Now let me see you smoke that cigarette and let it come all apart . . . Come on, sag down . . . Okay get it back together . . . Would you cross your legs please . . ." And so on, about being a slob and a lady. Concluded by a succulent film of an orange. Joe and George then bring on a Ping-Pong table and play Ping-Pong with Kleenex ripped out of a box apiece until the Kleenex is gone, accompanied by another sexy tape of a girl's voice talking about her mouth and her teeth and somebody's tongue making it inside her mouth. End of game, tape, the stage is set for the trial. Mary and Cynthia now face each other (still downstage but profile to audience) seated with a microphone apiece and a small table apiece upstage of them set with the silver pitchers and glasses. Joe and George sit just upstage of the two girls and tables, each holding a golf club. Further upstage and slightly left of center the defendant, Mrs. Wehrer, sits on a chair on a very low platform facing an upstage corner. She also has a pitcher and a glass set on a small table on the platform. There are three basic elements in the piece: slides and films pertaining to the life of the defendant projected on the back wall; six voices asking and answering questions, often simultaneously; the action of the two men occasionally getting up to stroke the strewn Kleenex with their golf clubs. Anne (Mrs. Wehrer) must answer the questions put to her by an intermittent taped male voice, rather deep and ominous. Mary and Cynthia function as alter egos to the defendant, answering as they think she might. George is most like a prosecutor. I suppose Joe is too but after all he's the defendant's husband. Given the format and excepting the taped male voice the whole thing is brilliantly extemporaneous. There's a terrific tension between the abstraction of a theatrical presentation and the stark realism of the subject matter. We learn a lot about Anne. She was a beautiful young woman (she's still very striking); her marriage, her five children, her aborted children; her weight, height, etc; her scars and diseases, her amputated left leg; her smoking and drinking habits, ideas about money and responsibility; her socialite background. Like newspaper clippngs of pedigree business and coming out parties. Questions: Have you been or are you now a communist?—Does this face (Joe's) have anything to do with the deterioration in your relationship?—A girl from Norfolk married a Hungarian?—Where are the keys to the toy kingdom now?—Do you find as time goes on you're more or less responsive to other people's feelings?—Do you feel responsible for events you read in the newspapers?—They're all talking at once. I'm amazed at the intimate stuff. Toward the end George is asking and answering for everybody including himself. Where does private end and public begin or vice versa? At some deep tacitly understood level it's about how we're all on trial all the time for all of our lives and possibly our deaths. It's about pricking bubbles of secrecy, seclusion, suspicion. Making explicit what we want to know anyway and then who cares since we all share these things nobody is supposed to know about much less perhaps ourselves. And so forth. Great. The trial is a success. Nobody wins or loses. The audience leaves. The equipment is packed. George passes out on the deserted stage. He's taken some pills for poison ivy that didn't mix with the alcohol. We go to a restaurant and back to the motel talking till 3:00 A.M. Breakfast at nine and decisions about driving on to Ann Arbor with them or catching a plane back from Chicago. I'll decide as we near Chicago. I change cars on the trip plying them with questions about the Group. I'm not satisfied but I make out of it what I can, beginning with my own idea that this is one of the most interesting provocative theatre groups in the country. Bob Ashley is probably the prime mover of the group. But although he initiates many of the ideas for the works the results are always out of a collaborative effort. They live and work together in a close community. The authorship is essentially collective. Ashley is a composer. Joseph Wehrer teaches architecture at the University of Michigan. So does Harold Brokin. Manupelli teaches drawing, design, and film-making there. Mary Ashley is an artist. Cynthia Liddell is a dress designer. Anne Wehrer is a mother of five. They think hard, work hard, and drink and play hard. If their theatre evolved primarily out of a music scene it was one of the important moves in the late fifties and early sixties in each medium toward a "total theatre" crossing all media boundaries. I'm pressing them for explanations of transitions but we're approaching the airport and it doesn't seem to matter so much. The academic stuff can wait. I'm too exhausted for Ann Arbor. So long, thanks for everything. Please conclude the trial in New York. I catch the 1 P.M. back to New York.

May 9, 1968

OKAY FRED

Our eminent photographer Fred McD. was exhorting me to tell it like it is baby so I asked him how he thought it was (I'm open to suggestion) which was unnecessary from his histrionic performance in the name of all that's given up the ghost. Maybe he's basically right, I thought, but he has the details wrong. No Fred, they're not amateur children, they're probably the best trained modern dance performers in the world. But they have no style, he says. Who has no style? Cunningham? Come on Fred you can't beat Cunningham for style. But his dancers . . . and I say well they do each in their own way have style but if they had Cunningham's kind of style they'd be Cunningham and it wouldn't do to have so many Cunninghams on the same stage together. I don't mean in the sense of being carbon copies of Cunningham but in being that distinctive each in his own way. If they were they'd have their own thing with their own troupe of beautifully lubricated flunkies. At the champagne bash after the concert I said into Merce's ear over the din of the Velvet Underground that I wouldn't last more than two days in his company. He took me several yards aside and got it into my ear that he'd make a special dance for me and then I would. I was delighted but still cynical. The next night I mentioned the exchange to Edwin Denby who said, "It might be worth it to join for two days." Oh boy. Well. How special a dance could anybody make for somebody else? How can anybody make your special thing for you? How special does anybody want to be? What's special anyway? The art game seems always concerned with constructing a pantheon of specialties. Merce is famous because he's special. He's modified the star system considerably but always at last it wouldn't be anything without this incredible man doing his special thing. Merce is master even when he's being upstaged by his brilliant company. And even when he's integrated in the cool classic deadpan anonymous business of any dance he has a certain careless edge to the way he moves—in the hands, feet, head— the self-confident abandon of being master. I like the quote in Calvin Tompkins's *New Yorker* profile: "I think dance only comes alive when it gets awkward again," implying that between being awkward there's a period of submission and conformity to professional training demands. In the solos he gives himself Merce becomes the divine shape of an ungainly tragicomic hero who could only be so superbly and intricately perverse with the discipline that makes him a virtuoso expert. Sometimes it's just undoing the precision of his precise choreography as in *Scramble* when the others are being predictably precise and he's stepping around there with no special steps elaborately and indeterminately shadowboxing with himself. I asked Carolyn Brown at the festivities how come he's the only one who's allowed to be sloppy. I didn't wait for an answer. Too complicated.

Fred said to tell it like it is baby. I've got so many "like it is" ideas I feel like a critical sieve. For instance, if the official position now on Merce is that he's great and he's finally made

it, as the *Times* man said, since I'm temperamentally inclined
to look elsewhere when things get very important, I could take
the logical position of reversal which puts me back in the underground where I started (with Merce, incidentally, when he
was underground). Or I could begin where I thought to begin in
this column—with an account of the social occasion attending
this opening of Merce's first New York season. (Jasper said the
Times already did that.) Someone described it as the social
event of the season. I could say I decided to go (I didn't) when
I read about it in the society pages of the *Times*. The paradox
is that I'm as impressed as I am horrified. They must be too.
Or maybe they just figure it for playing Robin Hood with the
rich—a worthy activity. Actually I'd like to see Merce be successful out of his head so I could in all conscience forget about
it. Or, putting it the other way, I'd like to see him be real bad,
I mean bad bad, so bad we'd all love him again, indiscrimi-
nately, like in the old days. That is you know it's so bloody
beautiful I'm bored with it half the time. I'm being sentimental.
Why should anyone expect Merce to be bad in 1968. What he's
doing now is in essence no different from what he was doing
when I first saw him in 1953 and later in 1957, when the message at last bowled me over and I understood what others had
before me—that Merce was a one-man avant-garde oasis in a
desiccated landscape of Graham cracker crumbs and other rem-
nants of better days. So now in effect Merce is standing still
doing what he does best ("remaining firmly committed to dance
as dance") while many of us circle around him seeing it in part
perhaps as great as it ever was and in part as belonging to an
archaic tradition which a new generation has challenged. That's
the way it works I guess. After you've had your time to be bad
you pass into the realm of the beautiful, you filter down into
the elite, who stick you up on their walls, and call you immortal names, and make up a fucking history to go with it.

Having once been problematic for unsettling cherished
customs (i.e., dissociating the music from the dance), Merce is
now controversial for clinging to customs that didn't seem so
customary in the late forties and fifties. I recall for example
that a lot of us were so impressed by the new ballet boom in
America that we were gate-crashing the City Center to see everything by Balanchine. Merce was close enough to the clean

hard extended technical look of ballet to satisfy one aspect of a reaction to modern dance. But further he satisfied the need for deviation from both departments of our tradition by reorganizing the spatial and temporal distribution of movement. Beyond or before (or within) that of course there was never any doubt he had a special way of moving, the mark of an individual that people craved from any descendant of the romantic individualism of Isadora. What the younger generation objects to now is the unfaltering good taste of the work, the virtuosic exclusiveness of the work, the balletic idealism of the work—in short everything in the work that doesn't correspond to the new attitude of the younger generation.

Telling it like it is means telling it like it was and how it is now that it isn't what it was to the is now people. A compendium of intermission remarks could provide an index to current sentiments, but I don't get around that much, and I tend to talk to people who agree with me. Anyhow one remark was that Merce is dressing up the same old dances with decorations by famous artists. This might be a new Diaghilev era in collaborations. After the earlier period of Benois and Bakst (artists he brought to Europe from Russia with him) and certain retrograde Russian composers, Diaghilev obtained the services of the more modish far-out Frenchmen. In 1917 *Parade,* with choreography by Massine, had a book by Cocteau, music by Satie, and decor by Picasso. There's no corresponding "early period" in Merce's career of collaborations. I think Satie is the only older composer he's used and Satie is considered perennially new in the Cage-Cunningham syndrome. As for decor and costumes Rauschenberg was a kind of resident artist between 1955 and 1963. The list of progressive composers contributing scores, endorsed I imagine by Cage, is impressive. Recently: Toshi Ichiyanagi, Gordon Mumma, LaMonte Young, David Tudor, David Behrman. (The music seems much more advanced than the dancing.) In decor there's been a transition from the "complementary interior" of Rauschenberg to the application of adapted work by accepted moderns, including another durably vanguard artist, Duchamp. There's Frank Stella's bright zappy geometric movable decor for *Scramble* and Andy Warhol's silver helium-filled pillows more or less all over the stage in *Rainforest*. Excepting those pillows languishing on the floor the rest are stabilized at various heights by nearly invisible wires.

At the premiere two floor pillows made it into the audience, who did the natural thing (bounced them around) until two responsible members secured them in the aisles, depriving the irresponsible of a distraction that might have been desirable. The dancing was fine but the dance was all pillow for me. Somebody said, take away the pillows and what you have left is a "modern dance."

May 23, 1968

TO WHOM IT MAY CONCERN

Okay Fred I have nothing to add or subtract, I mean exactly what you say that I mean. Having at first been distressed that the *Voice* plant lopped off that last line from my last column now I think it might be interesting to begin each new column with the tag line from the previous column. Followed by a quote such as I got from a cab driver the other day: I lost all my marbles and now I'm collecting buttons. I like to think of the critic as a corporate sensibility. Ideally the critic would be a transparent medium giving off vapors of ideas and opinions constantly passing through the body from street to concert to cocktail party. To mean exactly what you say that I mean is to say that I mean exactly what you say that you mean or any other variation on the phrase expressing the illusion of a single mentality. Collecting marbles and buttons (and losing them) is the critic as a scavenger of the junk-scapes of the mind, strung out from house to house in the telepathy of connecting clotheslines. Sorting out signals, selecting and rejecting, separating and pasting back together, is simply a compositional problem. The telepathy in various modes of activity in the world has often been noted. How, for instance, two or several scientists in different locations at nearly the same moment will arrive at the same solutions to puzzles kicked around by their colleagues laying the groundwork for the solutions. A singular achievement obscures elaborate networks of concrete and invisible collaborations. The puzzles and solutions in the world of art may not be so clearly defined as in science but the same telepathic situation is everywhere always in evidence. At some level it's called thievery. One of my favorite ideas is that genius is a faculty for clever theft. Since one solution poses further puzzles all creative enterprise may be viewed as either a succession of puzzles or a succession of solutions. They become synonymous. There's nothing so puzzling as a solution or vice versa. What's most interesting in any case is the form, or method, by which the whole thing is advanced. What is a puzzle or a solution if not an intriguing methodology.

Shortly after I left Merce Cunningham's concert on May 22, 1968, upon seeing the premiere of *Walkaround Time* I called someone to find out when the dance was made. *Walkaround Time* is a long piece, nearly an hour, broken by an onstage intermission. The curtain remains drawn, the houselights come up, the performers had been instructed to do what they would as though it were an intermission. Thus the piece continues but with a break in choreographic formality. David Behrman's score shifts from electronic manipulations to South-American tango music, the dancers walk on- and offstage, lounge about in leg warmers, practice their steps, chat with each other, etc. I don't think Cunningham ever presented "ordinary" movement in this manner before. It was too self-consciously casual to be very ordinary but it was a drastic cut from his high-powered dance routine, and it was, after all, presented as valid nondescript movement in the context of a dance piece. I'm guessing the audience was bewildered, amused, annoyed, or interested depending on what they know about where it comes from. The reason I asked when the dance was made is that I saw Cunningham at one of Yvonne Rainer's concerts in early April and Rainer used popular music for several of the interludes in her dance, including four scenes similar to Cunningham's in which the dancers remained onstage (as incorporated intermissions) with the stage black and the houselights up, which dimly lit the stage. The dancers were instructed to remain as far upstage as possible, sitting, standing and/or talking. I could make an invidious comparison but I'm not going to. I'm interested in telepathy, thievery, feedback, and insoluble puzzles. Since the world is in a convulsion it seems suitable to concentrate on these matters. Cunningham, as it turns out, choreographed *Walkaround Time* in February and premiered it in March in Buffalo. He might have done a double take when he saw Rainer's concert in April. No doubt Rainer flipped over a bit when she saw Cunningham's on May 22. Actually the date sequence is irrelevant. Who did what first is a game which obscures a much more complex reality of imperceptible communications in a common climate of profit by exchange through tacit collaborations. The question is always asked: Where did a certain ball start rolling? That's the game of history. The answer is lost in infinite regress, but we make arbitrary decisions to have something to talk about. Cunningham's *Collage* of 1953 for instance could be taken as the origin for that part of the Judson dance movement in which ordinary movement became a basis of operations after 1960. Cage's Black Mountain mixed-media event of 1952 has been considered a proto-Happening. In *Collage* Cunningham used about fifteen Brandeis students doing a lot of natural-type things. It's fair to say the Judson vanguard might well not have erupted without the sponsorship and groundwork of Cage and Cunningham. At its most obvious— Bob Dunn's courses in choreography which led to the concerts at Judson Church took place in Cunningham's studio at Cage's suggestion. What I've been talking about with *Walkaround Time* is an interesting feedback situation. While Cunningham has been unwilling to sacrifice an aesthetic he had become deeply committed to he's been more than sympathetic to a new aesthetic for which he was partly responsible. I think he makes occasional forays into a territory which he completely understands but which remains alien to the sweep of his classical purity.

One more blatant example: In his series just concluded in Brooklyn Cunningham presented *Field Dances* of 1963. *Story* was made the same year. The latter has been dropped from the repertory because Rauschenberg's collaboration was such an integral part of the piece. Both dances are partially indeterminate in structure. Generally speaking the dancers have certain liberties within a set of directives. Given a gamut of movement they're free to perform the movement in any sequence in any part of the performing area. Speed and dynamics are also included as options. The "look" of the dance remains a constant but the variable elements render a performance that can never be the same. In 1962 Rainer presented *Dance for Three People and Six Arms* in several places including Cunningham's studio. I've heard that Cunningham expressed an interest in how the piece was made. The structure was indeterminate in much the same way as *Story* and *Field Dances*. She called it "spontaneous determination." I call it "live chance." It was a way of transposing chance (hitherto a behind-the-scenes method of making a piece as fully set as any other kind of piece) directly into the actual performance. Now sometime before all this, in his musical adventures, Cage had altered his position by passing from chance operations to indeterminate structuring. It's amusing to wonder if Cunningham was waiting for a cue from another dancer to analogize the actions of his closest colleague.

Really I can't go on with this. It seems suddenly absurd. I'd like to say something about Jasper Johns's decor after Duchamp's *Large Glass* for *Walkaround Time*. It's a fine sculptural arrangement of seven varisized transparent rectangular boxes (heavy clear vinyl), two suspended, five on the floor, each with a motif (painted on one side, outlined in black on the opposite side) from the Duchamp original, his magnum opus (1915–23) called in full *The Bride Stripped Bare by Her Bachelors, Even*. I thought of the title as Cunningham jogged in place behind an upstage box while maneuvering a complicated striptease—removing and replacing tights and shirt involving a duplicate set of same. The bachelor stripped bare by his etcetera self etcetera. And Duchamp's work was also left in a state of "definitive incompletion." Which brings me to a final note: George Brecht has written from France, in a book just released by the Something Else Press, that "Marcel Duchamp plays chess and I play Pick Up Sticks." I'm adding to that: "George

Brecht plays Pick Up Sticks and I play in the sandbox." Send your additions (or subtractions) to whom it may concern.

May 30, 1968

CULTURAL GANGSTERS

To whom it may concern: Pardon me Jill or Okay Fred or Thanks Diane. Yours sincerely. It's all the same to me Alphonse. Really the incest in the world is frightening. I was on a very incestuous panel last week. We'd been making love to each other for so long I felt I had to invent a disagreement here and there to make it look good. (Someone noted that half the panel was or is married to the moderator.) Not that lovers don't quarrel on occasion but when the lovers meet in public they present a united front and it comes over quite cozy. I'm still mystified by the function of a panel discussion. Perhaps it's just another community get-together. That sounds vague enough to make it seem both essential and unnecessary. If the idea is to be instructive I don't believe in it. Nobody wants to be instructed. I think they come to see the famous people (har). I picked out the famous people in the audience (my friends) and felt more and more incestuous about it. In fact I began to think if things went right we could've had a gang bang on the spot without even knowing it. Possibly we did. Okay now I'm gonna be serious (not that I wasn't). I think the panel was every bit as world-shaking as that thing I read about where those cultural gangsters Mailer, Schlesinger, and Marcuse got together to straighten out democracy. They didn't have a Gene Swenson at their thing. Gene is a very disruptive guy but I'll tell you I was at a party once where Mailer and another guest were beating each other into a bloody pulp, and Gene is basically a harmless democrat with excellent vocal projection. He could improve his style but what he's doing is actively creating the kind of impossible situation that reduces all that talking to zero. Are you cats ready to plug your audio into the electric-circuit sound system? No we weren't. Frankly my sympathies were divided between Gene and my commitment to the panel protocol. One question might be how to make a lover out of Gene. We could've accepted the tootsie rolls he offered us in the beginning. But by some absurd reasoning, to embrace Gene would be to deprive him of his outrageous function. By another twist, to acknowledge Gene this way or that way outside the etiquette of the panel would be to subvert our own function. But then you might ask—what happens to the etiquettes when the people start storming the Bastille (by that time I hope to be squatting by the seashore mindlessly under the sun upon my knees in the sand). So at some level the panel was Gene the people raging against the authority of us the government. (Do not go gentle into that good night.) That Gene was ejected finally was the power of the law. Since I'm a minor criminal myself I felt uncomfortable about suddenly being on the side of the law. I would have objected if I hadn't been deadlocked as I said by my divided sympathies. When Gene was up there on the balcony screaming quotes from Mao or Ho Chi shortly before ejection Yvonne was sputtering to me to do something because I'd promised I could "handle it" but I thought it was handling itself. I mean it was just another Happening. Assuming authority is one kind of occupational hazard and Gene knows the price he can pay for being an uninvited bully. Artistically, we were a combine of two simultaneous events not brought together by single design. Audience participation in the form of questions from the floor belonged to our event in the accepted protocol of a panel. Another exception was a muted expression of Gene's vocal apoplexy. For a few minutes a young man quietly made his way through rows of audience members. Later he asked us what we thought of his performance. Meredith Monk said she liked it and I said I liked it too, that he was wearing a nice maroon sweater and a pleasant beard (moustache). Simone Whitman thought it was uninspired and unimaginative. (When does the government accept the people as inspired?) I might have added he neatly illustrated an issue posed by the panel. The title of the panel was "Dance and Its Alternatives." Robert Morris, the moderator, said he devised the title and that it wasn't especially relevant. I thought it was. Actually Morris disposed of it at the outset by defining it historically as the cleavage between dance traditionally based on studio techniques with concomitant "performing" attitudes, and dance reconsidered as a response to tasks, rule-games, objects, and the like. I thought of it also in a broader sense of an "alternative" being an attitude about dance as a constant activity in the world whether it's framed in a box or wandering on the streets. I suggested that if a groovy president proclaimed holidays like "tomorrow everybody will be dancing" eventually the population might think of themselves as dancers and so what. My panel companions have a greater vested interest in dance framed by a box to be viewed by invitation only (I could always be a "street critic") but they're completely hip to the nonsense of both the box thing and the street thing and I feel confident that as artists they'll continue to provoke controversy in their funambulism over the confusion of streets and boxes.

Meredith and Yvonne discussed a very interesting subject of static dancing and imagery. Like the difference between Yvonne's dancing as static in its repetitiveness and uninflected energy dynamic, and Meredith's "still" images as static in a more conventional sense. I liked Meredith's explanation of a recent event in her loft which consisted in part of performers in repose located within open white boxes, cubes, rooms (or what) —the sculpture of Julias Tobias. She said she was reversing the usual situation of a static audience and mobile performers. This reversal in one aspect or another is the beautiful controversy of the times. I'm quite happy about the confusion if it doesn't result in mutual extinction. The inflammable issue of audience interference is one vital aspect of the whole mess. And once an audience is mobilized how do they know where the artist's work ends and theirs begins or vice versa. How does the artist know? At last, who is the artist?

Possibly the discussion of training and body types was also relevant. How do you accept or deal with fat, ugly, knock-kneed, or involuntary tics. Steve Paxton's democratic people concert was commended or questioned as an example of sympathetic toleration of a variety of types as performance material. I quoted a story I heard about someone who wasn't eligible for the Cunningham company because her ass was too big. Simone was talking about being in shape or out of shape—an occupational disease of dancers. I wanted to know how it was possible to be either in shape or out of shape being as how a shape is a shape. Yvonne was talking about her need for exercise and I quoted another story about an organization in California called "Athletes Anonymous" where, say, if one member is seized by an urge to play eighteen holes of golf he'll call another member who hastens over with a fifth of whiskey. One member said whenever he had the impulse to exercise he'd lie flat on his back on the floor until the impulse passed away. Sounds like an interesting dance. I just received a letter by the way from John Perreault. It says: "Jill Johnston plays in the sandbox; I play in the sand." Lucky bastard!

June 6, 1968

RR

Some time ago I said the first time I saw Rauschenberg's goat I thought it was a Rauschenberg goat and it didn't remind me of any goats I had ever seen in the country. Also that the first time I saw Jasper Johns's American flag it reminded me of all the American flags I had ever seen but I liked Jasper's flag better. Further that Marcel Duchamp's *Urinal* is in a private collection. And that Robert Watt's heavy chocolates looked frightening for what they would do to your teeth. The name of the game is dislocation. George Manupelli just sent me a wooden sandwich (thanks George). A simplistic view of art is that artists are always wrenching things around to create novel effects. There may be nothing new under the sun but there's always a new way of rearranging the commonplace. The Rauschenberg goat, the Rauschenberg rooster, the Rauschenberg eagle, the tires, the bed, the pillows, the shirts, the ties, the photos, the fans, the chairs, the umbrellas, the Coke bottles—it's all been well documented. The high potential associative value of the images, etc., the celebration of the banal, the permission of accident, the breakdown of distinctions between painting and sculpture, etc., the juxtaposition of disparate elements in the best tradition of Dada, Cubism, Surrealism, etc. I was one who was knocked out by the retrospective in 1963 at the Jewish Museum. As a Sunday art critic I took it in stride. When Rauschenberg moved into the underground dance scene with his theatre pieces I was more perplexed, but I'll save the psychological involutions for my memoirs.

His first piece was *Pelican* in 1963 at a pop festival in Washington, D.C. True to form, the piece was dramatically aggressive. He took full account of the space, a huge roller rink, and furnished it with a basic appropriateness of roller-skating. The other properties included a beautiful dancer (Carolyn Brown), a tape collage, two pairs of bicycle wheels on axles and two parachutes stretched with spring steel rods to flatten them out, fastened to the backs of the two skaters with pack racks. I thought it was interesting enough to see a couple of his familiar images mobilized in a time-space continuum but the piece for me was just okay or not so okay. I didn't think about it much. His next venture was *Shotput* in the spring of 1964 at Stage 73. All I remember is a flashlight in the dark. Later it occurred to me that Rauschenberg was a frightened performer (after all he'd been associated since 1955 as set and light designer with the Cunningham Company) and a dance in the dark was a suitable initiation in New York.

The next one I'm really sorry I missed. It was presented in Stockholm later in 1964. It involved a descent into a big barrel of water and a slow processional exit accompanied by a cow. With *Spring Training* and *Map Room II* I'd say that Rauschenberg began to analogize in theatre the provocative complications of his paintings, silk screens, and combines. Both pieces abounded in striking images, just offhand: the turtles in *Spring Training* conducting light (attached to their backs) all over the floor; the artist in formal wear with dry ice steaming up from a bucket suspended between his legs; the girl in *Map Room II* squatting inside a truck tire; another girl changing positions on a contour couch ("the image wasn't couch and wasn't person"); or the artist traversing the stage his feet embedded in high clear plastic blocks, picking up and putting down two unwired neon tubes which lit up when he touched them. Rauschenberg has said that one performance of *Map Room II* was too stretched out, making it a linear piece. Stretched out or compressed it remained for me a linear piece and beyond the intrigue of singular combined images I couldn't get the whole thing together in my head. *Spring Training* was a long sprawling event which, again, aside from impressive incidents, was a series of parts that might have been a dozen different pieces. I could see them in *Barge* (his enormous silk-screen mural) unified by space but I couldn't see them in time. The problem was time.

In a series of four concerts recently given by seven artists at Bert Stern's studio Rauschenberg presented *Linoleum*. I didn't see its first performance in Washington, D.C., in 1966. *Linoleum* is also complex in its multiplicity of images but here the time-space problem, if it existed as I like to think, is happily solved. It's a terrific piece. With some linear overlapping, the bulk of the incidents are bound by a simultaneous presentation, and for all the weird coupling of images there are homogeneous relationships which also make the work coherent. In his combines Rauschenberg almost always somehow consummately organized, unified, the most heterogeneous elements. In *Linoleum* there are common vehicular elements, though each one is a unique entity with no logical relations to any other, and the three prominent images are a "combination of two independent elements being forced to operate as a single image." The girl in an old white lace gown seated on an old high-back chair with a pile of spaghetti on her lap is as wild as the fur-lined teacup, if you still think that's wild. Her chair is on a platform on wheels pushed around by another girl, in transparent plastic, who uses the spaghetti to make linear patterns on the floor, possibly ringing the girl-chair-platform, but that's unclear because she's always pushing the vehicle inside or outside the patterns. My impression is that she was outlining an object that refused to stay within its bounds. This space idea was beautifully projected by Rauschenberg who was walking around, also dressed in transparent plastic (I thought the semi-nudity in the piece was very sweet), outlining with chalk several small white objects (Robert Breer's sculpture) which moved quite slowly of their own accord, outside the artist's markings.

Another vehicle was a man lying prone inside a long low wire mesh cage (two hemitubular chicken-wire coops on wheels joined for a length of sixteen feet) also containing six chickens. Stopping occasionally to eat his supper (cooked chicken) he propelled the craft at random around the space with his hands. Another contraption was a man haltingly mobilizing a bed as he stood in the middle of its wire springs. At one point a white plaster schmoo-like container was placed over his head and torso, so here was this absurd man-bed-plaster image making the scene with the chickens, the spaghetti, and the whatnot. An important whatnot was a sheet-screen rigged up three times (beginning, middle, end) between the audience on a clothesline. The movies projected on the sheet, accompanied by a loud collage of voice-music travelogue stuff, were water and vehicle events—the first two of boats (like paddling in the rapids), the last of planes zooming off a carrier, with the appropriate supersonic roar on tape. A steady binding device in the piece was the constant buzz-whistle sound issuing from an electronic device that Rauschenberg wore at his waist.

My description is not complete, but I hope to convey a sense of the formally integrated bizarre juxtapositions which I experienced. Referring once to his collaboration with Cunningham on the latter's *Story,* Rauschenberg noted that in one performance, when he and Alex Hay did some ironing on stage, that it might have been difficult to tell if they were choreography or set. It was a kind of live passive set, like live decor. His theatre pieces are live collage, at once both set and choreography. There's an intimate relation to his early combines, to Happenings, to other intermedia work, and to the work of his dance colleagues.

June 13, 1968

THE GRANDEST TIGER

Prometheus stole fire from the gods for mankind and was punished by being chained to a rock and his entrails were constantly torn by an eagle. C'est toujours la chose, Monsieur Charcot, savez-vous les petits chiens dans la rue? Remember Renoir. Remember Pearl Harbor. Sometimes when I'm sitting all by my crazy self, it's perfectly true I don't bother about my groaning. I am no more philosophical than my legs. All general statements about truth are in the end amplifications of man's appetites. The soul of man is a memory and a handshake—sentimental spectacle in which to luxuriate. You can't hear God speak to someone else, you can hear him only if you are being addressed. That is a grammatical remark. The poetry of punctuation. The question Does something exist? is a declaration of its existence. Light is a lubricant binding everything into a visual unity. The limitlessness of the visual field is clearest when we are seeing nothing in complete darkness. Please take care of your servants strapped to the black caisson. Please take care of your servants rammed up behind the police barricades. The day was any old year when the leaves are getting pretty and looking old at the same time. So the tiger put on Little Black Sambo's trousers and went off saying "Now I'm the grandest tiger in the jungle." We should also ask if the crocodile means something when it comes at a man with open jaws. You have been chosen to play the part of a dead soldier. When the parts of a centipede are severed each part takes its own time about dying. When is the centipede dead? I just don't know what to do; I am falling apart. I was happy to have had the opportunity of playing a minor part in this project. I had said I thought the length of anything was just long enough. In partially unknown places . . . the flare-up and die-off, like like scenes lit by lightning. I did not want to see it, the blood of Ignatio over the arena. But this is history, lady. All of her leaned up against him at once. It was to have been a gay occasion. Crack-bones, rye-bones, mud-bones, flesh-bones, whole cities of bones and skies of hailing bones. Make mine manhattan. Wild roses for you, baby. A bird in the hand is worth two burdens in the bush. The captains and the kings departed returned today to the American earth. The day was any old year and Cobble Hill is not elegant bashed in against the rocks. If the people on the opposite side could look they would see only the backs of their heads upside down. Their hatred was frozen into a permanent depression. The movie shows that for them life has been one long rehearsal. There's so little to do and so much time to do it in. Is the length of anything just long enough? If you don't like the meat dish do you have the right to eat all the salad? Resist the poetry of punctuation. Eat drink and be merry for tomorrow we may hope to do the same. A pair of hands slithered around the gunman's throat. After we shoot you, we blow you up, then you go home and hang yourself. A sentimental spectacle in which to luxuriate. Someone who has just escaped the fear of death might shrink from swatting a fly, though he would otherwise do it without thinking twice about it. The social workers are going into the homes to teach the mothers how to play with their babies. Be it ever so humble there is no home like place. It was to have been a gay occasion. Everything, from that time, was settled by argument. The poetry of punctuation. In orgasm, all the splendor and misery of representative government. I thought the bathtub was broken. C'est toujours la chose, Monsieur Charcot.

June 20, 1968

DANSCRABBLE

The dancer stops short in her initial flight track, a full open run of high expectation, steps back slowly, a hand at the chest. Look down first, Madam, before stepping up, your hat is slipping. You're not supposed to smile when I enter the room. But I thought . . . You thought . . . All my trains left ages ago.

Just because you imagine you've nowhere to go. Why don't you write a book called *Supply and Desire: An Introduction to Economic Psychology?* A woman who wants to show off her furs will cross by the North Atlantic route; her figure by the South Atlantic. Does it hold your attention? Do you like to look at it? Do you dip the scent in the bottle before uncorking your pleasure? The least gesture is permissible. Walking on straight knees, on flat feet, twisted torso extended at a right angle from the hips, elbows sticking out from fists plastered against the ears. Her veined hands ran quickly over her pearls and the feathers around her neckband. She has a special way of cutting off an impulse with a fragile dab or jerk so that the continuity is oddly disrupted. She could be hanging herself—one arm stretched above hunched shoulders, head and neck pressed with tortured tension against the left clavicle. We even need volunteers to tell you how badly we need volunteers. I blow my whistle once for my butler, twice for my valet, thrice for the maid, six times for tea. When I blow something may happen, or it may not. I experimented with chance briefly and found that the possibilities are infinite, and that I am no more interested in infinity than I am in one given thing or another, or in no thing at all, than in a single way of arriving at one thing. I never noticed the clock lying in the crate and the lady who kept coming and going without saying goodbye or hello. Does the world live in order to develop the lines on its face? Do women see a uniform as a symbol of death? I can assure you I feel the visual image to be two inches behind the bridge of my nose. The torso and head thrown back, held there a moment, the arms angled, bent at elbow and wrist, up over the face, to reinforce the ecstatic arch. The romantic attitude is nowhere so clear as in the fall from that effort, for while the legs take the weight of the body into the floor, the arms remain stretched, the gaze follows the arms, and the torso sinks to one side, still hoping for the impossible. Advance token to the nearest railroad. Is this the way the world will end? I didn't get kissed nearly enough. What an old maid I'm getting to be, lacking the courage to be in love with death. Of course I couldn't risk opening the door. I try to reflect the flow and concentrated variety of the music through the interlaced bodies of the dancers rooted to a central spot on the stage. Don't music up no gravy on my spoon. I measure out my life in coffee cups. Genius is a faculty for clever theft. Martin Luther sat on a privy to tell the world the truth. Einstein had his in a bathtub. I'm reading Wittgenstein with great pleasure, not understanding a word. And I couldn't read a goddam comic book until I was almost in seventh grade. Are you hip to it? I have nothing to add or subtract: I mean what you say that I mean. The Ostiaks of the river Ob. The boobies of Fernando Po. Any time is a good time for a letter from you. He flashes a smile in all directions. She raises her hands with the palms outward and turns in profile. She says the police will never die properly until they are permitted to make obscene remarks like the others, inside the room with an unobstructed view of the landscape through the windows. They put her cat out on the street but fortunately she brought back a dying rabbit. It's impossible to please a satisfied woman. In her final pose, her head resting against the angle made by her upraised arm, there was the intimation of the acceptance of isolation. Should the raft be abandoned after the stream is crossed? It's wonderful the way I'm not interested. She does things like hitting herself into staggers and distorted backbends, or examining her feet as she lets her heels roll dangerously to port and starboard. Not much she can do to stop what's been done. She makes several footprints in dirt or coffee grinds by stepping in a small pile of it and using a brush to sweep off the excess to create the outline of foot and to push the dirt ahead for the next imprint. Mark a neutral area extending six feet on both sides of the net and prohibit throws and scores in this area. The player will find that the places in which he performs his actions will be determined by the wanderings of the other players. Did you realize that the Greeks dreaded the idea of a life everlasting? They never walk through doors, they pass through walls. Was my visit through a window an affront to your definition of a door? Should we reduce the universe to unexceptional exceptions by discovering laws of the correlation of exceptions? This whole business has been complicated by people who say all smart things. Look man, mind yer beezwax, I like to walk piggyback. They put platformate in my banana daiquiri and I crawled five miles further.

August 15, 1968

RETURN OF A PERPLEXED NATIVE

LONDON—June 27, 6:00 P.M. I'm in the Pan Am building at Kennedy. It looks like the whole world is going someplace. I've got a pocketful of vital documents including a round trip ticket to London. Two friends quite hip to my fatherland fantasies are dousing me with Bloody Marys. A few weeks ago someone asked me why I was going to England. I let off some crusty steam about Anglo-Saxons being snobbish about the place. I should've just said I was going to visit my father. Though he's long dead, that's perfectly true of course. I think I was conceived on a transatlantic voyage by a simple American country girl and a debonair Englishman who had a lot to do with making those big church bells. I was born in Finchley outside London. The last thing I don't remember was another journey—on the SS George Washington bound for New York. The memento was a faded photograph of me in the arms of one of His or Her Majesty's royal sailors. No doubt the only time lag between then on the big ship and now as I board the metal air bird is infantile amnesia. I mean when you return to the scene of the crime it's as though you never left. I never left England in my head. It's as archetypal as a Roman bathtub. With a few Bloody Marys under my belt I'd sing "Lloyd George Knows My Father" at a papal audience.

I'm imagining that as soon as the sun sets in New York the sun will rise over England. In effect it almost does and I lose a night's sleep. We're supposed to take off at 7:00 P.M. and arrive at 6:40 A.M. (midnite our time). We wait for two hours on the runway and I soak up three Martinis. A British lady across the aisle is hard put to amuse her two West Indian children. Everybody's drinking and getting hungry. The sign for smoking and seat belts flashes on then off then on, etc. The trip is a standstill. I'm driven to conversation with my neighbor, a theoretical chemist. He's also connected with nuclear physics and government defense. His righteous explanation finally of his lifelong dedication to the principle that "might makes peace" is lost in the roar of our takeoff. Enough of that. It's close to 7:00 A.M. The new sun was a dream. I'm drowning in coffee. I'm glued to the window. I see patches of land. That's got to be Ireland. The pilot says we just passed over Shannon. Next there's a glimpse of a coastline, very green and all jagged like on the map. The rest from there on is wiped out in cloud banks. I'm getting dizzy in the descent. Can't see a damn thing. They say it's raining in London. We land in the fog. Good show.

The airport scene is close to a psychedelic nightmare. The whole place is upside down. The mottled gray and white concrete floor might as well be chartreuse. The advertisements are Warhol in neon on Broadway. The passport man must be a Martian posing as a British spy. The customs man wants my life for the excessive baggage of 160 cigarettes. The bank man is taking my traveler's check for a bunch of phony-looking coins and papers. The accents and vernacular are coming at me like flak on a hot tin tower. I wasn't born here. It must be a joke. I'm tired. I'll fall down if I don't add some refreshment to the gallon of coffee consumed on the plane. I go to the refreshment place. The milk looks yellow and the cakes or rolls look as bad as the currency. I begin the charming helpless bit of extending one pawful of coins and the other pawful of paper and letting them take what they say it costs. I leave a couple of dimes and nickels in the coin hand to complete the identification. I'll be a foreigner with a vengeance.

Next thing I'm on my way to the only place to go: Victoria Terminal. The vehicle is a fire engine, actually a gorgeous red double-decker bus which you enter on the wrong side and which travels on the wrong side of the road. I'm glued to the window. It's raining. You can smoke in the bus and the strangers are being quite friendly together. The rows of houses I fancy to be Hansel and Gretel-ish. Like as not the doors and window trimmings are painted bright colors. The flower beds and box gardens are not what you'd expect of a city suburb. The grass is terrifically green. The bus stops are canopied. There's a huge ad of a multidecker sandwich in perspective. There's a Chiswick Maternity Hospital. There's a Surgery—an old fashioned name for a doctor's place of business. There's a hell's angel on a lavender motorcycle with a bearskin seat. I exclaim out loud when I see the first bobby. Best looking blokes around. The gentleman next to me says "and he hasn't got a gun." It's a long ride so we talk a while. He remarks on the violence in the States (they all do). Yes I reply, I suppose we're run by a bunch of gangsters. Cowboys and Indians and all that. Yes, a pity isn't it. Can't you take the guns away from the people? And the police? And the President? Then I'm a little defensive. Of course your history isn't so pretty either is it? No it isn't. Then he refers to "that colored chap of yours" who was done away with. I say he's something of a saint there you know, to whites and blacks alike. My companion is an English businessman who works in Thailand. He's just back from Chicago for a vacation on the Isle of Wight. I remark on a row of ugly houses. By this time I'm disappointed by anything that doesn't look Hansel and Gretel-ish. He says I should ask my taxi driver to go by Buckingham Palace. At the terminal I queue up for one.

Where do I want to go, the driver asks. To Russell Square. Any particular hotel? No, would you just drive around please and find me one. Really madam, that's impossible, we might never find one and the pounds will keep going up. Okay, I get out and go back inside to queue up at a tourist desk. They make a reservation at a National Hotel. The taxis are too much. They're narrow but roomy. They're all identical. They look like shiny black trunks. The windows don't roll down. You pull them down or push them up by a metal piece running along the top of the pane. We go by Buckingham Palace. It looks like the New York Public Library. We pass by the British Museum. Somebody had described it as containing the plunder of Britain's rape of the world. I'll have to go. It's around the corner from the hotel. The hotel is absurd but I pass out for three hours, then get up and drink some abominable coffee.

I decide to go on a "tube" to Picadilly Circus. I'm still disoriented. It's because I'm exhausted and all the details are different. The signs, the people, the traffic, the currency, the telephones, the butter, the newsstands, the toilets, the toilet paper. Two Americans help me on and off the tube. Lovely trains. The seats are like couches with red leather armrests. The windows are framed in old polished wood. You can smoke on them too. When I've "done" Picadilly, nearly bumped off by looking in the wrong (or right) directions for the cars, I'm homesick enough to walk into an American movie. I sleep on that and wake up refreshed at last, ready to be an ugly American tourist.

Back at the Palace I do what everyone else is doing: peer through the huge iron and gold gates at the bleak facade and the two toy soldiers in the red coats and tall black fur hats standing at attention in front of their boxes or stamping three times as they turn on their guard walk, right arm swinging much higher than necessary. I really know I'm a tourist when a lady next to me approaches a bobby and, visibly palpitating, asks if the Queen is in residence. Enough of Buckingham. It isn't old enough. Already I'm seized by the antique fever. The older the better. I walk down the Mall (I say Mawl, they say Maaal) toward Westminster Abbey. The Abbey is impressive. It's black from being so old. Inside a service is going on. We have to wait in a crowd at the back. I rest myself on somebody's sarcophagus. The Gothic aspiration in sheer height is staggering. After walking along the side looking at monuments and inscriptions for five minutes I'm saying to myself this place is a goddam cemetery. I ask a cleric about it. He says yes indeed this is the biggest indoor cemetary in the world. More than 2,700 people are buried here. They're stashed in the walls and stacked under the floors. I say to the cleric I'll bet these people paid plenty for the right to have their kin buried or monumentalized here. He says yes indeed, the Abbey for many years needed the money for building and restoration. Now they can get in only by order of the Queen or Parliament. The inscriptions for famous people appear in embossed gold all over the floor. "Hic Depositum Est Quod Mortale Fuit Isaaci Newtoni." Next to Darwin there's a William Herschel who apparently invented fingerprinting for Scotland Yard. As I'm walking over William Gladstone and his wife Catherine a lady exclaims, "You just don't know who you're stepping on here." In the Poets Corner I dig four of them right together: Eliot, Tennyson, Browning, and Masefield. As for the Kings and Queens, they're closed to the public right now. I'm thinking this place (and many others) must have been in a twit during the war. Yes indeed, another cleric says, that part of the roof was bombed to the floor, and the royal tombs were removed to the country for the duration. The whole architectural situation in London, by the way, may be viewed as "before and after" two disastrous dates: the Great Fire of 1666, the Great War of 1939. A particularly cogent inscription is in the center of a courtyard bounded by Temple Church and more modern structures: "Lamb building stood here, built in 1667, destroyed by enemy action 11th May, 1941."

Dear friends whom I miss: the above was written three days ago. It's now July 3, 1968. After Westminster I took a gander at the Thames and the Parliament buildings and went on a tube to Kensington to visit the wife of artist Joe Tilson. I've been to St. Paul's cathedral and St. James's Palace and the justice courts and Dr. Johnson's house and explored an ancient railroad station. I've had four different places of residence and am now happily at home in the liftlike flat near Regent's Park belonging to Yoko Ono, American-Japanese artist, daily appearing in the scandal sheets here because of her connection with John Lennon. I spent a discotheque evening at I.C.A. (Institute for Contemporary Art), an evening at the Arts Lab (for so-called underground film and drama), and an evening with the Beatles at their recording studio in St. John's Wood. I'll report on these next week. Also the Royal Ballet which I'm going to see tonight. I wouldn't be caught dead at the Royal Ballet in New York. Dancing here is nothing but royalty so far as I can see. I like London by the way. It's a big busy city, but it's gentler than New York.

July 11, 1968

GETTING BATTER ALL THE TIME

LONDON—Things can become more interesting here once you abandon the Palace and Tower tourist gigs. The Tower of London was my last jaunt on that circuit. Afterward I stopped by the Mermaid Theatre to see a rehearsal of a "modern dance" group from the School of Contemporary Dance. Actually the Tower was a lot better than whatever these kids were doing in some old-timey Graham and ballet style mix.

Much better than both was a visit after that to a place of business known as the Whitechapel Bell Foundry, the oldest foundry in England, dating from 1570. The present founder showed me round the various casting operations. The copper and tin bells are cast from molds, the bigger ones in a huge pit. They make carillon bells (played from a central keyboard) and bells for ringing changes operated by hand and rope. The establishment looked medieval to me. It's an ancient proud craft. They served tea in an old oaken office and told me a few things I didn't know about my father's foundry in Croydon, now defunct in bells but active in clocks. The beautiful coincidence was that I happened to walk in on July 4. Not hearing any firecrackers, I wouldn't have known if they hadn't said so since I'm not keeping track of the days. They mentioned it because they made the Liberty Bell for Philadelphia in 1752 and are now in process of casting 2,400 replicas of it, one-fifth the size, to sell in the States for the bicentennial anniversary of the revolution in 1976. On my way out I appreciated a large photo on the wall of the present founder as an infant in the arms of his mother playing hostess to Queen Mary and King George visiting the foundry on some bell occasion or other.

As for royalty in general here: what I gather is that there are those who will stand twenty-deep to watch a coronation procession and there are those living in 1968 who think it's absurd or don't give a damn about it one way or another. If the expense account for royalty were abolished the money would go for a Polaris submarine or some such. They don't think much of Mr. Wilson here either. I heard their equivalent of sending LBJ back to the ranch in a verse made up to the "Battle Hymn of the Republic": Send Harold Wilson in a spaceship to the moon. I hear it's impossible to starve in England and there are certain fine benefits like the free medicine, but their wages are outlandishly low proportionate to the prices of things. Backward in wages, heating, plumbing, dancing, and all sorts of royal bullshit, but advanced in subway upholstery, in general civility, in wit and humor, in rock and pop, in parks and fountains, in sex for all preferences. I'm enjoying some amusing juxtapositions and paradoxes. The censorship is tight for a play but nonexistent in the form of literally dozens of strip joints in the Soho district followed up by signs like "French instruction by Martinique." On Yoko Ono's wall here is pinned an old letter from John Lennon who offers sympathy for the trouble Yoko had in showing her film of bottoms. Still, he says, it's encouraging in a way, as he thought the Lord Chamberlain didn't know his arse from his elbow.

You walk out of the Royal Opera House into the stench of the flower and vegetable market. You walk out of the stuffy National Gallery into Trafalgar Square busting all over with pigeons and hippies and some charming pavement art in colored chalk. About the Opera House, by the way: its equivalent in New York is a brash monster next to this spacious but intimate warm elegant tastefully ornate expression of whatever it means to be there. I couldn't see the ballet for bathing in the Victorian luxury of the house. Somebody in the States should buy it in a package deal with London Bridge and I'd go to the ballet all the time.

About the National Gallery: I hadn't meant to go but after a pub lunch with George Brecht and his English girl friend my feet happened to take me to the vicinity so I walked hastily past all the suffering and suckling Christs and happily landed a fantastic Seurat I'd never seen in reproduction and three paintings I'd always much admired in reproduction: Jan van Eyck's *Marriage of Giovanni Arnolfini and Giovanna Cenami* and one of Uccello's battle scenes and Piero della Francesca's *Baptism of Christ*. If they burned all the junk in these museums and put the best of it together on a satellite show constantly tripping the world it would be a real study in sensible economy. Down with all these bloody awful mausoleums of indiscriminate plunder.

All right. I spend fifteen minutes worth of embarrassment at Arthur Kopit's *Indians* which opened here July 4. Really if this is the best the Americans can send abroad we deserve our vulgar reputation. It's a vulgar mock-up in skit style of a vulgar episode in American history. The Indians are still being shortchanged, even by our so-called enlightened intellectuals. By way of Pop however, which Kopit's play is I suppose, one of the zappiest things I've seen here is John Lennon's one-act Pop collage *In His Own Write* on a triple bill at the Old Vic. His play is preceded by an Elizabethan brothel farce, not very amusing, and a post-Elizabethan domestic comedy for two, very funny in rhetorical nonsense. The Lennon affair is a crisp, sophisticated production of exquisitely projected Pop Culture slides (including drawings by Lennon) and tape material and costumes not to be believed and plastic people arrangements— all in skit episodes tied together by a hero hippie representing the author taking us through magical subterranean autobiographical fantasy transformations. A critic here told me Lennon's stuff is infantile wordplay. That's just what I like about it. The absurdity of language is best revealed in slips of the tongue, in speaking with tongues, in garbled ambiguities, in the babbling of infants, in the dislocations of schizophrenics. What Lennon does essentially is to misspell words into their double or more meanings. ". . . my last will and testicles . . . I leave all my belodgings . . ." "Children should be seized and not heard" "They seemed Olivier to the world about them" "I trudged over hopping to be noticed" "Tell mawdle, what's the mater" "We have an unexpeckled visitor" "Can you hallucinate on that?" Someone should bring the production to New York. Lennon, by the way, is a local boy, and his verbal clowning is almost strictly colloquial. When somebody told him to read Joyce he did and didn't understand a word of it.

It seems the Beatles are surrounded by a lot of intrigue and nonsense, but they remain much what they grew up to be in Liverpool: nice lively kids. The evening I spent in their recording studio—after Lennon's white balloon Happening at the Frazer Gallery—I listened to the jamming and recording a long time but also had conversations with each one and altogether. Ringo was quiet, even subdued, said he was proud of his two sons, and thought I was a bit loco for asking "how did you guys get together." George was serious about drugs, revelations, relativity, and the Maharishi. John and Paul were cutting up in jokes and charades. They like Tiny Tim and Richie Havens and would like to hear tapes by LaMonte Young. Asked about John Cage, Paul shouted "Cage—he's a fucking nut." But then he got more cerebral about it with bright remarks on being "of two minds on the subject"—which corresponds to Cage's own mixed-up philosophy. Ringo described their success in America as the conjunction of the release of their first record, an appearance on the Ed Sullivan show, and $50,000 worth of publicity. My superficial impression was that they're very intelligent, friendly, relaxed, funny, and charming. Walking out at 3:00 A.M., a bunch of kids were waiting, as they do nightly apparently, to pay their sweet gawking respects.

Pretty soon I'm taking a car into the countryside. Maybe before that I'll go to the Tate, the wax people, the British Museum, some Happenings by Joan Littlewood at the Tower, and give a lecture at the I.C.A. Last night some artists took me to the Prince of Wales pub which they say is like our Max's.

July 18, 1968

HELLO YOUNG LOVERS

Thursday, September 5, 1968, 7:00 P.M., go to the Delacorte Theatre in Central Park to see the Harkness Youth Company and Rod Rodgers and Richard Kuch and Lotte Goslar. It's windy. The sky is overcast. I see big possibilities here with the lake water beyond the stage and a piece of city panorama beyond that. But then we're all stashed up tight among the dance enthusiasts. The trees outside the amphitheatre are incidental. They want our attention for what we agreed to come for. That's fair I guess. It's chilly so I'm snuggling into my seat and trying to overhear three fags behind me talking about what they had for dessert. You have to prime yourself for these things. When the business on stage begins I'm craning around admiring the flags of all nations or all festivals blowing about from positions ringing the outer limits of the theatre. Now I'm admiring five barechested sleek huskies doing a Spartan routine based on karate exercises. They're very serious about it. Mostly I'm conscious of the pretty torsos. The head of one boy lolls about more relaxed than the others so I'm thinking he might be the best one to go home with after the show. Next there are three routines based on swimming, skiing, and tennis. In the *entrée* for the first, two couples make like swimming, in bathing suits too, through some gauze or chiffon stretched from wing to wing upstage and undulating in the breeze. I suppose people are aware of the lake somewhat reflected by city lights behind the swimmers. But this is very unusual swimming fare. When the skiers come on I'm still thinking amphibiously. Now I have to adjust to a slope-and-snow situation. Next a tennis situation. This is a stage for all seasons. It's nice to be everyplace at once without being there or waiting for the seasonal cycles.

The audience apparently likes its sports spiced with its flirtations. Sports be damned. The love game is out in front. Cute teen-age stuff. They could be auditioning for the Ed Sullivan show. Especially since the dance people are showing us how integrated they are. I don't think the Black Power people would appreciate this at all. That black boy in the trio tennis game is already looking lighter than he is. He seems to be enjoying it too. I'm interested to see who'll get who, forgetting momentarily they'll have to end up the happy trio they started out to be. Clearly the two boys want to screw the girl in any case. She seems to be up to it. They're all healthy. Jesus what are they thinking about. At one point I'm rooting for the black boy, imagining he might be deprived of his innings when the white boy is jealously guarding his catch, leaving his competition to display nothing better than his splendid technique. I detect a bit of prejudice here. The white boy takes his turn, after all, for exhibiting his special tricks, but at that moment the black boy isn't as close to the girl as the white boy was when the black boy was doing his stuff. This is interesting sociology. Clearly the next step in trios is to have a black boy and a black boy, or a white boy and a black girl and a black girl, etc. It's very confusing.

The next sequence, the skating act, looks much safer. Lots of people. More possibilities in a crowd. I think skating is sexier on ice since the velocity is greater. Ballet might be the bastard child of skating. They say the skaters imitate the ballet dancers although it's obviously the other way around. But perhaps the skating profession could improve its costuming. I never saw a male skater in those almost transparent white tights so well made by the ballet designers. The white jock straps are nice too. White on white is always a pleasant surprise. I know the three guys behind me are digging that. Also, there's an outstanding trick in this number, as good as anything I've seen on ice. This fellow spins around in the air and at the same time his legs are going through some extraordinary pretzel mutations. I like that a lot. I never see the girls in these situations. Or else I wonder why they don't have any tits. My theory is that they have to be as toplight as possible to sustain their weight on the toes of one foot, which they do so often. They get rid of the extra baggage in school or maybe in a special place for that sort of sacrifice. It goes down into the calf muscle or something. Parts are shifted about to do the job. Dedicated kids. In the finale one chick loses her white hat too. They take everything in stride.

Well, I'm really involved in this performance. I've almost forgotten the trees and flags. The mopping up of the floor between the acts is especially interesting. They keep the lights dim for that. Not so dim you can't make out how the moppers are as integrated as the dancers. I'm getting color blind from all this integration. I like my black black and my white white. If they integrated the stop lights we'd be in trouble. Still, it's nice to see people getting along well together. One number on this program is all white and they don't get along together at all. The four of them are really angry about something. It's called *The Brood* and the choreographer is Richard Kuch. I never saw such an unhappy crew. The audience loves it. There's an old lady in it, and a young girl, and two strapping fellows. They're made up ugly as sin. A two-wheeled cart which belongs to the old lady is also quite involved in it, whatever it is. Sorry I can't transcribe the plot. I think it's about the end of the world. A real disaster. They're terribly mean to each other. One of the boys even seems to be raping the old lady. Anyhow he's sucking on one of her nipples. And she doesn't like that a bit. Obviously nobody's gonna be satisfied here so I concentrate on the lit-up top of a building off in the distance around Park Avenue. There're psychedelic possibilities wherever you go. The last thing I see, they've got the old lady slumped on a wheel of the overturned cart. I'm sure that's the end. It is. The audience applauds wildly and I recover during the intermission on a box of popcorn and other oral satisfaction available at the stand outside the theatre.

The next is a relief. A Black Swan or Aurora or what pas de dukes. The guy is a real queen. He's wearing a little pastel green skirt that almost covers his ass and a cross-torso sash to match. His hair is orange or straw yellow. He's strong too. The showstopper is a lift where he carries the girl off on one hand stretched straight overhead on a rigid arm. She loves it. They sprang right out of the head of Zeus, these two, or maybe a UFO, which has recently been identified as swamp gas. This is what all of us slobs could be like if we just tried harder. At the curtain call the girl gives her green Samson a pink flower out of the bouquet delivered by an integrated stagehand. This is going too far. We're being infiltrated. Or else it's a regression. They have to keep reminding us of our past. Really if the dancers are white the stagehand flower boys should be very white or at least computerized.

Never mind. They come into their own again in the final number. Lotte Goslar and Company. This is what I came for. I've heard she's very funny. She is. She's a riot. She's a stocky little middle-aged lady with a face of great putty mobility who could be anybody's peasant immigrant mother verging on the ridiculous. It seems I spent an evening with her last spring in the presence of mutual friends and I didn't know who she was and she didn't mention it either. In fact she didn't say anything at all. She got lost in the wallpaper. She must be a delightful friend to people. Maybe she saves it all up for her art.

They do about twelve short numbers under the general title, *Clowns and Other Fools*. Situation comedy. Lotte is most of the show. She even steals it standing stock-still as a "mushroom" in a scene involving the classical prince looking for his classical maiden in the classical forest assisted by classical hunters. One scene is Lotte enacting the life of a flower on a green mat, and in another solo she enacts the life of her grandmother as a lady who "danced her way through life" from cradle to heaven. I guess my favorite is the dancing lesson where a gorgeous siren of a girl tries to teach a recalcitrant Lotte the elements of grace and deportment. She's really a brilliant mime. It's clearly in the dance-mime tradition peculiarly American in the sense that Charles Weidman was at one time a famous practitioner of it and he came from Nebraska. Charles put the European mime tradition together with the American modern dance tradition (which he was helping to create) for a curious hybrid at once Charles and nobody else. Later, Katherine Litz, who emerged from the Weidman-Humphrey company, did her version of it: a somewhat nostalgic female humor, exquisitely subtle and delicate with shades of meaning impossible to catch and define. Lotte Goslar's humor is unabashedly theatrical. The comedy is often out in front with a slap-dash extroversion nobody can miss; but she's subtle as well, and a slow-motion film of a gamut of her expressions and gestures in just a short sequence would reveal a lifetime of arduous labor to accomplish what they call the mastery of a craft. Also, she has a keen grasp of sex types. She's got 'em all mixed up. A queen is a queen is a boy is a girl is a ballerina is a boy is a dyke is a fag is a butch is a boy is a girl is just a kinky son of a gun like the rest of us. Hello all you sexes. We're too good to be true.

September 19, 1968

LIGHT YEARS AWAY

Where does a story begin? Where does a continuation end? Having I thought said my piece on James Lee Byars last week I now must report on the true miracle of the red acetate. This story could begin anyplace. There's a book called the story of mankind. However, at various times I left the scene and later returned to it. It's every nervous system for itself. I had only to open a book at random at any page to find the desired explanation. When your ship comes in it may be a horse. Tell me a story: begin at the beginning and proceed until you reach the end, then stop. Shall I locate a point on the continuum? Where is a continuum interrupted? Is a phase a discrete part of a continuum? Is a discretion a social absurdity in a great vacuum? Is a vacuum cleaner a collection of dirty incidents? Is an incident a phase or an interruption of a continuum? Is a mile of red acetate the endless yellow brick road? Yes, well, I could begin where the night before I staggered home with twelve new books on witchcraft and related topics and stayed up till 5:00 A.M. reading in all of them and was wakened at eight out of deep slumber by Mr. Byars almost terrorizing me into appearing at ten sharp on Fifth Avenue and Fifty-ninth Street. Or I could begin at two years ago when I hauled LaMonte Young's equipment on the back of my car out to Bucks County for a week of music and connubial nature and one sunny afternoon sitting outside the house on the lawn facing the woods my eyes fastened on a small reflector light high up on a tree behind a lot of other trees and within moments every detail in the visual field, especially each individual leaf, blended into an incredible luminous allover web. I was, in fact, in a trance. I woke myself up because I knew I was "out there" and might not come back if I continued to travel.

Or I could begin with a painting by Lenny Contino hanging on my wall a month now. The painting has a bright red ground and four individual hard-edge shapes, off-rhomboid, off-triangular, in green and blue stripes. There are several optical kicks to this painting but the major kick is beyond analysis. Staring witlessly into its center you can dissolve or disintegrate the singular shapes into that iridescent continuum which might be the apotheosis of such an erotic geometry. One might begin right here to realize a reductio ad absurdum of descriptive analytical art criticism. For instance, questions of real or illusionistic perspective become academic nonsense when the entire visual field is mystically painted in a single plane.

So here I am still half slumbering on a bench at Fifth and Fifty-ninth with a coffee-to-go and one of those witchcraft books in my pocketbook. Byars had obtained permission from the Parks Department to lay down his mile of red acetate, a shiny red carpet, on the sidewalk from Fifty-ninth to Seventy-ninth. He had measured the mile foot by foot to cut the material in three sections necessitated by two traffic intersections over which the material could not be laid. One title for the event is "two in a mile-long dress." At each end of the mile of acetate would be a hole for somebody to put his head under. The two would communicate with each other! He had said I should locate someone on the street to get under the hole at the Fifty-ninth Street end of it. He had said to be there at ten sharp. He himself would be riding up and down the avenue in a taxi. At ten sharp I get off the bench and look uptown. In the distance on a corner I see a red blob and walk toward it. Two assistants are unrolling unraveling the mass of red down the sidewalk toward me. The people going about their business in passage are careful not to step on it, never mind their perplexity. I walk back along the carpet toward Fifty-ninth sometimes leaning over to pull it into the center. At the end, at Fifty-ninth, Bob Landsman and I are admiring the stretch of it off uptown as far as you can see. Now for somebody for the hole. Perhaps a wretched dirty lady babbling to herself on a bench nearby. No perhaps not. Maybe this lady now stopping to ask me if royalty just passed by here. I say yes it has. Really, who, who? Why you of course. No, really, who? Or an older lady with her grandson who wants to know what it's all about. Is it a play? Yes it is. What's the play about? Oh it's about Alice in Wonderland and St. George and the Dragon. Oh I see, you mean you were up in the park at the statue of Alice? Yes that's right, we were. Or an elderly gentleman who wants to know if it's a protest and I say yes it is because he likes protests. But then Landsman asks me if I'd like to get under the hole and I put down my coffee and pocketbook and do so immediately. At first I'm embarrassed. Making a spectacle of myself again. Besides, I've never been in such a long dress. Who's at the other end? Landsman says it's Roy Moyer of the American Federation of Arts. Fine, I like Roy. But I don't know about Roy. I mean really I can't see him and I'm not a clairvoyant. It doesn't matter. At this moment I'm having the true miracle of the red acetate. The red carpet begins glowing at the edges. It's glowing right out of existence. It's going to infinity in all directions. But the trees! You wouldn't believe it. All those trees in a hazy sunlight lining the sidewalk receding in perspective. They're blending again. They're a single tree, an enormous diffusing web of everything in all time. The people are little inhabitants of centuries ago or centuries ahead. I'm in a trance again. I'm de-focused. I'm a tree. I'm a heliotrope. I'm the endless red road. I'm not me. I'm blinded. . . . Landsman wakes me up and I relinquish the hole. He takes my place and I think he's doing the same thing, he's traveling light years away. I'm very excited, but we don't talk about it afterward. Now we have a friendly fellow here about six-and-a-half-feet tall. He agrees to wear the dress. He asks me what he should do. I know I shouldn't answer that, but with a sudden weakness for playing teacher, I instruct him not to look at anything. How do you encourage someone to go on a dangerous journey? He might never come back. He spread-eagles his arms and peers intently ahead through thick glasses. It looks good. Afterward he comments on the relative straightness of the red carpet. Did you want me to expand my mind, he asks. No, nothing at all, it was a pleasure having you with us. He's here on a field trip with other students from Iowa State University studying eastern urban problems. They were eating breakfast in Central Park when a lady informed them there was a Happening on Fifth Avenue. Later I heard that the rest of the students were sliding on the carpet in stockinged feet around Seventieth Street.

The assistants begin rolling the carpet back uptown to mass it together for a return trip to the League. Byars rides by in his taxi. He's a Siamese triplet in the back seat in his voluminous pink silk dress expanded to include two others. I get in the front seat and they drive me round to Seventy-ninth where other assistants are also rolling the stuff up. Byars is so excited he can't stand to hear anything about my end of it. Later I talk to Roy Moyer who says that at 10:20 A.M. precisely he arrived at Seventy-ninth in a cab, stepped out in his tails and top hat and walked over to the hole. Two assistants removed his hat, put the hole over his head and put the hat back on. Approximately fifteen seconds later they removed the hat again, pulled the material over his head, replaced the hat, and Moyer returned to his waiting taxi. Byars' final comment was: "now that it's over nobody is sure that it actually occurred."

October 3, 1968

THE UNHAPPY SPECTATOR

The "late" John Brockman said that anyone who gets up and does something these days is liable to be shot. He was right, although this is no truer for our time than any other time. Dionysus, for instance, was annually murdered and resurrected. To be successful means not only to "get up" (and do something) but to "get it up"—to erect oneself and then properly ejaculate. When the actor and spectator embrace in the ritual copulation of theatre nobody is satisfied unless there is mutual ejaculation. The actor who fails to bring it off is executed. When the girl in the Living Theatre's *Frankenstein* fails to levitate (to become a soaring phallus) she is executed. If she had in fact levitated she would have been executed just the same, as Icarus must fall in his presumption to fly. The program note for *Frankenstein* stated that if the girl, the center of attention in a hypnotic meditation to accomplish the miracle, did indeed levitate, the program would be consummated. The show would not go on. The girl would be the first and last erection. Once erected she must fall (ejaculate) in the consummation of self-execution; and the spectators would ideally participate in the ritual death. To ejaculate is to expire, to die. The consummation of a mountain is a volcanic eruption in which the lava falls and consumes all the inhabitants. After the ejaculation everyone goes to sleep, dies. The people leave the theatre and go home to bed, to sleep. When they arise they look again for the ritual of their own execution. If they don't find it there's hell to pay—a literal murder. "The world is governed by the badly fucked" (G. Brecht). —"There is no way to avoid murder except by ritual murder" (Brown).

Since mutual ejaculation (catharsis) in the theatre is very rare, and in fact impossible in any total sense, the antagonism between actor and spectator is an acute unresolved tension. Who's going to get whom? It becomes a sadomasochistic dilemma, a deadlock of mutual hatred. The actor, the hero, is the sadist screwing the passive spectator. Yet the actor sacrifices himself in the fiery outstretched arms of a greedy audience which desperately wants what it has for centuries denied itself —the right to act itself. The actor is that part of the organism (audience) projected outside itself to unfold the misery of its own self-alienation. If everybody is an actor there is no longer any need to act. We're all in it together. The revolutionary theatre of our time is an attempt to expose the farce of this separation between actor and spectator. When the collective authorship is understood, the projected author (leader, hero, actor) might also be understood as merely a practical expedient in a situation requiring a transient spokesman. In their playground games the children know exactly what they're doing when they alternate leadership as a formal expedient. The child who becomes a bully because of an acute daddy problem (daddy gets me at home so I'm going to be the daddy here) is expelled, exiled, executed by the rest of the group. If the demands of the bully are accepted and complied with the children are doing precisely what we adults do in the larger political arena. Mutual hatred (sadomasochism) is the only outcome. And the bully, the leader, will murder the people if the people don't get him first, or we all go down together, which is the genocide, or giant suicide, now facing an unhappy world.

The theatre must go. There is only one theatre. We are all actors and spectators simultaneously upon the stage of the world. The argument between actor and spectator is no more nor less than an attempt to dominate the proceedings. When the argument evaporates the actor and spectator become one.—The audience at Loeb Student Center of NYU, on Sunday, October 6, 1968, got the idea very quickly. The confusion was very intense. Last spring six of us agreed to collaborate on a performance to take place on October 6. I'm hazy on how it actually originated. There was a phone conversation with Janet Solinger of NYU about a possible panel. I suggested a "panel performance." For three years I've nursed the notion of a "panel caricature" without any specific idea of the form it might take. I asked sculptor Les Levine to participate and Levine and I then asked Allan Kaprow, Gordon Mumma, and dancers Barbara Lloyd and Meredith Monk. When Meredith couldn't do it dancer Trisha Brown Schlicter agreed to collaborate. Each person would contribute his own thing involving all of us simultaneously in one way or another. It was quite vague. A month ago we met to bat it around. Les said he'd bring in his videotape equipment for some sort of television feedback. Gordon said he'd manipulate the voices with his electronic gear. Trisha talked about doing something outside the windows. Barbara wanted to manipulate the audience somehow. If they were in groups designated by number or letter she would suggest a shifting from group to group. Allan was thinking of engaging the Telephone Company to pipe in some of their public service numbers as answers to questions. And I said I'd provide the script, the written stuff comprised of questions and answers. We were still searching for an overall form to the event. At that first meeting I believe it was Allan who picked up on Barbara's audience involvement idea to push it into the brilliant conclusion of the audience replacing us as panel members. The key word became "disintegration." We had no idea the extent to which a disintegration would be fulfilled. If we had we might have worn bullet-proof vests. But as one of those Kennedys said, there's no safety in retreat.

No doubt the initial question was: What is a panel? The word panel is derived from pane, meaning a piece, and pan, meaning a part. A panel is a piece of somebody or something. Panels are a big drag, that's what they are. They're a tribal council of elders meeting to decide the fate of their subjects. They're a corporation board meeting to do likewise. They're an official organ mouthing the dogmas of the current style. A few people are erected, elevated, to pontificate the agenda of the day. They're the authorities, the experts. They're the publicity agents for themselves and what they represent. The people come to get a "fix." The people are antagonistic but they submit the way a child submits to the classroom situation. A teacher up there is going to tell you where it's at and if you're well behaved you'll get a chance at the end to be a Mickey Mouse yourself by asking a question which has already been asked. If you're not polite you'll challenge somebody and then the whole place gets up-tight and perplexed. Everyone starts looking for the exit. If the teachers stand their ground a battle is in the making. The issues are irrelevant. What's at stake is the question of authority. Traditionally a panel is a serious affair. People expect serious answers to serious questions on what everyone has tacitly agreed to be momentous issues.

So I suppose the idea of our panel was to undermine its seriousness (in terms of settling any issues) by exposing the emotional roots of any authoritative situation. The panel is a conventional public structure as good as any other for revealing the raw nerve of the unhappy spectator and the presumptuous authority. I must say that I don't believe the mob of people who came to Loeb October 6 expected a panel of any sort. The final publicity for the thing simply identified it as a "program" to be given by these six people. But there we were behind a long table on the stage looking like a panel. So I can't say if the convulsion that threatened to finally seize the event was in part a result of an initial disappointment over a structure (panel) that a lot of these people, like myself, don't ordinarily attend. It might be a moot point. There was a huge crowd. I could swear that 2,000 people were there. Enough for a political convention. I asked Janet to close the gates before the Fire Department descended on us. As moderator I introduced the panel members, forgetting to introduce Wilhemina, a sweet friendly pig whom Barbara had brought along to participate by being there. Les, by the way, was invisible to the audience, although he was seated at one end of the table. When I introduced him he turned on his image in the form of three television sets arranged in pyramid in front of him on the table. He also had a French interpreter with him. After introductions I asked each member a conventional (somewhat impertinent) question related to their respective professions. To Gordon: Would you comment on the axiomatic advantages of electronic sadomasochism? To my own confusion my collaborators began immediately to reply with the prepared nonsense of the script. I had hoped the thing would begin more conventionally. So we were plunged into our own confusion at the outset. The more I pressed for a conventional reply the worse it got. Moreover, with Gordon's electronic sound-modification system, our voices were turned on (up) or off, and sometimes made unintelligible through distortion.

The script was in two parts. There were about eighty short answers which members could speak or yell at random at any time in response to a question or to another answer. Samples: It strikes me as absurd; Let's start from the beginning again; You're interrupting me; You're full of shit; You trumped up that question to confuse me; You must be out of your mind; Let's change the subject; Phrase it differently; I was always vague on that issue; Do you think you're ideally suited to ask these questions; That's not a real question; That's an interesting question, I'll give it some thought, etc. There were also some longer involuted answers providing the opportunity for an oratorical delivery. Each member had an identical script. Deviation from the script was possible at any time. I had a separate script of questions, although some of the questions were answers (or statements), just as some of the answers were questions. Samples: Can anyone else add to that?—You're repeating yourself—You're putting me on the spot—I'll try to clarify the question—I'd like to get a concept of the whole before we go any further—Do you see anybody in the audience you'd like to make it with—etc. Some longer questions, like the longer answers, were convolutions, plays on a single subject, like about exits and entrances. The short answers and questions were the kinds of clichés that people often speak in these situations, sometimes as preface to a serious remark. Or they are the unspoken clichés of an emotional response that people feel and don't express. They were loaded on the side of repressed hostility.

To compound the responses were a set of about thirty-five gesture possibilities, identical for each member, from which to choose as the moment seemed to dictate. They were the physical counterpart of the verbal material. Tyrannize someone on the panel; crawl across the panel table (Trisha did); embrace someone; pretend to have a headache; make wild oratorical gestures; look omnipotent; yawn extravagantly; wrestle somebody on the floor; become confused, etc.

Trisha had abandoned her plan for action outside the windows. Allan was unable to secure the cooperation of the Telephone Company. And Barbara had abandoned her plan for manipulating the audience, although we retained the essential idea of gradually relinquishing our panel positions. In any case the audience became involved almost instantly. The first invitation for license was my announcement at the outset that a vacant chair on stage at the end of the panel table was there for anyone from the audience to occupy at any time to ask or answer questions, etc. Even the explicit invitation was probably unnecessary. After several minutes of our own confusion, both real and planned, and my constantly stepping into a real or imagined vacuum with a commandeering aggression that might have unnerved an elephant, the audience assumed its proper role of the enraged spectator. I'm speaking in general, knowing that there are always some, especially your friends, who will come to celebrate anything you do as your thing of the moment, offered in a spirit of celebration. I'm speaking of the general sickness of the resigned passive spectator, rendered impotent by his own repudiation of responsibility to act, to participate, to become himself the center of his own attention. Who has never felt this impotence and the repressed rage which accompanies such a helpless condition? To be enchanted and mesmerized by a special theatrical event is not an answer to such a sorry plight either. We've all been thus pleased. This is the romantic illusionism of a mutual ejaculation which creates the next anticipatory anxiety for a successful conclusion. You out there, the better part of me projected to fulfill my fantasies, you'd best not let me down, etc. The critics are always murdering some poor bloke who doesn't quite make it on the stage. The critic and actor alike are educated to expect a successful conclusion. The critic is the angry spectator wielding a wicked pen on behalf of his fellow spectators. The critic is the medium between actor and spectator to convey to each the success or the disaster of the attempted copulation. The critic is as screwed up in his presumption as the actor is in his role of the sacrificial lamb and the spectator in his role of the suffering nobody.—The theatre must go.

Someone said the situation at Loeb October 6 was a historic occasion. If so it was only because a breakdown of actor-spectator boundaries took place under the guise of a panel idea, and through an agony of extreme confusion in which an audience encouraged to express its hostility had to fight its way through to the recognition it has always been primed to reject. (If you cease to be the authority, who are we going to attack, and so on.) We didn't make it that easy. Nor was it easy on us.

I can't speak for the others, but I felt on fire from the intense concentration of dealing with flak from every direction, and converting the flak (by the reversal we had planned) into the absurdity of an antagonism that had no place to go once the antagonist found himself recognized. As an exercise in emotional conversion the situation was different in kind from certain participation events in which the artist instantly recognizes the spectators and robs them of their passive role by seducing them into a game of total participation. Moreover, the panel event remained symbolic from the view of total participation. The take-over was incomplete. Ideally, if literally enacted, the panel which succeeded us (whom we found at random to supercede us) would have been replaced by another panel, and another, and so on until the ritual was completed. The murder of each successive presumptuous authority. The irony was too much. Barbara found our first panel replacement. He was Willoughby Sharp. He couldn't have been better. I'm not sure how long he was with us when he lunged, and I didn't know what hit me as Willoughby, my chair, and I went crashing to the floor. I'd forgotten that gesture instruction to wrestle somebody to the floor. I returned askew to the mike and announced I'd been raped. Earlier, in response to a panel question about who gets screwed in the theatre ritual, a man in the audience yelled "We are." After the event Les remarked that perhaps everyone stayed to see who else might hump the hostess.

But Willoughby wasn't done yet. At some point I was dimly aware of a white form looming up next to me. Willoughby was standing on his chair removing all his clothes. Again, I'd forgotten there was a gesture possibility called "undress." Everybody applauded the beautiful gesture and I think at that moment we were going into the final phase. Wilhemina the pig was being much appreciated. The children were wandering onto the stage to be where the action was and to add their two golden cents. One small boy toward the end took charge of a mike and called for order and asked the man shouting "Fire" to shut up, among other things. The mix-up in people's heads over what was real and what wasn't was as perfectly expressed in the continuous fire episode as by anything else. The man incessantly yelling "Fire" might have been immoral in the situation, but he was saying the word which struck home as no other word might have. Fire means to be burned up, inflamed, angry. Fire means to be fired from the job. Fire means to fire the cannons. Fire means execution. Fire means sex and war and total holocaust. Fire means to be immolated altogether in the flames of disintegrating boundaries. Fire is the word of panic when everything is at stake. Yes. Then there was a real fire on stage on the panel table. Gordon put it out with two glasses of water. Earlier he had gone into the audience to give the "fire" man a glass of water and to light his cigar to boot. Back at the table he told a story about his grandfather who once fell in an old outhouse hole on the farm and shouted "fire" to attract the attention of possible rescuers. Later, asked why he yelled "fire" grandfather said, "how in hell far do you think I'd have gotten if I'd yelled Shit."

But the fire which must have moved everyone was the unhappy desperate girl who mounted the stage at last to burn the place up in a plea for love. She was absolutely for real. She was signaling through the flames. Steve Paxton and Barbara Jarvis became her immediate rescuers, finally easing her down between them, after encouraging her to let it all out, holding her hands and rubbing her back. She was everybody's transfigured sacrifice. She was the crucible of the day. If she wasn't in fact, resurrected, I think we all wanted her to be, to be resurrected right there out of the center of her own catastrophe.

She was the real echo of Trisha earlier following instruction at the table by "leaving the proceedings angrily and returning with denunciations." Trisha screamed and crashed her chair down and left. Again the confusion. Two days later she called me to say she was following instructions, since she had heard I thought she might have been actually upset. And that's true, I thought perhaps she was. Perhaps she was.—And Barbara, by the way, was very involved in the mythology of the pig, which was a sacred animal accompanying the Greek earth goddess Demeter.

The pig, the children, the dog. My moderator replacement, David Bradshaw, has a lovely dog called Sumi. They're very close friends. In between moderating, I think, David was lying down on the stage in front of the table being humped by Sumi, who enjoys humping her close friends. This was near the end, which you might hardly call a conclusion. I recall that a lot of people had left, but the place still seemed jammed. Allan, Les, Trisha, Barbara, Gordon, and I shook hands with and congratulated our panel replacements the way they do after the Tonight Show or something and gradually at this point much of the crowd appeared to be massing toward the stage, and in fact the stage became a swamp of people, talking, talking, and looking over the equipment and making off with some of it. The milk and yogurt I'd consumed during the event was sustaining me in a dizzy spell of exhaustion and exhilaration.

October 17, 1968

TORNADO IN A TEACUP

Last spring I was talking about hoping for a new funk dance. It may be upon us. A new metaphor might be sexier in the long run than the thing a metaphor is designed to conceal (among other functions) but there's no question that at certain historical moments the people can be heard to be yelling "Take It Off" so they can see what the metaphorical fuss is all about. Steve Paxton's comment on *Paradise Now* was that it didn't matter about the show too much, what you thought of it, when you were standing on stage there and happened to see one of the actors going down on the directress. Steve didn't pay for his ticket either. The best things in life are free. As for metaphors, you can get weak in the head thinking about what a metaphor is or isn't, or if there is such a thing, so I'll try to stick to the facts. A few weeks ago, visiting a couple of friends, I suggested or announced at random that there isn't a thing on television that isn't about fucking, so we promptly repaired to the bedroom to play with the set. First channel we got was one of those jungle dramas at a moment when the gorilla was squawking off a tree about to molest the young lady in a hammock. Next I think we spaced out on an advertisement for eye drops. The screen was filled with a big eye. The better to see you with my dear. And so on.

At the New School on October 15, 1968, Steve gave an *Untitled Lecture* on a mixed-bag program including Stuart Hodes, Margot Parsons, and John Wilson and the 1950 movie of José Limón's *Moor's Pavane,* which Betty Jones was on hand to talk about. Fortunately I'd been to Steve's rehearsal the day before—and saw the pornographic movie which was censored for the actual performance. Steve substituted a Biafran documentary. His piece consists of four simultaneously performed parts. It's a kind of illustrated lecture. Steve is talking on tape about sex and ballet; he stands downstage left making slight hand and pelvis gestures (also mouthing the lecture) stolen from Yvonne Rainer's *Body and Snot* piece from the week before (at the New School); and two films, several yards apart, are projected on the back wall. At the question period after the concert it seemed almost the whole audience was bending on Steve about his piece. Yvonne, for one, was outraged at what she thought to be a glib substitution of the Biafra film (notwithstanding the necessity), saying it destroyed the unity of the piece. I think she was really outraged at the theft of her *Body and Snot* material. Anyhow—the association of Biafran obscenity and *Swan Lake* (the other film) was certainly not as pointed or dramatic as the juxtaposition of *Swan Lake* with the pornography, especially since the lecture was about sex and ballet; but it was announced as a disappointed substitution, so I can't see how it mattered if you knew what it was supposed to be. My analysis of the great attention focused on Steve was that the audience felt deprived of the real thing, thus they were trying to find out what they missed exactly, and in detail, even if the question was about the weather.

If the definition of pornography is that which arouses prurient interests, I suppose the film was among the best of its kind. It's a Forty-second Street stag movie, nothing to do with tender sweet that I could see, just good old-fashioned mauling sucking and fucking. The way it worked with the *Swan Lake* film was staggering to my way of seeing it. There was nothing in between. Bang naked dirty funky low-down primal scene—

next to the polite etherealized de-corporealized all-dressed-up insanity of the good fairy godmother ballet. The balletomanes would have Steve's neck for this sort of proximity. I don't know if Steve had such a head-on impact in mind. I do know he already had the film (he used it in a rather obscured fashion last year in another context), and that he thinks a lot about all aspects of human physical qualities, in dance and otherwise. What interested him to explore here was a certain energy common to sex and ballet, as he sees it. The key sentence perhaps in the lecture is: "I speculate that some of the qualities which have made ballet, in spite of its practitioners, the second oldest professional physical tradition, is an early infusion of physiologically basic modes of energy use which I find similar to the ecstasy of stretching such as is experienced during certain types of orgasms . . . a positive and energized stretch." He seems to undo his little thesis at the end with the question: "Why are we in the West so hung up on orgasm?" The implied judgment throws the theory into a department of complaints, which may be more pertinent to the wild proximity (stunning) of two cultural physical extremes, one private and one public, than Steve himself realizes. I think any analysis of dance techniques in terms of basic sexual energies is both fascinating and important. Everybody knows what Graham's "contraction and release" syndrome is all about. A sex physiologist could probably make a critical contribution to dance literature with some scientific analogies. Anyhow, Steve upstaged me with his lecture, since I've been thinking for some time of developing the idea of ballet as a rigid erected phallic art. This is not what he had in mind in his lecture. We had a near knockdown controversy over it in Boston last week. For one thing, I said, how can you speculate on these matters without having read the classic essay on the orgasm by W. Reich. One's own experience may be sufficient for a theory (I accept it) but there's a point at which an experienced clinician can enrich a generalization by more inclusive evidence on a subject that's more scientific than poetic. Reich has been much criticized (before and after his death) for his single-minded concentration on full orgastic potency as the sine qua non of a healthy life; but his detailed description with diagrammatic support (regardless of opinions about his therapeutic conclusions) of the physiological process of orgastic excitation must be a masterwork of its kind in the field.

In our argument Steve said that although the motives are different, the pervasive "stretch" in ballet is similar to the orgastic stretch, not only in position but in the energy employed to get there and stay there. No question but what they both involve "a positive and energized stretch." Beyond that I disagree. I can't find anything not to agree with in Reich's description of orgastic potency as consisting of involuntary pleasurable contractions radiating from the genital to the whole body in a total surrender to the flow of biological energy. I'm not impressed with the ballet as an art of surrender. Our early modern dance technicians were much closer to an organic base for dance movement. Their revolt against the ballet, after all, was more than a historic rebellion in the interests of advancing a backward medium. Isadora set the scene. She predated Freud in her crudely expressed ideas about repression and liberation. Whether her successors knew it or not, they were expressing the temper of the new psychology. I think Graham was the only one to literally plunder the available literature. They all must have sensed that the ballet was a sick Western mode of physical discipline. Eventually they got trapped by it themselves—but that's another story.

What I see (and have felt) in the ballet "stretch" is a *rigor mortis* of painful extension. Those ballet dancers may have their ecstatic moments but nobody can convince me they don't in general suffer the tortures of the damned. There's no keener self-flagellation in any of our Western disciplines. If Steve were right I think they'd all look a helluva lot happier; furthermore they wouldn't be doing that in the first place. Ballet and pleasure are mutually exclusive activities. I can't think of a thing in the ballet repertoire of action that isn't an unrelieved exercise in phallic erected exhibitionism. There is a ballet here and there, like *Scheherazade,* which deviates somehow into something sloppily organic. In any case, the classroom technique itself is nothing short of a borderline psychosis in rigid repressive control. The paradox of the ballet, by the way, is in its phallic nature masquerading as a pitifully romantic searching etherealized unearthly body. There's iron and steel and plenty of clenched teeth in every flight and facility. Another interesting paradox is that the ballet is rampant with representational orgasm. There are climaxes by the dozen in any one ballet. These are the traditional maneuvers of the choreographer to keep the audience awake with shifts in pace. An ascending accumulation of energy is a favorite device. The movement gets faster and bigger, etc., as the plot, the music, and the attention span of the audience all dictate. The ecstasy of the ballet is a giant put-on. A fanfare of unhappy instruments. A fountain of ice. A tornado in a teacup. But this brings me back to Steve's concluding question: "Why are we in the West so hung up on orgasm?" The *Swan Lake* and the pornography movies are hopelessly off base from opposite ends of the pleasure spectrum. Somewhere in the middle is the continuous uninterrupted pleasure of homeostasis best known to the Eastern mystics. Pornography is real hot stuff. The ballet is a frigid witch. The Eastern mystics know it isn't necessary either to have or to deny the orgasm to solve the anxiety of unrelieved tension. For them the surrender is total and constant . . . there's no such thing as unrelieved tension. They live in divine relief. The energy that Reich called orgone energy and which has been called divers names for centuries is a cosmic energy coursing into and out of and through their bodies in a flow that can't be separated into states of tension (anxiety) and discharge (pleasure). This is the psychosomatic totality of a self-contained grace which we reserve for the ecstasy of a specific tyrannical experience known as orgasm. Definitely hung up.

Various writers have touched on or explored the broad changes in Western art since the turn of the century. An outstanding essay was by Leonard Myer in *The Hudson Review* a few years ago. He developed his thesis in terms of the end of teleological (purpose-oriented) art in the West, especially citing the chance methodology of the Dadaists and some contemporary composers as examples of the new purposeless, anticlimax art. In my opinion the most advanced art of the century is a conscious or unconscious attempt to eliminate not the orgasm but the orgasm anxiety complex. It's a complicated subject that I can't go on with here for reasons of space, except to throw out a few typical words used over and over to describe certain work in certain mediums: diffused, allover, ready-made, synthesis, de-focused, equal value, etc.

October 24, 1968

ANGEL ANYONE?

Wednesday, October 23, 1968, 7:30 P.M., I take a taxi to the Americana Hotel. This is Fred McDarrah's doing. He told a Ted Lorenz up there to call me to come see a Ken Dewey Happening in connection with something called The Society for the Family of Man. I never heard of this organization. Maybe it was named after the photo exhibit at MOMA. I've scanned the release sent by Lorenz for a clue. They started the thing in 1962. They say it's about doing good works for ghettos and such: "funds directed toward ghetto'problems through the nonsectarian community services of the Protestant Council." But according to Dewey they're running competition to the Nobel people, giving out awards every year "for excellence in the fields of Art, Education, Peace, Human Relations, Science, and Communications." I've pieced it together before getting in the cab. Briefly: six famous affluent people are receiving the award, which includes a $5,000 grant. They're the kind of people who are on other award committees to give the same type of grant to other famous affluent people. The shindig at the Americana is a $100-a-plate dinner in the Imperial Ballroom to make the award presentations. The six recipients are Norman Cousins, Mrs. Coretta King, Lady S. D. Rama Rau, Hans Bethe, Gunnar Myrdal, and Martha Graham. Other recipients have included Eisenhower, JFK, LBJ, and Lester Pearson. The master of ceremonies is going to be Douglas Fairbanks, Jr. Lorenz told me I wasn't invited to dinner, but I might think anyhow about my outfit if I wanted to since it's a black-tie affair. Couldn't find a black tie so I've got my blue and pink one on. I feel pretty respectable. The cab driver thinks so. Got my black shiny boots from London, black vest and black culotte skirt and black leather jacket, etc. The Americana has other ideas. I don't imagine an entire lobby turns round to gape at someone unless they think you belong in another place. Never mind, I walk briskly through like I have ten important business engagements. I fancy they think I'm a cousin to Barbarella on a mission to open an invisible door with an invisible key. Now I'm stuck. Scanning the directory with haughty concentration for notice of the awards dinner I don't see it listed, so I'm forced to speak to someone. The uniformed cats never heard of it. They look like they want to call for the bouncer. Maybe I'm in the wrong place. No doubt of that, but I press forward. Someone mentions the house phone and calling the banquet headquarters. Approaching the four white phones on a counter along a wall, I'm up against this blond buck-eyed business nut who thinks I'm Barbarella for sure. He wants to know if he can use my silver comb (just visible apparently at the top of my right boot) and then makes sure I have the worst time calling the banquet headquarters by leaning all over my field of vision making sloppy passes. I get the information I need anyhow and leave that one sprawled on the counter. I walk over across and up (one flight) to the warfare clatter of dishes and silverware signifying a dinner for more than a moderate number. Inside a door I case the obscenity. I'll admit to being prejudiced. I ask a securities man if this is where I want to be. He doesn't know. He grimly indicates an information desk. Yes it is, and here's Ted Lorenz, who suggests I go up one more flight to the Chambord Suite where I can look down on the situation and have some soda and sandwiches. No sign of Fred, but here's photographer Peter Moore. It doesn't seem the most inspiring set for a photo, except maybe the huge chandelier. A few thousand people at close-packed round tables and about thirty elite at an elevated table overlooking their contributors. I think I've seen this before in a Roman history movie. I look over a set of brochures on the dinner subject, including typed copies of the recipients' speeches, then go in search of a bar. A waiter says it's in the Georgian room across the way. It's a huge plush room one-quarter filled with a private party, a man smiling ear to ankle tells me from a chemical company that makes napalm. Lily-livered bastard I think, as I head for the drinks. But I don't look chemical enough and a big man says I'd better get out of there right away before he calls a cop. I take his advice after telling him he'd better loosen his grip on my arm before I give him a potch in his chemical belly with my invisible weapon. I go downstairs to look for Ken Dewey. I'm a bit agitated by now. I'd like to see the Happening and go home straightaway. But the guests are just lapping up the last course and there'll be lots of speeches to follow before Dewey does his act. Now I'm talking to him and a Mr. Kerr from New York State Council on the Arts at one end of the ballroom near the stage and outside the door leading into the kitchen. Kerr seems upset about one of Dewey's tapes (Vietnam sounds, etc.) that a technician toned down or turned off to satisfy a few complainants. I ask Kerr if there's a drink to be had. He says why don't I sit at his table where he has a bottle of bourbon. Now I feel invited to dinner. The guests seem a mixture of Westchester and Dewey's friends, so I'm wondering if I should address my hostile remarks to anyone in particular or just shut up which would be the tactical maneuver, specially since they've already noticed I'm not dressed properly. But I say all the wrong things anyway. Dewey advises me not to go up on the dais and remove my clothes. That would be upstaging him. Agreed. He says that all the photographs on the tables, of ghetto children, were his idea. He wanted each guest to be observed eating by a poor child looking at them out of a cardboard frame. This blows my mind a bit since at first I thought it was the obscene idea of the Society of The Family of Man to display in this manner the so-called objects of their goodwill. Both possibilities seem equally appalling. Dewey goes off to work on his performance. Kerr is holding his head. His wife is quite furious, apparently at me. The Westchester types all around look happily stuffed and pleased to be there. I tell one of Dewey's black friends that she's very pretty. I change my seat to sit next to a white one to see if she'll commiserate with me. She's okay but a lot cooler than me so I try to follow her example and make myself more comfortable by slouching into the seat, rest my boots on another seat, and appear to be listening to Douglas Fairbanks, Jr., talking about humanity and stuff like that. Presently I'm shocked into an erect position by the appearance of Martha

Graham. She's being ushered into the ballroom by devotees or security agents. She looks regally tragic in a modest way. She's still heavily made up from her opening night performance at Brooklyn Academy. (Maybe I should've gone there.) I guess they whisked her off after *Alcestis* to receive the award. I'm impressed. Soon they have her on the dais to join the fishbowl. The speeches are droning on. Lady Rau is very attractive. Gunnar Myrdal is handsome. Norman Cousins sounds authoritative. A friend of Mrs. King is receiving for her. And Miss Graham says the nicest thing of all, about how her money will go into a fund at her school to help indigent dancers. Now they're winding it up with thank yous and bless yous and I feel unhappy again so I'm daydreaming about the invisible door when my eyes catch on that acreage of chandelier and I'm spacing out beautifully until a shift in the atmosphere indicates the end of speeches and the beginning of Dewey. I leave the table to circulate. Dewey's performance lasts about fifteen minutes at the most. Tapes of conversation are amplified (he said they went round earlier to ask the guests questions so I presume this is the result); there's a large slide projection of the Empire State Building and next to it a movie I can't make out too well, maybe a documentary of poor people; and some action involving a man on stilts in a monk's outfit walking through the table scene toward the stage, also a few girls at the far end possibly in bridal gear likewise walking through the guests. On the stage the stilt man dons his robe, appearing in a shimmering cascade of silver mylar strips, walks across the stage. That's the end. I can't believe it. I do something I've never done before. I collar Dewey near the kitchen and start raging like a woman gone mad. For Krissake I'm yelling, you've got the opportunity of a lifetime to turn this goddam imperial ballroom into a shambles and look what you've done . . . nothing . . . etc. Poor Ken. I don't really mean it. He's a good man. A friend of Ken's is collaring me in turn to want to know who the hello do I think I am giving his friend a hard time like this. I do really mean it. But he's right I guess. I get lost in the crowd and find a telephone for someone to come rescue me. They're coming pronto in a cab and meanwhile I head for the bar two flights down. I'm Barbarella again. The boss of the bar says I don't look right and I don't have an escort. Okay I'll sit at a table. He doesn't like that either but the waiter takes my order and a dollar fifty. A besotted business nut is lurching over my head. The boss looks murderous. His cronies at the bar are shooting flames out of their nostrils. The waiter returns with my dollar fifty on a platter. Better get out of here madam. Great. I'm ready with my invisible key. Where's the bloody invisible door? This is the chamber of ultimate solution. This isn't a poetic enough way to die. They don't even know my psychocardiogram. You mean we're living in a primitive state of neurotic irresponsibility? I pick up a big handful of those little round peanuts and heave them into the bar. Have you seen an angel anywhere? I'm breathing easy now, out on the avenue hobnobbing with the chauffeurs. I'm waiting for an angel in a visible yellow brick cab.

October 31, 1968

HEADS—TAILS

November 3, 1968, Meredith Monk gave an afternoon called *Co-op* at Loeb Student Center of NYU. Meredith had a few simple oppositional ideas in mind, but I think the afternoon was basically united as a body show. Strange to speak of a dance event as a body show since what else ever is it; but aspects of Meredith's presentation concern the show of the body as a body more related to the body as seen perhaps by a painter, a sculptor, or a lover than by a dancer or a dance-goer. As a medium idea dancing can become quite removed from the everyday functioning body; so much so that it begins to look like dancing and people forget to see the body which is doing all that stuff. Possibly the dancers forget about their bodies too. Thus I see the three aspects of Meredith's body show as three contemporary ways of revealing the solid shaped-as-it-is body and the body as an essentially erotic being. Other than how I see the bodies around me from house to street everyday, I've been thinking sometime how a body looks better to me in an old-master painting (an Ingres, say) than in a modern traditional piece of dancing. Maybe Robert Morris had that in mind when he set up the nude female as replica idea of Manet's *Olympia* in his dance piece, *Site*. She was all body and didn't move around thank god. Morris did a lot of static and relatively static body things as perhaps in part ironic commentary (and reaction) to dancing as an art seemingly involved with disguising the real body in a whirlwind of movement and technically distorting configurations. There's a new demanding realism in the dance art of the Sixties.

Meredith had two static presentations of the figure in her *Co-op*. In the main theatre auditorium were four cubicles, two on each side of the room flush to the walls. Each wall of cubicle consisted of stacks of ten beach umbrella boxes, six-feet long by eight inches square. Within each cubicle a clothed person or people assumed ordinary relaxed positions which they occasionally changed. A striking idea was the cubicle filled with people, maybe ten, all standing and facing the wall. As the audience freely mobilized around the room, like a bazaar, they might at some moment be standing behind the ten cubicle figures, and I don't have to make the visual irony explicit. The single or double figures clearly cut a scupltural idea in a space partially enclosed to set them off in that fashion. But perhaps Meredith's dominant idea in this exercise, bodies notwithstanding, was to reverse the actor-audience relationship by immobilizing the performers in a space where the audience would have to mobilize in order to see the presented objects. Extending the informal idea, Meredith hoped the people would feel they could leave, have coffee, come back, etc. As further extension: downstairs in the Loeb lounge was a six-and-a-half-minute movie going forward and backward to run continuously for the hour and a half of the total performance time. The movie consists of six body sequences alternating with five ball bearings. Three nude men and three nude women are the subjects of the film. One sequence is seen as a single body in the same reclining position in each of four frames, but they're facing different directions in each frame compartment.

The formality of the cubicle and film presentations was offset by the informality of free mobilization by audience. Yet a limitation was superposed on this particular situation by the program indication of specific shows taking place on stage at precisely 3:17, at 3:41, at 4:05. If you wanted to see the shows you had to watch the clock and interrupt your nonchalant itinerancy. So there was this theatrical thing mixed up with a bazaar thing.

The theatre shows were of three elements. Meredith did her hippie love dance (in front of a psychedelic backdrop) with William Dunas, originally performed last summer in San Francisco as a nightly night-club act. Meredith here conformed to the crazy New York State laws about not moving or touching while naked. They did a lot of straight charged sex stuff avec clothes, then stripped to G-strings and stalked each other a bit, then dressed quickly and attacked with a pelvic grind and thrust that looked as much like the real thing to me as being properly undressed. Simultaneously, a movie of the original San Francisco version was shown below the stage on the floor in the middle of the audience. In that space the film was postage-stamp size. Not many people saw it. But it was shown three times. The second time, at 3:41, with the second show on stage: Meredith and Bob Wilson bouncing lightly on a long low board suspended a foot or so above the floor and between two boxes, wearing winter hats and heavy long fur coats. The juxtaposition was funny and good. Who cares about clothes or not if you know what they're for.—The third time, with the third show, at 4:05, the hippie love dance again.

The hippie love dance is a corny name for where dancing is at for a lot of people these days. I meant to say above also that a body not only makes more sense to me in an old-master painting (not that either really) but also in any discotheque where the body as erotic being is displaying itself even if straining after this erotic heritage denied it by the bullshit of Western body sickness. Maybe the best of it is the best black dancing and the white dancing which most looks like black. The white Negro. I saw a black chick at Max's one night knocking me and a friend of mine out, and this friend said to me what would you do with her in bed. Clearly she wouldn't have too much truck with a stiff white.—As an artist Meredith is trying to resolve a conflict between concept and physicality, between art and fucking. She says she's tired of lying in bed conceptualizing a dance. She's a pretty bubbly open-ended girl anyhow. I never thought of her work as spineless or juiceless, no matter how static or conceptual or imagistic. But now she wants to be more physically direct, meaning in part not to set a dance into a piece recognized as an indeterminate moment (the complexity of a spaghetti heap) caught in an angle and a step the same forever. The hippie love dance is as indeterminate in this manner as a body in a moment or an evening at a discotheque, or a body in a moment or a night of fucking. They could only be immortalized on film. Who wants to immortalize anything? It's all over. Why do you think that the very thing that holds our society together is the most appalling aspect of living here? As for your concepts, etc., Meredith, I gotta assure you that as Yvonne said of Martha Graham—What's between your legs is no more interesting to me than what's in your head. You're good because you have an interesting head and a healthy body. Did you know that the French never got over the loss of their head? And the Africans in America are suffering the loss of their bodies?

November 14, 1968

NOT IN BROAD DAYLIGHT

I wanna tip my bangs to that man in the *Voice* last week saying nice remarks about me. But I must assure him I don't have an interesting life at all. I make it all up. For instance, last week some very rich people flew me in their private jet down to Houston and I had such a spectacular time I couldn't find anything to write about it. Whereas that Americana Hotel deal was just another ordinary evening in the life of a lady gangster. And this morning on my way to a dental appointment I was minding my business on Twenty-third and Park looking for a subway when a taxi swung by with a male face in the back seat doing wild happy expressions of recognition at me, which made me wonder who it was since he was going by too fast or else the taxi window was too dirty; whereupon I noticed the cars stopping at the red light up the block and ran that way to the lights to try to satisfy my curiosity and found I thought what I was looking for, opened the yellow door on a beaming bearded face I'd never seen before who asked me if I was going uptown, to which I replied yes and got in, thinking he was the guy originally gesticulating but just someone who knew me perhaps and not me him. Much to my pleasure, however, he wasn't that guy at all. But he had seen me the night before at Longview's and happened to know who I was when I mentioned my name. His name is Gary Dobosen. The moment I got in and grasped the situation I was craning ahead to see the taxi containing the first mysterious character. I told the driver to give chase. So we did a cops and robbers act from Twenty-third to Forty-ninth where we turned off to go west. Would you call that an interesting life? I told the driver I had to overtake that cab to make my story for a Friday deadline. He said listen madam there's millions of stories in New York every day. I felt somewhat humbled. I've even lost interest in the identity of the mystery man.

Maybe the great thing about life is a bag of popcorn in a lady's room. I went rather dutifully last night to the opening of Anna Sokolow's evenings at Brooklyn Academy. Miss Sokolow is an excellent choreographer with a death-rattle message. She's been doing it since the thirties at least. I go once in a while to give myself a break. I'm always thinking or hoping someone gave her a break in the meantime, like a trip on a carpet to dizzyville damascus dateline dionysus, or just a cup of hot tea in a Japanese bathtub. She's clearly missing out on something. Where does she go after the show? She might be whipping out *The Sickness Unto Death* on the subway back home. I'm gonna send her my psychedelic Yo-Yo from Houston. These and other thoughts were bumping about in my head during the first number when I repaired to the ladies room at the curtain call. And there on the counter running the length of the mirrors was a large unopened still sealed bag of popcorn. You can imagine my relief. There's always something makes the trip to Brooklyn worthwhile. I wandered back into the lobby for the intermission with all this buttered popcorn in my mouth looking for a couple of people I wanted to see. I asked Lew Lloyd four questions in a row and received no answers, then found Edwin Denby, probably my favorite gentleman over forty east of the Mississippi, who was about to share my popcorn with me when I gleefully mentioned I'd located it in the ladies room whereupon poor Edwin looked horrified and threw up his hands and said to reply to my "what's the matter"—and assurances that the bag was sealed when I saw it—after recovering his composure: "She might have died before she was able to open it." People like Edwin make life interesting indeed. Later, in the bar across the street he gave a beautiful condensed exposition of how he saw Martha Graham flower and decay from about 1930 onward. I wished I'd heard it before writing the 3,000 words I had crammed in my pocket ready to mail to *Ballet Review,* called "Martha Graham: An Irresponsible Study: The Head of Her Father." Edwin doesn't think libelously the way I do. I guess the thesis of the piece is a silver platter idea about Salome not knowing the difference between a head and a penis. And was it Freud or N. O. Brown who delivered us from the misconception that Salome was thinking of a head in the first place. I don't think either of them were interested in Salome at all actually. My own Salome trip is through Oscar Wilde. Can't recall if I read the Wilde story before or after a stunning essay by Arthur Michel (German dance critic–historian, died 1946) on the iconography of Salome from way back in Bible times through Graham's *Herodiade,* which was the subject of the essay. Anyhow Salome was a dancer. Before I forget it I'd like to take small issue with my admirer by saying I think I'm writing more intensively about dancing than ever before.

Speaking of platters, maybe the great thing about life is a platterful of artichokes on a table in a rich house in Houston. On our way to the museum opening there we stopped at a patron's place (friends or acquaintances of my host) for drinks and appetizers. It was a party really. Simone Swan, organizer of the whole trip, was less than keen on the hostess at this place and didn't even want to go there, but as long as we were going she gave me explicit instructions to misbehave. I said I'd see what I could do. I didn't see any opening at all (except the way I looked I suppose) until I hit the artichokes. After some sexy stuffed oysters I couldn't keep my hands off the artichokes, which felt like wet clay or whatever you like to squish around in some inspired excremental moment, and just then a lady vulture guest fell into Simone's trap by flapping down on me all red-headed auburn-eyed rage with instant denunciations. Her eyes were huge. She was a kind of vulgarized Scarlett O'Hara. Artichokes in hand, I saw her right off in my mind's eye, in the Atlanta bedroom being trussed up at the bedposts into a huge red corset by a contingent of sadistic black mammies. Well Simone was right there and she calmly asked the lady if she was the housekeeper. Gregory Battcock further compounded the issue by saying he'd written a book on etiquette himself and didn't know what the lady was talking about. I don't remember the rest, until I was about to leave later on and she came up red curls flying to demand a few moments with me in a corner and without my shades so she could have the benefit of my naked eyes and please to tell her where the hell I came from, etc.—at which I hastily reassured her I was from Corpus Christi and flew in especially for the party. Phew. Two pals rescued me then for the trip to the museum, although I thought to invite the lady to my room at the end of the evening's festivities in case she wanted to know more.—Dynamite you know immediately when it works (Bradshaw).

If you're losing sleep because of our laughter a sleep inducer is what you're after. I'll save your mother for you if you'll keep my sister for me. You mean I wouldn't have to go so far to get serviced? Yes, Lumumba you have reached is not a working Lumumba.—And Levine was playing with my Yo-Yo the other day when it flew open on the floor, the batteries falling out of its sides, and I said, "damn it Levine can't you be careful," and he said, "never mind, it didn't break, it just fell apart." A moment later Byars called me to inform me that the history of the atomic bomb was written by a Mr. Blow, published by American Heritage. In Houston, having lunch in a seafood place on the Gulf of Mexico we discussed the possibilities of people living out their names. We got deep into the name thing. I said my name is the feminine contraction of Guillaume and that I'm thinking of a corny new title like Jill the

Ripper. On my way over to the *Voice* just now with this copy my cab driver opened his shield to have a conversation. He said I didn't look like the type who would rob him. I said not in broad daylight anyway.

November 21, 1968

CREDO QUI ABSURDUM

I thought *Duffy* was as good as *Barbarella* which Paxton thinks is worse than *2001* which I liked even less than *The Fox*. Last Sunday my kids took me to see *Duffy*. When my kids dig a movie I know it's good. They understood the complex old-fashioned psychology and wouldn't think it unnatural if the heroine, whom I thought at first to be the sister of two of the heroes, was making out with one of them, which she was. Realizing my mistake, I continued to think she was a sister anyhow. It seemed like a healthy relationship. Why did Durrell have his Pursewarden in love with a crippled (blinded) sister? And why did Bergman make the attraction of one sister for another in *Silence* such a morbid unrequited obsession? An East Indian I know says that the only thing against incest is the possibility of a genealogical impairment. Clearly this is not entirely what the British had in mind when they drew up the ninty-ninth canon of the church, "A Table of Kindred and Affinity" "wherein whosoever are related are forbidden in Scripture and our laws to marry together" and listed thirty forbidden possibilities (i.e., a woman may not marry with her mother's sister's husband), which I saw in fine print hanging up in a cathedral in Salisbury last summer.

Possibly the mistake I made over *Duffy* enhanced my outlook on the picture, which Andy Warhol and his crowd think is a bad flick. I didn't know why until I'd seen the premiere of

Andy's *Lonesome Cowboys* in Houston on November 19, 1968. I made another Houston scene because the week before my host John de Menil suggested maybe I cared more for airplanes than for his company since I was leaving in a hurry in order to catch the private company jet and avoid a commercial flight the next day or the day after when the little jet wouldn't have been available. That's as good a reason as any I suppose —both for leaving and for going back. Anyhow, on the return trip (to Houston) I told Andy in the airplane I was happy to be going to Houston to see one of his movies since I never see them in New York and in fact I think perhaps the last flick of his I saw was the one he made of me and Freddy Herko dancing on Wyn Chamberlain's roof before Andy got famous for those things, although he was famous on the soup cans and such. I think that was even before he made the *Sleep* movie. And around that time, right after JFK was shot, we were out in New Jersey in the woods around Billy Klüver's house, for an afternoon of television (funeral) and filming (shooting) in which I was pretending to be a hoofer who was a good shot, improvising steps in the fall mud and leaves under the weight of one of Billy's rifles. I wore the same outfit back to the city and a Park Avenue party Andy had been invited to, where we saw Larry Rivers who thought I looked perfect to model for a new painting he had in mind about a moon man and a moon lady. Andy's movie and Larry's painting may not be the best of their kind. But the way one thing leads to another and often the time lapse in between, like Andy in Houston, five years later, is the subject of his piece, or perhaps any piece these days, considering that's as good excuse as any for the pleasure I get shoving words around. At lunch on the patio of John's house, a real fine sexy Phillip Johnson house by the way built twenty years ago, I forgot I'd told one of my stories the night before, at dinner after Andy's movie, about how last week I found a Ping-Pong paddle and a Ping-Pong net on the back seat of a taxi. I said I might make it the central story of a next *Voice* piece. The trip I got into over it, was a domino thought pattern involving the mathematical probability of playing Ping-Pong again somehow many years after being a champion at it for six years in a sports-oriented boarding school. Very simple. Buy another racket, a little white ball, a five by nine foot sheet of plywood and three horses to support it, and bingo I'm a Ping-Pong player again. But I mean, what was the mathematical probability of locating any Ping-Pong gear abandoned in a taxi to bring the game into my life again after just happening to mention the find to Alex Hay who suggested the plywood board as a table.

For instance, right now there's a charming bearded man in my house making me a book. I don't know how he got in here. But I think I know how I met him. I was sitting on a curb one night waiting for a bus when this fellow came along in shorts and bare feet tripping out with a much younger "guide" who offered me some French cheese tasting like wild cherries. Later the "guide" called me and maybe two months later this bearded David, an elderly flower child who spent a year in jail for indecently assaulting his eleven-year-old daughter, also called me, to make a book, but I was in Houston when he got in. Anyhow, he says he makes instant rare books. It's a portable publishing house, every book being a limited edition of one. He puts all these words together in some random fashion on his beat-up portable typewriter after asking you to select (at random if you like) fifty words from two piles of one hundred and twenty-five cards. He says that if Random House publishes some version of his book it would be made at random and titled *At Random.* It's an exquisite perfectly-bound one-inch square book, by the way and it took him seven hours to make two of them. And so on. And on the plane ride to Houston Simone Swan asked me if I had a compact. I said I never touched the things. Then I recalled a little gold compact I'd swept off the car seat in Houston the week before with a bunch of stolen toys. I reached in my bag and produced the little gold compact. Oh wow, Simone said, that's mine. At which moment I recalled sitting on the bed where Yves Klein died, in 1962, last summer in Paris. His young widow told me he didn't die ordinary at all. His heart exploded from excitement over his immaterial investigations. And behind me on the plane Andy reading *Esquire,* alive and well five months after I saw him at a party one week before l'affaire Valerie and listened to a few of his stories about female fatuousness at the factory. I said I was certainly happy to be seeing his new movie in Houston. He said he'd like to shoot my friend who walks on her hands (how'd you know that, Andy?) and maybe I'd like to write a script. Later at Maxim's or someplace I said yes I'd like to write a script, but for a Christ on acid great trip thing. I said I'd like to see his *Imitations of Christ*. The Christ bit is far from exhausted yet I think. He was a sex meanie of the lowest orgy (Lennon) . . .

Andy is really too much. After the museum opening the night following his movie premiere we were having a two table crab meat dinner interrupted by musical chairs organized by John when at dessert time I was conversing with Andy next to Ultra Violet carrying on with a middle-aged Houston chick wearing a deep cleavage, and Andy produced a silver autograph book which he asked me to present to Roberto Rossellini across the table to please ask him to sign it for him. I did so in broken French with a little Italian thrown in, and said to Andy "boy Andy I'm gonna write in the *Voice* about how you wouldn't ask me to sign your autograph book." Also, the day before, debarking from the plane, a photographer jumped out of no place and herded three of us together with Andy for a photo, after which Andy remarked that he was making me famous. I said, listen Andy I was born famous. There was another of these scenes at the museum, with cameras clickety flash-bulbing and after all sheeeit I had on a pink gold and blue cowboy suit and a ten-gallon hat plundered that afternoon (courtesy my host) in a polite stampede through Houston's big cowstore, and so I say screw it, I mean it's all about "project ego destruction by overexposure." Or, when in Texas do as the Texans. Beside, my image doesn't register on film. Jill the Nipple strikes again. Bob Ashley has said of Anne Wehrer that no matter how much she exposes herself there's always something left. Amazing. She stayed overnight at my place couple of months ago on a trip from Ann Arbor and she was still talking when I went to sleep and she was talking when I woke up. She must've been talking in my sleep. Someone asked Helen Keller once if she closed her eyes when she went to sleep. She said she didn't stay awake to find out.

I woke up in Houston in a room with a Max Ernst and little Napoleon busts and a Napoleon Solo game in the closet. But I think cowboys were the order of the trip. I walked round all one afternoon from desk to trees to kitchen etc. thinking to write and get the benefit of all that outdoor nature stuff plus the indoor overgrown tropical forest stuff at the same time, but mostly feeling like the Lone Ranger and the rest of those birds in my pair of chamois ochre chaps. And I already said I went down there to see Andy's *Lonesome Cowboys*. This is about a bunch of beautiful randy young cowboys out on the ranch screwing each other and playing with Viva who wants a "real man" I guess but whose constant companion is Taylor Mead whom you know well to be everybody's favorite mythical underground poet fellow traveler poet jailbird poet queer and superstar extraordinaire. Taylor plays peekaboo with the cowboys, pimping for himself by the ruse of appearing to set them up for Viva, who is beaten, raped, and otherwise indignified until she gets hers at the end by seducing the most beautiful of the cats, the one who doesn't know what he wants, who doesn't know how to do it either, but who responds with dour Olympian passivity to Viva's incredible mixture of outright commands (take off your pants, etc.) and soulful rendition of the Catholic Mass. Wow. I told Andy it was something, the whole thing. As for *Duffy,* I can see now how Hollywood tunes in late on everything, and might come up with a flick as sophisticated as *Lonesome Cowboys* in three to ten years or more, if ever. Still, I liked *Duffy*. I'd like it even without the incest mistake I made for which I like it more. And what are all those cowboys doing in Andy's flick by the way. Aren't they a primitive ancient fraternity? The primeval horde? Aren't they properly renouncing all the chicks (including the in-laws) who caused so much trouble back on the ranch when their common father hoarded them all to himself? And why was Viva doing a Romeo-and-Juliet bit (lovely camp style) with her cowboy god about the necessity of dying after so beautifully screwing? He says he doesn't wanna die. Viva says she'll die alone then. "I do everything else alone. I might as well die alone." And why was that young girl at the museum opening getting me alone in a corner to interrogate me on my sex habits? *Credi qui absurdum*. I told her I'd send her a special rare edition bound in velvet and leather about my sexual exploits in London last summer.

November 28, 1968

HOLY CHRISTOMETER

A lady at Jasper Johns's house last night where a black-tie thing was going on as benefit for Merce Cunningham, who also danced for the contributors, told me "they" didn't understand my writing anymore. I used to be so good. At the black-tie dinner beforehand, uptown, the president of the Whitney said "who reads *The Village Voice* anyway." He didn't care for my velour Garbo hat or my crushed velvet pants and he tried to take my drink away from me when we were going in to dinner. At dinner I was stranded with five of "them" all bending my jugular over the goodwill cultural intentions of their money organizations (Whitney, etc.) and trying to find out at the same time if I could possibly be happy in a pair of silly looking pants. I wanted to tell that story about Jung telling Joyce that the difference between him (Joyce) and his daughter was that he (Joyce) was jumping off the bridge and his daughter was falling off the bridge. But I got to thinking instead about what my friend Ann Wilson said of how she suddenly understood what the South American coups were all about. She said it must happen that the governor of a province is giving a dinner and six revolutionaries walk in and the governor doesn't have enough dessert plates and pretty soon the governor isn't running the mansion anymore. Something like that happened at Ann's house one night when six of us were gorging ourselves on a French friend's cuisine and six other wierd-looking people, Latin types in low hats and wild colors, unexspeckledly entered and appeared to feel at home. We offered them some food.

They accepted. We got up so they could sit down. They accepted. Then a little later we could be observed as a party of six Anglo-Saxon types enjoying ourselves talking on the floor about ten yards from the table where our new Latin friends were holding forth with food and conversation on their own. At that point Ann gave us her astonishing revelation on the nature of a coup d'etat. I also thought to tell my black-tied dinner companions about what I read in the *Times* on the German Krupp dynasty. How Alfried died, was succeeded by a son Arndt, whose principal interest in life is to have nothing to do with the family firm. But I didn't say anything interesting at all. They knew I was a bad dream. Tomorrow they'd forget. For myself I made two pleasing discoveries there. I walked into the master bedroom (the master hot on my boots to know if I was a spy) which I thought was very yellow. The whole thing was yellow. But as I walked out I thought well maybe it was green. The master asked me what I thought of the colors. I said it was yellow. He said no it was green. Anyway how could I tell with my shades on. I said I could tell fine. The room was yellow but possibly it was trying to be green. Then I recalled a pair of pants I have that I can't wear anything on top with because the pants are green trying to be yellow. I was always putting a green top but they really need a yellow top to match the color in the green which is trying to be yellow. Terrific. New color revelations. My other discovery was a Dubuffet in the living room which the owner said was 1947. When I expressed curiosity my host inquired if I was interested in the visual arts. (!) The Dubuffet is a child's Dubuffet. Now I want to know more about Dubuffet and I never did before. This picture is not better or worse than some paintings in a children's book of paintings I have, done by ages about eight through fifteen, and they're all beautiful. I understand that the Smothers Brothers show a film consisting of all the great art of the world. The film lasts three minutes. A great painting is flashed at every one-sixth of a second. That's six paintings a second and 1,080 paintings in three minutes. I heard this in Boston last week at a luncheon after a special television preview at WGBH, Boston's educational station. They must've been excited about this show because they were flying people (press, etc.) in and out for it. I was supposed to fly up from New York but drove down from

Hommage à Duchamp.

George Segal: *The Girl Friends* (retitled by the author *Jill and Polly Entombed*). 1969. Plaster. 41″ x 72″ x 42″. Photograph courtesy of Sidney Janis Gallery, New York.

New Hampshire instead. Hearing the story about the film of great paintings I meant to say I'd slept in a house in Boston that night with two Monets in it. Not one, or three, but two. They were early Monets, before he went rather daft on the light of day hitting haystacks from sunup to sunset, It might be just as interesting that all I saw of New Hampshire was a place called Squam Lake. That's because I arrived at night and left in the night. It's also occurring to me that I'm not sure anymore about my trips. I mean the difference between a head trip and a road trip. The confusion became very apparent the other day when I was supposed to make another Boston trip. Les Levine had offered me $50 and round-trip fare to play my Yo-Yo at a lecture he was giving. We had it all worked out. Rent a car. Arrive at 11:00 A.M. for the lecture. Eat lunch at the Oyster House. Try to meet the WGBH man. Look at another big Boston house with great paintings in it. Maybe even sleep there. And go to MIT to see the Centre for Advanced Visual Studies. Fine. Levine said to rent the car at night so we could leave early in the A.M. I picked it up at Alexander's at 10:00 P.M. A spanking new white Pontiac with twenty-seven miles on it and a pickup like a clown out of a cannon. Driving downtown my friend with me said let's go around the island. Okay. Heading into the tunnel connecting the FDR drive and the West Side Highway all the lights on the dashboard flashed red. Right, the damn thing stopped dead in the tunnel. After more events I won't go into we wound up back at Alexander's in a cab, leaving Pontiac in tunnel, and left Alexander's again with spanking new Ford Fairlane, color also white. It got me home all right, but it was late. Levine woke me up at six. I said yeah the car was outside but I wasn't going anyplace in it. I'd take him to the airport if he liked. No he'd take a cab. Great. I slept till 11:00 A.M. Holy Christometer, have you ever rented a car you never used? No kidding, it sat on the street all day and I brought it back at 6:00 P.M. before going to that black-tie deal at the Whitney people place. My point is that it doesn't matter anymore about whether you're actually on the road or not. I must've made dozens of trips in my house all day. And possibly the people on the street were enjoying the car.

But my first Boston trip was excellent (too). I mentioned about the TV show. It was a double-channel affair. Gus Solomons, Jr., had choreographed a program called City Motion Space Game. Gus danced and did other activities on two sets separated by a few inches as we looked at it in the WGBH studio. Different things on each set, but basically all about Gus in action in the city. On the sound track sometimes Gus would say "any two events occurring simultaneously are related in the perceiver." Yes man. The idea for people at home would be to get their living room and bedroom sets together close to each other so they could watch the double-channel broadcast as a kick on related-unrelated visual occurrences. I watched the election night results on two or three (I forget) sets at once, in color and black and white. What I like best in this kick department is turning off the sound and playing rock, for the ads especially and also for Westerns, soap operas, and cartoons. Anyhow, we had a good time in Boston. Gus looked great (in person) in a tan corduroy suit that didn't zipper or button down the front. It sort of sticks together from neck to navel like wall and masking tape. I asked him how he felt now, not being with Cunningham anymore. He said fine; although he broke his back when he left Merce. I said never mind I broke my foot when I left Limón. We were talking over sherry and Cheeze Whizzes around a conference table at least fifty feet long, before going to the studio to see the show. I saw Stan VanDerBeek there. I jumped on his hips to say hello. And I saw Steven Smoliar who was representing *Dance Magazine* although he's actually a math and computer nut at MIT. He looked seventeen if a day. I asked him what he wants to do in life. He says he wants to be the first dance critic with a Ph.D. in mathematics. He's an unusual guy. Another unusual man, whom I met at Squam Lake, told me the key to a healthy life is plenty of sex, lots of Scotch and salad. Every so often it hits me, wow is this the only thing to be doing. Is Fred Asparagus the only guy who is long and green and dances beautifully? Did you know you can open a wine bottle with an umbrella tip? Are you still lying on the unemployed side of your body? You know they say when you're duckfooted you should try being pigeon-toed for a while. And when your feet are sore try walking on your hands. Did you know there's a new dance called "The Mess" where you put your feet together and move your bowels? L'enfant abdique son extase. Am I talking too much? In Boston they gave me a name

tag identifying me as The *Village Voice*. Friend Polly didn't
think she wanted to be there but after a while she went to the
name-tag desk and made out a tag identifying herself as the
Village Listener. Driving back to New York she left it in a ladies room. I retrieved it and changed both tags so the *Voice*
read *Listener* and the *Listener* read *Voice*. Am I still talking
too much? Listen, last night after Jasper's I ruined my crushed
velvet pants by falling asleep with a glass of milk on my stomach. I must've been dreaming about my concern for the Whitney
gang. They're not awfully happy. Are they in league to do the
same to the people they're philanthropizing and so on?

December 19, 1968

ALPERT'S THIRD LIFE &
THE CHEMISTRY OF DIVINITY

I feel a bit clumsy over saying anything about Richard Alpert,
now at least, especially since till recently I knew of the man
only as "that other man" who was expelled from Harvard with
Timothy Leary. But I think there should be some initial report
here, with hopefully more to follow. Returning recently from
India, Alpert is now known or wishes to be known as Baba
Ram Dass. I'm going to refer to him as Alpert because I don't
know why I'm going to. On December 4, 1968, I went to the
Universalist Church on Seventy-sixth Street to hear him speak.
He sat lotus-leaf on a cushion for a long time in a long beard,
wearing meticulous Indian white, accompanied by incense, a
watch, three candles, a vase of flowers, a photo (maybe of his
guru), and downstage of a mural of Christ in a washing of the
feet scene. He spoke into a mike in deep clear resonance, sometimes pausing, often smiling, occasionally chuckling. He has a
real big head, or prominent forehead, and crystal-blue eyes. His

face looks drenched by wind sand stars. Terrifically clear. He speaks a mixture of the University scholar, the psychedelic hippie, the more recent holy man still a bit nonplussed by a role we Westerners don't take seriously, much less consider a reality.

I was happy to hear him, although I didn't need to. I like churches, but never to listen to someone. The smell of worship turns me into a dead-eye dick. The atmosphere at the church there wasn't my idea of a picnic without a chief exactly. There's this incredible misunderstanding in the West over divinity. Alpert may not be divine yet, I don't know, but he's certainly beautiful. He's been someplace. He's not coming back either. And as he said at the lecture, he wasn't even there.

A lot of people know this. A few people in the West are charting the spaces Alpert is also navigating. Most people at the church lecture I guessed were people experienced in the use of the hallucinogenics as therapeutic agents. As such they know about how we are all divine if we would but know it. The terrifying confusion in the West over divinity is the reason why people become divine in the megalomania sense and get shot for it and why people don't become divine and shoot the people they think are presuming to play the god they too believe they could be if only they had enough money. Given our origins in the primitive tradition of the blood sacrifice, both aspects of a distorted divinity are understandable. It was both fitting and misleading that Alpert should have been speaking in the shadow of a Christ picture. That Christ was a savior there is no doubt. That Christ cast doubts on the potential divinity of his clients is a statement of fact putting it mildly. After all he was the Son of God. Who else could be the Son of God and not be murdered for it as well. Wilhelm Reich wrote a book, maybe his last, called *The Murder of Christ*. A totally nutty book. Ostensibly about Christ, he was speaking of his own murder. The ultimate paranoia of Christ's own next to last words, My God My God Why Hast Thou Forsaken Me. By that time Reich had lost his cool. You can't be god in the West when there is only one god.

In a midwestern loony bin there are "Three Christs of Ipsilanti." These three lower-middle-class fellows think they are Christ. I imagine they are. But the "treatment" there has involved the staff pointing out the absurdity of their position to each of them since the two others obviously like them (incarcerated, dispossessed etc.) also believe themselves to be what they claim to be. The staff wasn't successful and they continued to be held prisoners. The ironies would be funny if they weren't tragic. One aspect of the tragedy is that these fellows aren't divine either. Or you might say they are as we all are but know it only through a glass darkly which is to remain confused. Or let's say they might have been, or had a vision, but translated the vision and possibly feelings of great power into our literal tradition of the super hero, the final master and judge. That is our idea of Christ developed by a power-mad institutional church. These three men are not being shot for playing god on a big expense account. They're being shot (imprisoned) for claiming outright to be the one figure whom Westerners still view as he who must die for us who cannot die within ourselves to become transfigured and resurrected on our own cosmic responsibility. Christ was the last great blood sacrifice in the West. Even to think it anymore is to rob ourselves of a paradise on earth, in our heads and bodies, which is our cosmic right. Because the human condition has become so hopelessly confused, the more utopian you sound the more tragic you sound.

The true revolution is in the head, not on the streets. The people on the streets believe the myth of the West about paradise looking like a dollar bill. They want to repaper the shanty back home to resemble the White House. Once the shanty resembles the White House, or looks even better (an old rags-to-riches story in America), the owners are still stumbling around bumping into the furniture of their cluttered unhappy brains. The revolutionaries think they'll make things much better for a lot of people. But some other heads have to go in the process. Whose head is more valuable? Are the cops and the industrialists less valuable than the flower children? As groups I'd say they're a good deal unhappier. That's all. In any case the equal distribution of wealth wouldn't solve the head problem—either the head on the block or the head as a god head. What we have now in the West is a very limited paradise of people like Alpert doing that difficult navigation into realms of consciousness best known to the holy men of the East. The closest we have to such a tradition in the West is among the American Indians, disclaimed by their invaders and conquerors as primitive stock not worth the time of day or dollar. I always recommend *Black Elk Speaks*—the story of a holy man of the Oglala Sioux, introduced to me three years ago by artist Robert Whitman, who is a descendant of Walt. Bob was always buying the book to pass it around. Lately I've been doing the same.

Alpert is giving his talks to tell us of his journey. I think he's on his third life. I think he wants to get off the karmic wheel of rebirth. His second life in this life occurred between 1961 and 1967. That was his life as a psychedelic drug man. The reason I didn't need to hear him is because I heard it all from Shyam Bhatnagar (an Indian yogic therapist in America) and Shyam's friends one afternoon last summer over tea and coffee, in a few sentences. Shyam's friend George said "he's the most beautiful American I ever met." I was impressed. But what told me all was the short tale of Alpert's meeting with the guru in India last year after a fruitless odyssey many a moon in a Landrover rather comfortably looking for he probably wasn't sure what, armed as well with his usual battery of drugs. The return of Richard Alpert is about his return, for a short time before going back, to tell us of his new life without drugs. The media which grabbed up the drug explosion several years ago to grind up in their money mill (*Time, Life,* etc.) won't be interested in Alpert's conversion. It's much more dangerous. Or if they do they'd try to make him a sitting duck on a Carson show after which Carson would do another Maharishi type parody (cackling about "flower power" as he bashes a bouquet over the head of his assistant).

Alpert's new life without drugs began in a hippie restaurant in Nepal, India, after he laid eyes on a twenty-three-year-old American boy from Laguna Beach, California. They got to talking and Alpert said it became apparent within moments that this boy was very special. He was the first person he'd met who looked like he'd found something. "Everybody else seemed to be looking for something." The upshot was that Alpert abandoned his Landrover and traveling companion to follow this new friend back into India by foot. He was sick and confused a lot of the time, but he kept going. He said at one point he experienced the humor and the horror of being mistaken for an itinerant holy man. The people kissed his feet and gave him money ("It paid to be a holy man") but of course he had no illusions about what he was. He said the young Laguna Beach boy gave away his money and kept cutting off his game, like his habit of discussing the past and the future. "Just be here now," the boy would say. At last they came to the place of the boy's guru. The boy's face was streaming tears as he loped up the mountain to see his beloved. Alpert stumbled after him, thinking I suppose on the absurdity of lurching on the bare heels of this six-foot-seven-inch long beard from the States with a high school education. Sitting with the guru, Alpert got the "cosmic put on." You came to India in an automobile? Would you give it to me? Etc.—But the real stopper became the moment Alpert entered upon his third life. The guru told Alpert about a revery he (Alpert) had had the night or so before about his mother. He told Alpert of how his mother had died of spleen trouble, of a swollen stomach and so on. Alpert's mind raced for an explanation of how the guru could know these things. He said there was no earthly way of him knowing. Only through his Laguna Beach friend, but they were never parted. Alpert cried then, he says, not out of joy or sorrow, but out of the feeling that he was home.

They brought him to a temple for the night. In the morning they brought him again to the guru. The guru asked him if he had a question. No, no questions. "Where is the medicine?" the guru inquired. Alpert misunderstood, thinking he meant vitamin pills and the like, but produced a palmful of what he had, including the acid. The guru sorted the stuff out and swallowed nine hundred micrograms of the acid. Alpert awaited results. Nine hundred is plenty. Nothing happened. This fellow had been "happening" on his own stuff (head) for years no doubt. That was enough for Alpert. He had his answer, he says. The guru was a living breathing statement of the special being he knew it was possible on earth to be. Soon thereafter Alpert received a teacher, a fifty-year-old Brahmin who weighs ninety pounds, whose total food intake is two glasses of milk per day. "The World Health Organization says he's dead."

While he's in the States, aside from giving seminars, Alpert is doing what he did in India, following his yogic pursuits, living in a small cabin in New Hampshire. He describes his present state as like being on a mild hashish high, continuously, twenty-four hours, free, no paranoia. He talks about the master and servant relationship as one of lover to the beloved, not as in the movie *The Servant*—which is a good enough example, by the way of what I meant about the revolution in the streets. The servant takes over (if he can) because he was taken himself (or thought so). In the religious sense, master and servant become one. The student becomes the teacher. Didn't Socrates even sleep with his male students?

Like everything else our education in the West is based on the principle of hierarchical domination. The one and only father as ruler, master, judge—until or unless overthrown by an ambitious rebellious son who is so angry as to enslave the former father, the other sons, etc., after enduring so much similar injustice, only to be overthrown by his own evil by the next son turning father and so on in the sad cycle known as Western education. It takes place at home, in school, on the job, on the street. A somewhat mellowed or mollified son will come to be known as a benevolent ruler. The project is to do away with the rulers. The students in our universities are roaring for a restructured university. What they should be wanting is to abandon the universities. What they really want is to take over in the manner of *The Servant*. Once they take over, who is going to be taken? What they really want is daddy's head. But daddy's head will multiply as their own heads once they get daddy on the block. The closest we've come here to a nonstructured (anarchic) university so far as I know was Black Mountain College, which folded in the fifties. These rebellious students of ours, most of them, wouldn't be happy with a Black Mountain. They want the laddered structure they were brought up to believe in. As students, they're just a bit more precocious in wanting a higher rung sooner, faster, than formerly. And if they talk socialism, whatever they call it now, they're still stuck with nothing better than the idea of equal distribution of benefits.

Alpert is one of our heroes who abandoned the universities. And Alpert is a standout for reasons he develops in the first part of his talk about how he was well into being an exemplary empire builder of the West. He had plenty of money and quite a few important positions in his role as expert in the field of psychology. One might ask if Harvard expelled Alpert or Alpert expelled Harvard. It always works both ways. Alpert's second life began March 7, 1961, when he ingested psilocybin with Tim Leary. The big drug experiment was launched. His university days were then numbered. For instance, shortly after the psilocybin experience, he was to deliver a scheduled lecture at Harvard—a lecture on motivation, theories of ego psychology, etc.—but that place he had gone to, on the psilocybin, he couldn't find it in a book. Before this, Leary had told him that he'd learned more on the peyote he'd taken in Mexico than in all his years as a psychologist. Alpert was to discover the same. There was nothing in the Western psychoanalytical theories to account for the altered states of consciousness under use of hallucinogenics. And the schizophrenic experience was (still is) regarded as a breakdown and not a breakthrough. The correlation, by the way, between insanity and the high states induced by outside agents has yet to be explored. The bad trip aspect of insanity, for instance, is the same bad trip as an acid high when the preparation and environment are inadequate to meet the demands of a mind thrown into outer (inner) space.

Much of Western psychoanalytical theory devolves upon definitions of abnormalcy in relation to something conceived as a rational functional mind. Artists are "abnormal," but they get away with it by calling themselves artists. Deviations in expression (i.e., a person decides not to talk for a few days) are suspect for what they can do to a well-organized society. Psychoanalysis doesn't have much of an already shaky leg to stand on unless it can define states of abnormalcy which require treatment and readjustment to the nine-to-five job. Presently the most advanced psychoanalytical thinking is beginning to line up with the heresies of the hippie drug revolution plus deeper renewed excavations into mythology and increased interest in the wisdom of the East. People like Ronald Laing and N. O. Brown are mixing up notions of sanity and insanity such as to throw our "therapies of adjustment" into the kind of disrepute which should shatter the entire psychoanalytical profession. To become truly healers our doctors would have to abandon their offices (and the money game) just as the students and teachers and trustees should be abandoning the universities. They are no longer, and never were really, equipped to deal with the altered states of consciousness which they have defined in their books and clinical practices as abnormal. What they have been calling abnormal is ironically the one spontaneous way a totally screwed-up animal in a screwed-up society can break through to the normalcy of a cosmic ego-less consciousness. Freud's "unconscious" is really a state of being (buried by centuries of rational thought, behavior, etc.) and not a repository for repressed unfortunate childhood memories.

The drug people have discovered the horror of sanity and the pathos of insanity. The latter as a heroic pathetic attempt to reunite the inner and outer worlds. If it's pathetic it's because the attempt is usually unsuccessful. The rare case survives. The confusion of insanity needs a proper guide. Insanity is too often a way out and not a way back in. Or you could say that it's a way in without a return-trip ticket. If the trip is successful the traveler will know he's been someplace and a good deal about where he's been and how it's possible to be there without being insane, which is one kind of distorted divinity.

This is what Alpert discovered in 1967 about the drug experience. He says he never doubted the psychedelics as agents, keys, to another state. And still doesn't. He says he wouldn't be where he is now without the drugs. But he didn't know enough (no one in the West does) to maintain the states of altered consciousness. No matter how many trips he took, and he took about three hundred altogether, he always came down. Going up and coming down, even when some transformation has been achieved by the insights on a high, remains the manic-depressive cycle of a confused human animal.

Alpert is now on the kind of high that could only be called high by a Westerner thinking of high distinct from low. His high is our cosmic right. Still, he speaks of himself as a beginner. In his third life he is doing the discipline as natural to the East as gravy and potatoes to an American. But drugs versus discipline is not an issue. There is no moral issue. Nor is the discipline viewed as a task or as a punishment, as we here view the idea and practice of discipline. Alpert's main quarrel with drugs (I think) is that their effects are discontinuous. For this reason, Alpert's new-found discipline is more dangerous to this society than the drug idea, which has been under constant attack by the media since its first exposure as good copy. The threat of drugs to a normally sick society is very apparent to those who've used them and to those who've suffered the economic etc. consequences of being in the path of their users.

The therapeutic effects of the hallucinogenics could be far reaching. Like any other agent, they can be abused. But under the right conditions (different for everybody) they can do for a body and head in a trip or two what an unusually good psychoanalyst (rare animal) can do for the same guy in several years. In short, a few good trips can project a person beyond psychology and open the lock to understanding, which is the embarrassingly simple fact that the world in its diverse forms is incredibly beautiful. The drug people have discovered the riches of the world. One reason they come down after a trip is that the rest of the population is still sleeping. Still tied in knots by an imagined psychology. We could be through with psychology now. If administered properly, the drugs could begin the work of release from this bondage. Yet it is now known that the chemistry of the drugs is also spontaneously manufactured in the body. You can't give somebody something they don't already have. Alpert is working on this natural chemistry, to release it. The East holds a few keys to how to create this continuous chemistry (without drugs, without insanity). This is the chemistry of divinity and it isn't any secret and it isn't beyond any man.

December 26, 1968

SOFT IN THE HEAD

Recently Yoko Ono's ex, Tony, was in New York with their daughter. Tony does make-believe business. I've been trying to get a tape of LaMonte Young's into a Beatle's bare hands, preferably George's. Tony said I should stop at Bob Dylan's farm in Vermont where George Harrison was hanging out. I said oh sure Tony. Next thing he said he set it up with their business agent in the city here and that George was waiting for me all one Saturday afternoon, but Tony forgot I told him I wouldn't be here that weekend. So later when I got back I called the agent, whom you reach by being very clever, who said George never heard of this LaMonte tape thing and I replied of course not he wouldn't remember that conversation five months ago when I told him about it in London. But still I wanted a Beatle's bare hands and over anybody's dead body please and he wanted to know what did I think was so special about all this that I needed such special attention, so I got really exasperated at last by informing the ruffled man I'll bet the Beatles' mothers can get in touch with them, at which he yelled YOU'RE NOT THE BEATLES' MOTHERS—so I hung up. I guess when you get famous you don't have any mothers either. (Jesus said to Mary: what makes you think you're my mother?) Anyhow if it's that much trouble I'm sure the *I Ching* would say to forget it. Besides, LaMonte even in his poverty must be better off than the guys you can't reach. I visited him and his wife Marion Zazeela recently. I went to see Marion's slides. But when you go there you don't get a piece of anything. The whole place is buzzing all over, vibing up your organs and such, from LaMonte's generators. Marion's calligraphy is very apparent at the end of the loft where you don't eat and drink. The turtles are prominently big in a child's inflated swimming pool fitted out with the best sewage system. Marion and LaMonte always talk on the phone together, when someone calls. And on the wall there's a news photo of a two-headed turtle now inhabiting a zoo someplace. This turtle sometimes tries to go in two directions at once. In the loft all directions are one by virtue of the sound. According to James Byars you can hear the roar of insects above the full rush hour freeway traffic in Los Angeles. I wonder how many watts a person is worth in LaMonte's loft. James says everybody equals about one hundred watts. Three mathematicians at the Rand Corporation in California told him so. Byars is interested in what would be the wattage at half-excitation of the entire population. He says they don't know what the exact wattage is for self-electrocution. I mean how much would be required. A mouth kiss, by the way, is one hundred and twenty-five to four hundred and fifty watts, and kissing anywhere else is general excitation wattage. I wonder what happens at the Watts Towers. Or what would be generated by a school of whales screwing with a bunch of kangaroos looking on. The Rand people also go out on a limb with a "partial process definition of electricity that is occasionally true":—any two or three points in space that have some attractiveness. While being charged at LaMonte's by LaMonte's singing plus generators and Marion's superposed slide projected calligraphic designs I thought of James's big brother type question: what would it mean to have all human attention called simultaneously on earth to a single focus, or sign. I suppose the planet could get so excited as to wander into another orbit. But I think the off-white meanies have something else in mind with their nuclear reactors. On Marion's and LaMonte's terms it would mean a world immobilized in trance. I like that. The Atlantic Ocean, where does it begin and where does it end? Every dwelling can dissolve around us while still remaining there. Déréglément des sens! But afterward Marion and I academically discussed the optical effects and properties of her beautiful calligraphy. I'm not going into it here. I have an optical piece in mind. Larry Poons told me he became a painter after reading *Lust for Life*. I'd like to have more information on this sort of thing. I'm becoming more interested in the found art that I find. LaMonte was never any better in a concert hall. He's good in my head at home too. And I was thinking just today how that *Times* art critic might not go to so much trouble getting so hot and pothered making out a case for and against George Segal if he took off a few hours to visit George at the farm (in New Jersey) and see how it all goes together as a style of life. George upstairs in the studio where the man and the plaster make a transaction with the live models, and the rest of the stuff, all finished, lying in funky state outside the house in endless low dank rooms of connected chicken coops through which George must've made hundreds of happy guided tours these many years after having once been a chicken farmer. Jesus who cares about his or anybody's contribution to or subtraction from the aestheticks of contemporamiable sculpchur. All it has left to do is to become meaningless. I like Gregory Battcock's recent criticism of a Bob Dylan painting on a Bob Dylan record jacket. It was a point-by-point psychoanalytical analysis which Gregory claimed had no justification.

I went to the Whitney Sculpture Annual opening last week wearing my ruined crushed ultra velvet pants and most remember seeing Lil Picard wearing some tin armor of her own making I suppose, around her back and bosom. It was kind of formidable in a sweet way. I was saying how delectable a low floor sculpture looked, an oval shaped thing called *Decomposition*— all the materials used to make the Whitney in their preconcretized crumbly form, arranged looking a sort of early-American rug, although Lil said it was a cake. I said I wanted to walk through it or roll around in it. But guards would shoot me I guess. And Lil said "they shoot you, I protect you." I also saw a big motorized silver aluminum cock and a white structure I thought to be a Broken Pyramid by I. C. Morewhite. And Claes Oldenburg, who said he guessed I'd been told I was the Hedda Hopper of the art world. And a nice McLuhan man who wondered if I knew I'd quoted McLuhan in a recent piece to which I said no I didn't. I don't know anymore what belongs to who. Recently someone asked me if I was quoting Jill Johnston or speaking for myself. Putting down my immortal thoughts daily I'm not sure which peoples are entering and leaving my brain at random. Before going to the Whitney where I saw Lil I saw Howard Smith at the *Voice*. I'd like to claim him as my discovery since I laid out about thirty of his three-by-five white cards filled up with his telephone doodles on a large piece of black paper and then triumphantly called him to come see the layout to point out what a terrific doodler he is, which he must already know, but meaning more than that about how he could be a collector's item within days by proper application of art world tactics. Right, he said, I just construct an ethic around the work and so on. Right. Like you send off an article to *Art forum* on the subject called "The New Yankee Doodle." Stick a feather in your hat and call it Beethoven's last movement. That's what we used to call our butterscotch pudding in boarding school. I sat in a pew last week to celebrate Beethoven's birthday anniversary one day early. He was a lot like he is now, but nobody paid much attention then. The pew was a row at St. Peter's Church and the author of the celebration was a young composer by name Kenneth Werner whose lower lip hangs down away from his upper to complete a relaxed deadpan physicality but who otherwise resembles the great man he was celebrating.

I enjoyed it a lot. Yvonne says I'm getting soft in the head, enjoying all these things. They want me to shape up and talk business. You gotta be extracting a success from somebody else's failure or vice versa in order to qualify as a good grade giver. The winners make history baby. And Beethoven was probably an okay guy too. Pretty wrought up for his time. What would the wattage of an *Eroica* be in 1968? The wattage of Werner's first piece, called "birthday," was such a light touch as to be almost a child's story about lying on a puffy cloud with an angel feeding you a sponge cake dressed up in blue icing. They served some vile tasting stuff like that. Sky cake with cloud puffs or shaving cream. It looked real pretty before it reached my mouth. Anyhow the setting was gentle and affectionate. Werner's assistants, including a little girl, lighting and blowing out and relighting the candles on the cakes, and wafting bubbles and making balloons and a few audience people singing happy birthday to Ludwig and a pacific disintegration as everybody got messy on the blue icing and felt free to do anything with the balloons. The rest of the program was more formal I think. An "air" for Marcel Duchamp (wonder if Ludwig played chess) included TV mileage of *Peyton Place* plus slides of people, places, plus Charlotte Moorman properly dressed for church she said playing nostalgic on her instrument while Werner draped her and cello with blinking Xmas lights. I liked it. Also an impressive assemblage of screen images (real-time TV and double-screen film) accompanied by siren blooping over and over sound electronic. But that was nothing. On December 16 in 1770, Ludwig was born. On December 16 in 1773, there was on this territory the Boston Tea Party. On December 16 in 1631, Mount Vesuvius erupted, killing 18,000 persons. And on December 16 in 1809, Napoleon was divorced from Josephine. On December 16, of this year I don't remember a thing because it was one day after Werner's birthday celebration for Ludwig. Next year I might remember Ludwig on the 15th. I hope Werner was thinking up a new scheme for impressing people. They say everybody was born, but I don't remember it. I must've been having one of my blackouts.

December 26, 1968

TELL ME THE WEATHER

I read somewhere about a man dying of being snowed on while he lies with his head stuck in a dog door. Possibly that's an apt metaphor to describe the general condition. Often I wonder how it's possible to keep moving without going anyplace. That seems the ideal position. Yet I'm hearing all the time about people actually going places. David Bradshaw goes hunting for deer in Vermont. Jasper Johns leaving for the Carolinas to spend time around some Bucky Fuller domes. Rosalyn Drexier off to London or Edinburgh to see about her daughter and one of her plays. Peter Hujar just back from Little Rock, Arkansas, having taken some photos of a football game for *Sports Illustrated*. Ann Wilson also back, from the Virgin Islands having baby hauled a small boy to his grandma altogether a thirty-hour trip. Henry Martin just in from Italy for a week to see about a book about art on somebody. Steve Paxton out on the coast right now having no trouble showing his pornie movie although that's where they banned *The Beard*. And Ralph Ortiz with the scariest story about Vancouver where he short-circuited some head fuse by smashing a Beethoven symphony cum record player and also a grand piano stuffed with mice and getting the whole place wherever it happened bloody absolutely messed up read bad from being so destructive. Then, Ralph says, on the plane trip back he saw a Canadian newspaper with a big photo of himself looking fiendish wielding overhead the axe the weapon he got everybody so upset with. I asked him if anyone on the plane recognized him. He said no he was cowering under his lapel. But also on top of all that the Canadian Parliament in Ottawa was discussing him because they wanted to know how it happened that the Canadian Government would be donating the money to a gallery in Vancouver for this sort of unfortunate event. No doubt Ralph doesn't need Canada for awhile. If he did he might be asking how to get back into the palace this time without attracting attention. It's curious, by the way, that some American TV people think the only clear ap-

proach to the problem is to cut down the sheer number of kill-
ings, beatings, burnings, and flesh wounds per show. But did
you know that the scientists detonating the first atom bomb in
the desert had no idea the extent of damage to occur when the
thing went off, that the calculations were all on paper? What I
think sometimes about a guy like Ralph is that he's one of our
socially concerned artists who likes to stagger, snort, and swing
one leg over the top of a house to clean the air of invisible spir-
its. A man on stilts, they say, can cover more ground faster
than a man on foot. I have a friend about forty years old who
still shakes her legs when she gets excited. What do they mean
by that expression shake a leg? I'm not going to feel badly until
after I have my coffee. Are we really brought up to keep on the
move? Recently Hannah Wiener was talking about paying the
rent when I suggested a poet act to tour the colleges, like putting a package deal together. She said yes she'd been considering that. "Have package, will travel." Whereas Barbara Stacy
told me she was thinking of leaving New York (forever) but she
wasn't financially prepared to do so. Feeling confused about it
she consulted the *I Ching* and threw the number which led her
to the text on waiting and it said when there's an obstruction
and you can't move or make any immediate changes make the
inner trip, concentrate your attention inward. That's precisely
what an Eighth Street Bookstore salesman was telling me one
day when I asked them for a book by a turn-of-the-century
French psychologist on the interplanetary travels of a Helen
someone and I said wow that's a pretty expensive book, for
which I was rewarded by a twinkle and a suggestion that I
could probably take the trip for much less money. I thanked
him and left feeling I'd accompanied this Helen someone for
several interplanetary trips the cosmos over.

Driving through a snowstorm to New Hampshire last week
we got a buzz on the radio which friend Polly said was the sign
of a UFO in the vicinity when you heard this buzzing in a
snowstorm in New Hampshire and friend Gene said I wish
they'd come and take us away. And all Ann could say was that
she wished she could see a neon sign of a cock in various stages
of erection. We didn't see any of those unidentified flying cup-
cakes. But the snowstorm was a scene and a half. They were

talking on the radio about the astronauts going around the moon. Don't tell me the news, tell me the weather. I had that sexy feeling of being taken someplace on a weather report. Meredith Monk told me about some college kids at a college where she performed where most of the kids were like you'd expect but some of them looked like they wanted to be taken someplace. Which reminds me of a perfect story about a David who used to look very all right working here at *Harper's Bazaar* when one unsuspecting trip he was hitchhiking to San Francisco and happened to be picked up by the Grateful Dead on their way to the same place. They were traveling in their hearse as always and everything was A-1 okay until a fuzz car seemed to be trailing them and the leader, who was driving, commanded his whole car to swallow all the stuff they had. And thus beganneth the story of a David, whom I saw in London leading life of happy ne'er-do-well wearing longish hair and rough looking outfits. So whattya gonna do. Thousands of people are now looking for what only a few of us once looked for. The only thing disappointed me about this last New Hampshire trip was drawing a blank on a possible gondola ride up and down a mountain. I went to a ski slope without any skis. They said on the weekends they wouldn't permit gondola trips for tourists minus their skis. I talked up a storm about getting a whole piece out of such a trip, but they pretended not to understand. I tried the same lady at two windows with different stories without realizing it was the same lady. They must be short on ladies. That's what the fuss is over the gondolas. However, it's an expensive looking slope. And I made plenty of discoveries there. For instance, the worst skiers dress the most ostentatiously. The good skiers can look like ordinary bums walking around in the coffee lodge. Skiing is just like dancing. Either you can do it or you can't. Over cups and cups of coffee I watched all these stick figures spilling or zigging down the last run of the slope. I guess each sport is all about using mostly one part of body and the rest of the body falling in line. No doubt skiing is the big knee sport. Badminton is the big elbow and wrist sport. Dancing is supposed to be an allover sport. I imagine whatever you do though you'll have a similar style. I noticed how fancy some of those ski bunnies are. Like in the parallel action how the torso will swing gracefully but much more exaggerated than necessary when it goes in opposition to the knee movement. They'd probably look the same in a discotheque. I told an elderly skier I could feel the slope even if I wasn't doing it. He said could I know about sex just reading on it in a book. I replied he had a point there. But I have a theory about how we have archetypal knowledge understanding feeling of our former lives as fishes and birds and so on. Skiing is a big flying sport. I'm a high flier. I fly in my dreams a lot too. How much do you have to know to fly properly? What's a proper flying dream? What's the proper method for flying down a mountain? Why couldn't I be flying in my coffee as I space out my eyes up the slope through a picture window lightly? One of my most beautiful flying dreams was up against a ceiling in the breaststroke. Anyhow a little eight-year-old girl skier, probably an expert, told me the proper method for flying down a slope. According to her there's only one way to do it. You have to take lessons. I asked her why. She said otherwise you won't know how to do it. Oh I see. For example, she explained, it's wrong to come down doing the snowplow. Why? Because it isn't right. I see. You mean you have to do something else besides the snowplow I said. Yes, that's right. And you have to take lessons. Otherwise it's wrong. Her father thought I was raising philosophical questions, but we continued the conversation. I asked her if you have to learn how to fall. Naturally. And what's the object in learning how to fall? She didn't know. She was just certain there was a correct way to fall and someone had to show you how. One time I fell out of bed and split a cartilage in my knee. Maybe she's right. But I dunno, I just don't fall out of bed anymore. And I don't recall taking a lesson to fall off my first roof into a deep snow just for the helluvit.

January 2, 1969

CASTING FOR '69

My story begins with some unfamiliar handwriting on an envelope. I pulled a little red string which tore the bottom part to make fall out a shower of confetti and happy new year. I had a love letter from a guy wants me to marry him. I don't know him. Anyhow sorry, I'm like a nun, I'm married to Mary. Well at least the Xmas is over one more time. Everywhere you go you see Mary and her kid. How many independent researchers have come to the same conclusion? It doesn't matter. My lord returned from the wars today and pleasured me twice in his top boots. I've noticed if you just pretend you're a girl everything will be okay. But he gave me no quarter; if I made a foolish move he'd wipe me out instantly. Then, at some age or other, for lack of any good reason to go on living, he committed suicide. And I was enjoying it and not knowing it. That's the worst. But now it's just Twinkin' Blinkin' an' Twat and I hope you kick your garbage around until it gets lost. And I hope you grow up after you get married more than an inch. I got there by the northerly route twenty kilometers southwest of Saltandpepperland. I'm really wishing you a happy 69. I'd like to give out some prizes. I'm thinking about it but I woke up three hours ago after having a brilliant time in between. First for prizes I'd much appreciate myself receiving the distinguished flying service cross. I like Janis Joplin's movie choices. Did you see it in the *Times?* She said *2001, 2002, 2003,* and *The Yellow Submarine.* My choices would be *The Fox, The Canary,* and *The Yellow Pajamas* (by U. Betty Takemoff). And I'd like to give a prize to dancers, all the toe, tap, and other various types. After all this is a dance column. Shall I go in for points or for beauty? For 69 I'm looking forward to anything what's quivering motions intended to titillate and to reclining in any positions in an indecent manner such as splits on the floor making shivering up-and-down movements. We don't know what to do with a phallus so we send it into space. In 69 everybody will be determined to enjoy life. So much for prizes. I was happy to learn in England a while back how my once alive father was a

Commander of the British Empire, just like the Beatles. Except my father was into bells not songs. Anyway I think C.B.E. is their big prize. That's why I want the distinguished American flying thing. You've gotta have something to be dismembered by.

I'd like to ask anybody a civilian question. What's the insignificance of locking yourself out of your house New Year's Eve? My friend Laura said she couldn't call me because I'd locked myself inside out. This got to be a whole trip and a tailspin. Is the world meaningless if we don't invent explanations for it? Why should I lock myself out of a pleasant home? I'd even want a new wife my home wouldn't be ashamed of.—If it came to that.—I'm attempting a transition here from prizes to revolutions. I'm making a New Year's revolution to write a sincerious dance column. That's because upon leaving my locked-behind-me house I went several places and happened to see John Perreault at one place in a furry beary vest saying here's to bigger and better gossip columns. It's getting so I could trip over a dance work and think it was a picture collection. But I heard more thought invoking revolutions than mine. I wasn't going to bring up George Segal again for at least until another life if I had one. But I have to. He did it again. He'd invited a good friend of mine to pose and somehow we survived with the loss of everything but our heads. (Don't lose your head, your ass goes with it.) Can you with impunity confide in someone and not give him weapons? All the initial elements have now undergone a mutation. I first went to see George many lives ago when pretending to be an art critic for *Art News*. I conned him out of two pastels which I later sold to pay the rent. From Mark di Suvero I just took the money itself. The economy of the art world is an encyclopediatric study. I was determined not to enjoy life. But my story begins here with a new year's visit new year's day quite sensibly. I was happy about 69. I'd forgotten my locked-up-tight house. I was wondering where the centenarians are this year. I was wondering if I'd do a 69 for George to get his year off to an interesting start. I told him he needed a shocking sculpture to celebrate our only 69. I felt funny not having my keys in my pocket. But I wanted to know about their new year's revolutions since I was all set into with mine. Helen said hers is not to talk to her mother-in-law about anything, not even the weather. And I think she made one up for George how he should try minding his own business, not his mother's. The way it was going it was such a mother thing I asked Renie aged fifteen if she had a mother revolution. She said no and I said please go in your room and don't come out until you have one. She obliged by coming out after a minute with another no and so I had a new idea about going into the room again to find the revolution by blindedly picking out a book at random then just as blindly pointing a finger at a word or passage in the same book. This produced beautiful results. She happened on the Thesaurus Theorifice with "Pacification conciliation accommodation compromise and adjustment." So much for mothers. I'm attempting a transition here from mothers to something I wouldn't talk about if I'd been brought up nicely, which I was. Maybe it began with a discussion about the meaning of a reproduction on the cover of a recent *Art News* of a slice of George in person in red lumber jacket regarding a sculpture of himself holding the head of a seated figure separated by a foot or so from her head which George was holding. A mother erected is a mother decapitated. What is George up to out there? Why are his white plaster-casted people lying dismembered around the studio? Why does he mummify his guests and family and let them lie around the floor like that? Why does he painstakingly and with love I think put all the parts together back again later after you've left yourself behind in all those pieces? An accident at the crossroads. Who was it got torn to pieces after a reign of a day and a night? The queen for a day I guess. I'm not making an issue however over what sex it could be. I could stumble over a female and think it was a female. So the reference to queens is purely accidental about how I happened to sacrificially offer myself along with my friend and to also have the organisensations most clinically visually accepted as female, like the female on the cover of *Art News,* probably his wife. There's a story about the English duke who was to inherit his rightful dukedom but somehow was once registered at birth as a girl because the doctor thought his short penis was a long clitoris. After some lengthy litigation it was declared he she could acquire attain to his her dukedom since it was distinctively proven that his long clitoris was really a short penis.

I felt funny not having my keys in my pocket. How many independent researchers have come to the same conclusion? How many people grow up after they get married more than an inch? And I was enjoying it not even knowing it. That's the worst. Somebody forgot sex is all in the head. Coleridge said great thinking is androgynous. We're raised on realities not illusions. Does George know what he's doing out there in New Jersey besides literally doing it? Isn't this true art from the ritual act? Why do they keep talking about the actual sculpture? Can you know what any man's sculpture is all about if you don't get inside it? I'm almost ready to say no, although I never like to sound so conclusive. The experience was a cataclysm. We left the house a carnage of plaster and pieces and unmade beds and half drunk coffee cups. The murder went on for hours. It was too late to come back to my locked-inside-outside house. In the A.M. I said well now the kids were gone to school we had the run of the house. I was kidding. I had a big foot out the door with the last part of me bound up encased entombed embalmed absolutely Vesuvisized except for my nostrils. That was the last act, the head. By then it was hilarious. George said I'd ruin the cast if I laughed. I tried not to. But a radio announcement broke me up. Something about "art news." Anyhow I laughed when it was hard already, I mean the wet stuff was set, so that George got his plaster head intact and I got my amusement as well. Removing the damn thing, George held it up for inspection. I said yeah it looks just like the last one (I did this five years ago see, but not in my altogether, and if you want to know where I am I'm at Schwebbers Electronics factory sitting at a dinner table with George Lucas and Allan) but I think it's somewhat bigger actually. One day I was exclaiming to Ann Wilson over the size of Gertrude Stein's head I saw in a photo in a book by Alice or somebody and I said boy what a big head (it's even been likened to a Roman Emperor's), do all great people have big heads, and Ann said listen some great people also have little heads like Francis Bacon for instance had a pin head. I'd like to know George's inside opinion on heads. He seriously by accident tried to put an extra head in the form of a hunk of white rock between my legs, and my friend's too. You see when you're sitting there with say your whole back chest arms inside yourself, inside your white plaster cast yourself, and you're dying from singing to stay alive because you're all trapped first wet soft then dry hard in this living grave of a George Segal immortal picture collection; when you're like this it's really essential that the technician the artist who's doing it to you becomes a good plumber and makes sure the excess gooey wet plaster doesn't drip down right down through the plastic sheet he's rigged up around your waist for protecting you, and into your crotch your cunt. So that's how I got an extra head I don't need. I noticed long ago how if you just pretend you're a boy you don't need what they say you gotta have to make you look that way. It's all in the head. Pretending to be both a boy and a girl I have it every which way not being anything in particular. Well all the king's horses and George's helpers including me made sure upon my instructions to totally circumcise the extra head with hands pliers and razor's blades and all equipment on board ready for emergence. I told George this was the second and last time. I'm happy about 69, happy new year, and I don't believe any more in mothers erected is a mothers decapitated. I'm quite self sufficient. I mean I'm not up for erection. I enjoy my horizontality. Still, I'm happy I went and did it since I feel much closer to George, and to Helen too, and to everybody no doubt, having been locked inside myself and inside his sculpture in that particular incredible way. For 69 and every other I'd wish to quote Lincoln Scott writing to his draft board: Truly then, did I plunge my soul into existing with the grace of light in my being.

January 9, 1969

ABOUT THE ASH TREE

People say sometimes I talk only about famous people but all I know is famous people so I don't know how anyone distinguishes between their famous people. Maybe some people are in hiding. I know occasionally perhaps too often people die in a

broken face even in their living from not thinking they are famous or from thinking they are famous and that nobody knows
about it or from thinking too much. The question is it seems to
me shall we call everything famous or shall we say everything is
not famous. I don't care this or that way about the calling or
the naming for if we call everything famous it is just the same
thing as saying everything is not famous. The infamy of it all
could be a side or central issue. I think they mean that when
we're infamous we're badly famous. Let them be known by
their works. Can you go anyplace these days on end for two
cents a night where you can meet everybody who is anybody? I
like to think so. Last week a nice young man told me I was
swearing and I said okay although I'm not interested in convincing anybody of it. I enjoy my talking for the sake of my
talking until they say to shut up and then I get funny on my
thinking which can get you in trouble too. What I'm saying if
you don't mind, and this is a serious article about criticism, is
that I'm not talking about anybody ever in particular actually,
only myself, and I don't exist either, except in my imagination,
or yours, although just at the moment I'm riding on a train, I'm
not sure to where I think they're picking me up at the lost and
found when I get there, riding along with a lot of famous people I haven't looked at yet because I'm inside myself and this
yellow paper and that isn't true either. I asked a sweet Spanish
couple and their eleven-day-old infant swaddled in pink which
smiles in between sleeping if I might sit with them a time and
we did some smiling together along with gesturing and admiring of their infant including an exchange of my paper he asked
to read and some food he offered which I didn't accept. Their
last name is Class. I found out by noticing the name tag he had
on his army uniform. They seem a great deal in love. Now
they're gone. I'm seeing things out the window. I'm thinking
about my pals in the city. Now I'm not. I just saw a bare chest
through the window of the door which I'm facing beside the
empty seat of Mr. Class. The world train is spinning out to be
more surprising than I thought. This train might not be going
anyplace. This is a gentle and sometimes amusing horror story.

I made an elaborate prison escape out of our great city. I
never saw so many assassins in one day. And all so helpful. I

even discovered the fundamental nature of employment. At Grand Central after a tour of midtown looking for the right station, having become insane again, or having the flu the Hong Kong Bolshoi Washington variety, I was really keeping my cool although I was burning holes in my hands and eye sockets, feeling like a knight after the grail in the form of the correct and safe manner of departure, I spoke in undertones with a ticket window seller for my ticket and wondered at the same time if he could inform me the number of the track the train was leaving. This poor fellow mumbled incoherently and twitched a part of his chin or jaw over his shoulder in the direction of a higher up a manager who seemed retreating and advancing at once in their common cage. I understood instantly. I said whisperingly you mean you know the track number but you're not supposed to tell you might get in trouble. He jumbled his words and gestures about how did I guess. He had a secret code. I said I wouldn't tell if he told me the number, I was still whispering, but he tactfully demurred again so I glanced round at the information booth where I didn't want to go (the information all around the station was staggering) and knew again instantly the entire employment system. We create jobs for each other in a pathetically beautiful way. A computer, a single tiny computer, could run the world and possibly all the cosmic enterprises when it comes to that. Then after I knew the track number I was steered away from two conductors by themselves to the conductor at the track itself to indicate the train itself, the final information, although the first two conductors also knew the train itself, which was what I was hoping for in the first place. Each person in the station knows everything about it and they're there to help you but they have to respect each other's duties jobs employment livelihood family situation. So I didn't get impatient for a change. I just wanted to get the hell out of there. They have a mutual protective system. All of us in our groups also have it as I see now and if there's a problem it's the translation of the secret code to die it takes only twenty-one days. One time they even showed me to one of Nijinsky's doctors, now an old man, who saw me and he shook his head perplexedly although he seemed interested and sympathetic. I tried to get some private information out of him about Nijinsky, the doctor the old man was into the records naturally, but he kept his professional cool about how another man would jump so lightly through a window just as in *The Spectre of a Rose* and land up so darkly, which might have been lighter happier than we are led to believe from the history books. I know more about Nijinsky right now than I care to tell. By the way, to add to Mr. Zolotow's tale about Joyce and his daughter, Ann Wilson told me the daughter burned herself up for good immolated in a mental place at last.

Well I purged my head and my body of its sadnesses. I brought my head down from a windstorm to a breeze and my body up from a silent lake to a still ripple. I know that a breeze makes a ripple and it's all the same thing now. I am willing to serve man, but not in a way that would suffer unto men. The illness in the city is a gigantic safety problem. I don't want to hurt anybody's otherwise okay feelings either by writing about them or not since I don't know any more about importance, I see everything equally important, or equally unimportant, how can we any of us bear to live this way, not to mention the safety of employment in which we must appear to be serving a higher or a lower interest, to sometimes appear dumb and at other times smart when we know we are all one to another most inside and outside too when it's clear there's nothing more beautiful than a silly old tree. And even so, a fine lady up here by name Mrs. McQuaid tells me I could get in a mess for sure writing more about the ash tree than the maple. My friend Sheindi in New York thinks it's okay to write about trees period. I guess everybody who said it was right to say it's just as well to do nothing to say nothing to simply exist as it were and evermore since if you are doing anything special you might appear to be convincing somebody of it which is instantly political and of course of one group by another in order to interpret safe passage. Boy was I relieved to sit inside the train.

My body was slow, my mind very fast. I was burning up. Without knowing it I was on my way someplace to convert the process to bring the two back together even again because you get sick if one is too much or too little for the other and vice versa. I was sick anyway but I had an idea what to do about it. Don't count your goings before your comings. I was a mess. Now I'm resting in an octagon of a house all wooden with beams and everything and six picture windows glancing at some trees and snow on a lake they say although it's all snowy looking in at me as I'm inside myself and this yellow paper and that isn't true either. I'm thinking of the windstorm last night. Somebody was huffing and puffing to blow the joint down. I stayed up in my bed. Somebody here, Polly she told me, made a tall sculpture of seven chairs piled high perfectly balanced and extremely precarious looking. That's how I felt in my escape from our great city to slow down my head which was knowing too much and to see what my body might do about the whole thing. My head was a windstorm. My body a silent lake. This is not good. Unless you want to die. My legs were stopping still as a rock that isn't falling anywhere. So I tensed up my neck and upper back and decided to suffer. It's the damndest way to get better. The true wind, the velocity in relation to yourself when you are moving, is the velocity when you are standing still, therefore I couldn't let myself be carried away into my increasing speed. If I were a photographer I'd ask someone to superimpose an X-ray type picture of a football player or you know one of those athletic sorts on a stretcher in pain with a broken kneecap on top of a picture of himself in that exquisite speedy action we all like so much. The sports news is half and half about who won or lost what and who got an accident. Competition makes a man grow quicker and more likely to fall down very hard. I know so many dancers with the same afflictions. I used to do it myself. Progress is a cracked head on a game field or a war zone. How much you should drive off in what condition and how much additional distance you can afford, I've been told, is a matter of judgment and practice. And if someone puts you away someone else will liberate you. I think I had every possible disease for three days, including infantile paralysis. I was on the critical list, although a hospital wouldn't take me, because I didn't go to one, nor to one of them doctors. Nobody would know what to do anyhow. Later after I got better I spoke to Dick Alpert who said if you decide economical. I got involuted here in this octagon of a wood house making my head dumb and my body smarter. There's a book called *The Thinking Body*. Laura told me about it. Or June maybe. Or Steve. I know a lot of body people. Some of my best friends have bodies. And I must aggressively announce to anyone mostly myself that it's not that there is no right or left, therefore up, but that there is no right or left, only center. The body head is dead alive center. Should the wind be in any direction or other you can just sail away. And if your speed increases and the apparent wind moves farther and farther forward, you could trim your sail tighter and tighter until it becomes flat as possible. I also drank a lot of liquid matter and cried it out that way too. And I slept a while to get my waking dreams back into my sleeping dreams. Sally McQuaid aged twelve says if you lose all your problems you lose all your money. But nobody has any money to speak of. Something else I discovered is how even the Queen of the Isles doesn't have any. She has to ask somebody for it like the rest of us. Since we're all asking each other we should have as much as we need. If we think to be needing it something must be wrong. Thinking such ways I'm not standing still enough but attempting to progressillate myself someplace where it's necessary to be if I'm not contented with where I am. Progress is a cracked head on a game field. Once I fell down hard trying to be a good writer. How can we be what we are if we're trying to do it somehow? When the water could be flowing along both sides of our rudders or udders. When we left the octagon Polly said now we're going out of our way four- or five-hundred miles, just down the road a piece, to return to the great city for a business trip.

January 23, 1969

WHAT SIN A NAME

Every medicine is good if wisely used. Every medicine is bad if not used properly. I'm happy about being a westerner. Although I also appreciate the East. I've read into Eastern thought and find especially in Zen the kind of thinking what seems good medicine for the West when the thinking here is too right or too left. Every man in his deep unconscious wants every woman, all women, to himself. Every woman deep in her unconscious desires every man, all men, to herself. To bare the unconscious is itself a sin if to reveal nothing but the murder in the cathedral inside each of us all together. Why didn't the Russians leave the Czar alive the way the British did, the way the British left the Queen alive if merely as a beautiful emblem? Why didn't the Americans all the former Europeans that is leave the Indians alive the way the Finns left the Laplanders a Mongolian race throughout history, to do their own thing, to play around in their reindeer in their tents. All together. I'm sitting now deep inside my black corduroy pants and red maroon shirt at 5:00 A.M. inside Mary's Motel on Route 95 south of the border meaning just into South Carolina having crossed the dividing line the boundary the Great Wall of China. These speculations may be relative to the times. This column down the coast down the spine of Eastern America is a collaboration between Kari, me, and Polly who is sleeping right now in her original bom name, Mary's Motel. I know practically all the derivations of Mary, including Maggie and Marguerite. I had enough in my own family to know not to mention a couple of Pollys and Paulines. But don't ask me what Kari's name is. He's a beautiful Finn about twenty-three weighing at least two hundred and thirty pounds and really twenty-three, he just told me today's his birthday. No, I know his last name now, I've only known him three weeks if a day, he used to know only Polly that I'm certain of myself, I saw his last name on a shaving kit he says, belongs to him, it's Siirala. Also on top of himself a big hunk of a guy his father's a theologian, a Finnish theologian as good as Tillich one of the top-ten bracket they say all over the black-and-white intellectual world, and he once told Kari that he (Kari) was the product of the best screw he dad ever had, which Kari said wasn't bad for a shot in the dark. I never saw the name Siirala. I never learned Finnish, most of all Latin "Gallia est divisa in tres partes" etc., and French "dans l'école pour six ans, mais conversation rien" etc.; but Kari knows four fluent languages in all accents dialects vernaculars and drawls, which is coming in handy-footy right now in south of the border in Georgia land where it looks to me the Negroes are reclaiming Savannah (savior Annah?) which could

be a silly good reason for the governors to be so upset. Kari
says we gotta drive fast through Georgia. He's going 65, I'm
still in black corduroy and wine red shirt but out of a black
leather jacket into a soft blue light number and I'm still watching the signs when not poisonally addressing for you writing
letters like this, to see how to read the territory to see if they
like us or not in order to interpret safe passage to a possible
stopover near St. Petersburg where I stayed once aged eight
with an arthritic grandma named Pauline, her last name being
Crowe, as the bird flies, and I was reading *David Copperfield* at
the time. Kari eats a lot. Polly sleeps a lot. I read the signs and
think too much. Right now I'm at a Pigadilly Restaurant Bar-
B-Q run owned managed worked by whites not far out of a
black Savannah the blacks quite subdued but running the town.
I forget my American history. Except for the names. I only
went through here by train those few many great deal years
ago, seems a short time now. There's a big yellow tractor on
my right, as I'm sitting into my shrimp basket, and a bunch of
piglets in the poke in a medda to my right also but off the road
where the tractor just finished noisily passing onto the bigger
road we ourselves came down away from only twenty minutes
ago. I left our great city in a hurry. But not to be sick again, to
lie on a beach a coupla days and sweepstake the countryside
South to central to West to far West then back straight across
to fair Michigan why not why can't we. I'm much less paranoi-
dilyzed. I'll be back later. Someone asked me if I was moving
and I said no I was traveling. I'm inside my words again too. I
wanted Mary's Motel instead of Hank's or Mack's or Stonewall
Jackson's or even a Dixiedream place where I wouldn't 'ave
been able to sleep well wondering if the Confederates are still
after the other guys or vice versa. For to bare the unconscious
to a Dixiecrat even by now after how many years the catastrophe, just sleeping there, would be a sin to reveal nothing but
the murder in the cathedral inside each of us altogether. The
speculations might be relative to the times. Were they ever?
Can I wear my black pants and my red shirt and also something I love I received recently before leaving from Remy,
Remy Charlip, a Star of David or a starfish, or some sort of a
wheel a rusty old thing with eight spokes worn around my neck

held up by a lanyard made by my son Richard last year in a camp?

Maybe easterly. For East is East and East is West etc. and we hope the Twain Mark to meet. South Carolina's a friendly state. I can tell by the signs. I like to think of my star as German. Possibly Jewish. Freud is a favorite Jew. He wasn't such a fraud. He was inside himself into a brave new world of a personal life study. Also a great many pals I know in New York. Like Sheindi. I like to think of her as a half-and-half something or other just like me, since in any case her kids are all mixed up, I mean territorially. She told me her name means beautiful little girl in Yiddish or Hebrew (I don't know myself which), although she's a lot bigger now but only about five foot three. If you wanna be taller taller than she is speak to Kari he's about six foot five and once played football in Texas among other shady hustlings in the hintervind lands, like Canada, far from the madding crowes. My grandma I loved she was a Crowe but also a German before that. In Florida here they got a Messiah Lutheran Church. I was born a Crowe and they changed my name to Johnston. I liked or like now also the Pauline concerning Christianity for at some time someone decided no doubt in a dream to add the last three letters "ine," like in praline a good southern sweet, to the Paul who was either distressed I've heard, so it was a good thing I suppose I'll bet to adulterate his masculinity with a piece of the female, the way I've just added a neck piece to my star in the form of a name tag reading Pauline after my first dancing teacher in Boston whose name was Pauline. But only in a name! No more formulas for actuality please! The Spanish moss may be killing the trees! Now I'm riding by in this dark blue VW station wagon darker than the color of my royal blue jacket I'm leaving on forever since it's giving me no trouble, even with the rusty wheel showing quite obviously on the red shirt. I'm riding along quite safe with Kari and Polly looking straight ahead neither to the right nor to the left, passing some sand castles or pyramids in a desert or a wasteland of another part of Georgia which was once a sweet place, Sweet Georgia Brown, just like Florida now north of Miami or excluding whatever Kari and Polly are hip dating updating me to in the way of what to avoid for funny-looking tourists. Mistah Kurtz, he dead. But the sun is bright. I'm hot. I'm sweaty. I'm enjoying it. For a change. We also had a break our fast at Florence, right inside Florence, possibly another Little Italy. We went straight through the lady but stopping at a cheap place, very cheap, nice too, waited on by a big mother red lipstick all hot and vermilion ready to smile for us early customers. Kari looks okay. A real heavy. Pink to red white cheeks. A health bastard. They say I'm an older woman. Can't make it out. Kari is a good lovin' character anyhow, straight out of a brother Theo (logy) college close to following dad's steps behind him but too smart appearing dumb to finnish up the last six months; therefore he's not being his dad at all but a finished something much altogether, a delightful bum. All I've done is to change his life. Every man may in his deep unconscious want every woman, all women, to himself. And every woman may in her deep unconscious desire every man, all men, to herself. Down to the sea in shippies again across the bridge we go. Only into Florida halfway. That's enough for a beach or two before Houston I like too. At five years of age or so I'd take my dollie walking out to an ocean at sunset before bedtime at Nantucket to say good night to the sea. Just read it like a lullaby. The Western type. I'm not into the Eastern music much. Nor am I into their dancing techniques although already I've made an alarming discovery this trip. First night out after traveling down the spine of the coast not far from the shore stopping at Mary's I got involved in my exhausted back and recalled at least a year of intensive anatomical studies learning all those names the skeletal names for the skin covered bones and I found out that a vertebra is a chukra, which is the East Indian name (I'm not even sure how to spell it) for a vertebra, the cervical (neck), thoracic (torso), and lumbar (pelvic) variety, the whole bunch of them constituting a total spinal column and terminating in between in the center of the pelvic bones in a pointy bone called the coccyx, the vestigial tail of a human body, and in between each vertebra is an "opening" meaning fluid tissues etc. Flowing like a river current from top to bottom, head to foot (New York to Florida) without blocking as in a dam where the water stops up and maybe trickles down to a dry part of its natural current river stream bed dying from the lack of vital sustenance. Reich, Wilhelm Reich, used to call this damming up of the human body an armoring process. The East Indian and other Eastern like Japanese dancers have a fluid spine in their dancing everybody can see it, like one of our predators, predecessors the sexy snake a model for a dancer wishing to enjoy a spinal trip down a coastal stream all winding and undulating not even with a head or a foot since a totally energized body begins and ends absolutely nowhere but continues into the cosmic unconscious, not desiring any man or woman but happy in harmony with itself the universe. When I became insane all my chukras my vertebrae opened up totally all together. Every medicine is good if wisely used. Every medicine is a bad deal if not properly used. But when it's inevitable relax and enjoy it, the sign says so far a place like Pedro's south of the North Carolina border. We didn't stop there. Too psychedelic. They have twelve honeymoon suites heir conditioned. We liked Mary's. Possibly what's relative to the times is a celibate situation or at least an unconscious situation where we all know each other inside to each other as we know ourselves our deepest desires thus we may enjoy ourselves together even knowing horribly the origin of our persons deep back in history terribly upset at the separation the original sin which caused us to look for each other as Plato said it in the *Symposium* on love which may be the only answer now.

February 6, 1969

TAPIOCA STATE PUDDING

ANN ARBOR, MICHIGAN—March 3, still 1969 I'm told. I know it's March because of the wind and we have to be in Ann Arbor on March 11. We decide to leave Taos. It's been great. We stayed in the whole time looking out the picture window. Mr. Vallier the owner and/or the manager of the Inn says did you ever stop to think that where you're sitting right now is higher than Mt. Washington, about 7,000 feet above sea level. No I didn't. But I know I know, that's why I sit by the fire. Now we have to leave—Mr. Vallier mentions the Sangre de Cristo, the blood of Christ range of mountains we'll be going through somehow, a pass I hope, I have my passport too, the American plus the British one, the latter guarantees safe passage by His Majesty now dead, the former's a green rag more official not so impressive in these parts nor to me. The Spanish type would do better here. August comes in. He's an old Indian, looks like the guy on the nickel. I don't know how it got in my pocket but I have a Canadian coin, haven't been there in three years, which says Dei Gratia Regina, 1954, with a picture of Liz II as a teen-ager maybe on one side, and a beaver on the other. Thanks a lot. August works for Mr. Vallier, who says August makes the fire by rubbing two gringos together. I like August but he thinks we oughta have our tourist cameras taking his picture. He's trilingual and doesn't really care, I guess he can't place us. I think he's got a good life up at the Pueblo up the road, from whence they import him every morning by taxi. Mr. Vallier, originally from northern New Hampshire, thinks the Pueblo dates from A.D. 900. It looks it. The adobe stuff I saw in England, the old Tudor houses, like the Hathaway cottage, with the zigzaggy beams, dated only 1480 or so. I dunno what sort of mud 'n straw they used before that. Nor the Indians before 900 although at the Pueblo, where you spend seventy-five cents to be a tourist, we spent ten minutes at the place exackly, there's a more ancient structure, we call it a ruins, you can't hardly tell now what it was, maybe a religious thing, tumbling down around a cemetery of white wooden crosses. I call it a Stonehenge. All across Arizona I saw Stonehenges. I couldn't tell if they were natural or man arranged. Clumps of red rock. Sandhills of pale white dark stone. Plateaus of lime rock of a meteor who knows maybe a tourist attraction near the Grand Canyon, roped off in a curio shop and identified as a Paleolithic geographical wonder of a find, I thought it was a lunar module with tiny craters or a smallpox. Kari used to say the rocks outside the car window were mounds of woman with big boobies, that was in southern Texas on the way to El Paso from Big Bend. We laughed about it. I could care what we call them. But in Arizona I always said Stonehenge because I saw the rocks by that name in Amesbury about 100 miles southwest of London on a gray morning rising up all majestic mysterioso, I was all alone or with Charlotte Victoria a New York photographer a walking sex encyclomaniac very informative, out of a misty mother of a magical ancient times and did those feet walk upon England's mountains green I loved it and drove back to Salisbury to a cheap hotel room near the Cathedral. Stonehenge the original Minimal sculpture. They said the Druids or some other animal lugged them the stones, maybe twenty feet high y'know, the lintels, the cross horizontal part, the original post 'n lintel (soup) structures I've also heard, the lintels about six, seven feet across, they lugged these monsters across the rolling greens from a lake a river an ocean or something to erect them on the plains there in Amesbury for religious and/or astrological purposes. The scholars are still busy at it. They wanna know who really did it. Here in Taos New Mexico there's no question since the Pueblo Indians, the most peaceloving of all the tribes according to Mr. Vallier, are still living in their architecture. It isn't even a reservation. A.D. nine hundred although a few adjoining adobes are slightly modernized. August lives there. So does Jerry, alcoholic, an old one like August, he sits and laughs at us the tourists, asks where are the cameras, we didn't have any we said, but could we buy the beads please, sure my wife makes them, okay good, where's your wife, she's inside all secret, Polly says she's looking at us behind curtains in a modern outfit, so what, we purchase the beads and laugh on the way back to the car about how we could buy the same thing in the town of Taos but for the same price and we couldn't get them from Jerry, whom we like. Who called him Jerry? August is closer to a Red Cloud a seasonal a weather a place name like the old Indians Black Elk or Crazy Horse of the Sioux tribes. We're going up there. I wanna find Black Elk's son. Bill Meyer a New York artist told me he's an old man now, his father long dead. I've been sleuthing. I picked up the white bleached bone of a sheep's jaw in Texas the desert, put it in the glove compartment. Jerry's beads made by his wife he said we strung up from the visor next to the right-hand passenger window along with some rosary beads from a mission church another pueblo, but a reservation unlike Taos, a Spanish-Indian church built 1595 the most beautiful still untouched, not a modernized interior, little église, a basic rectangular shape, I ever saw. The reservation was sad. The adobes spectacular, old as the Taos ones, as the hills. At Taos the adobes resemble apartments, tiers of buildings, baked tan and pink, rising in four or five banked stories, with tiny rectangle holes for windows. In the sixteenth century for a while it became a fort, when the Spaniards invaded. Another reservation, unlike Laguna of the beautiful church (west of Albuquerque also New Mexico they say) between Santa Fe and Taos was even sadder. The church was Spanish completely, nothing Indian about it for a minute. Also modern. Ugly. Also an inscription Yo Soy Immaculada Concepcion. Oy Vay! Also a boy Andy a Bowery-bum type we wanted to be friendly with, he was too drunk. Almost stuck his whole body in the car reeking of the stuff, hands hard scaly from labor, skin broken from diet, eyes blurry bloodshot from not seeing correctly, how could he, a delinquent Indian whom the Taos Pueblo Governor would have the right to punish and reprimand, since the Taos Pueblo, unlike any other Indian peoples remaining in our country, is independent of the Federal Government, therefore not a reservation. Amazing. Mr. Vallier is telling me all about it. Polly is packing. We're leaving. Taos is muddy, dusty. The people are crazy. We're reorganizing the car. Thinking about going north through the Sangre de Cristo. Then Colorado Springs, Denver, then east straight across Nebraska. We might change our minds. Never know. All I'm certain of for sure is when we hit Sioux country I'm removing Jerry's beads from the visor. The dingle dangle of a rosary will do, should be okay in any country. It's cheap lavender. The nun at the mission gave it to us for nothing. Said they were made in a factory. She was a Franciscan. I'm a Martian. Polly is writing about the contents of the car. I'm saying about the Greeks again how Socrates didn't know nothing actually. His mouthpiece his mentor his soothsayer his know it all his real teacher was a woman by name Diotima, the Delphic Oracle, or one of them at the time and he got the good word from her. That's how nutty our Western philosophers have been for all these centuries. They pretended it all came down from Aristotle. Helen help us! Oy. Old Aquinas was mistaken too. He should've heeded St. Augustine's *Confessions* more close more careful. I'm thinking because it's sad to move on. We might see another sign Behold the Lord Cometh Soon! Where Will You Be in Eternity? Now Mr. Vallier is showing me an incredible poem written many years ago by the late Mrs. Kate M. Chapman, whose father, when she was a girl, was honored by his own sect, the Penitentes, a fanatical group what whips themselves with cacti and other flagellentable material, early Spanish-Americans, by being crucified at Eastertime. His daughter wrote this poem very moving, it's hard to take over my morning coffeepot, like how she knew, crouching at home with her mother in the dawn, how the cross had hung from her father's shoulders, how it was bruising his flesh, crushing the side of his head crowned with thorns sending hot streams of blood down his cheeks staining his white mask crimson and so on; and how the knowledge was passed between her and her mother that this was the thing long looked for, long dreaded by her in silence, the thing her father had always meant when he said "Follow me! Some day you shall see the glory!" Then she prays: "Senor Cristo, Mother Maria, if there is no middle road, help me to choose!" Phew. I'm glad she ended up a Chapman. Gotta get out of here. I tell Polly to pak up real fast now, pak up yer trubbles in yer old kit bag, I even help. I didn't like the Spanish church down the road anyhow. Polly wants to see a college near Denver where she spent three months. I wanna see a college in Minnesota where I spent eight months. We're on the road now. So long Taos. I call Ross on my way out to say please change that other title to Pubis Est Veritas. Wonder if he did. Haven't seen a VV in a month. Hope the proofreaders are in good health. The mountain air is sexy. So was the ocean. Now we're going down. I stop at the bookstore and buy up everything documentary on the area including the autobiography of Kit Carson, whom I thought was a girl, a golfer like Babe somebody, not a Daniel Boone type an early scout in these parts. Listen New Mexico is crazy. The poor hippies are out to change the world and the rich hippies are buying up the property. No soap. Argh. We're driving in the snow, climbing to 9,000 feet, that's a lot, this is what I like the best. No more Jack Rabbit sculptures poised on a big hill or a low mountain a mess of rocks. Geronimo! And here's looking at you. No more half breed hot rodders the ass of their souped up cars very ob-

scene sticking up in the air. Chasing two innocent girls. No
more foreigners peering suspiciously at two strangers. On the
road the worst can happen to you is you'll fall off the mountain
into a gorge a gulley a valley a chasm of the blood of Christ,
very scary mountains. Don't look back or you'll turn to stone
by looking at the burning city. Polly says that I learned by accident and she's learning by faith. We're wearing our cowboy and
Indian jackets from Houston. Even in the car the people like
the dingle dangles. In the back there's a duffle bag of books I
never read. I'm still osmosing them. The hippies are mooching
off the Indians. Those Pueblos at Taos will always survive.
They have horses and buffalo. They get water from the river.
They pee in the corrals. They go underground for the kiva the
tribal council. They do their special dances no gringos around
to buy up their phony beads. They're really hip. They're better
off than their neighbors the Navahos, who own lotsa land but
who stay poor inside themselves, also better, much, than some
other Pueblos, also the Zuni the Hopi the Apache the Coman-
che the Dakoti the Sioux and the Squamis back East. These
Pueblos were great arbiters, conciliators, etc. Terrific statesmen.
When a young brave of theirs transgresses the law, gets drunk,
and calls upon his civil rights, appeals to our Government
against his own chief the "Governor," the Pueblo makes sure
they can punish their own man by somehow forcing the Government to amend the laws to exclude them from whatever it
was. Fantastico. I'm impressed. Now we're passing a point of
interest. I notice my writing changes with the changing weather
the temperature etc. I'm excited about Colorado. Now we're in
Nebraska. Fast trip. An old man a gas station attendant says
Pine Ridge South Dakota is where we'll find Black Elk's son.
Black Elk was called a Holy Man, he was a medicine man a
Shaman etc., a doctor a healer not a lawyer or an Indian
Chief. Before the Indians got it from us there was the Governor, the chief inside the grounds, a law giver, and the War
Chief, a protector a sort of nightwatchman, outside the
grounds, and the Holy guy, and the elders and so on. A strict
hierarchy still obtaining at the Pueblo although the present day
Pueblos have a mild system whereby the two chiefs are re-
elected each year by a foot race among the three clans, the win-
ning clan then choosing the new chief a man at least 65 years

of age. We met Adam's wife. Adam is an elder but not a chief. Adam was underground when we met his wife, who showed us a buckskin dress. I said I like pants. She understood. Her son, Adam's son, fought in Korea. They said he'd never walk again. Wounded Knee is a town or a point of interest we're passing on the map right now, it's perpendicular to our route about five miles, that's where Crazy Horse a great Sioux warrior killed one of our guys, maybe Custer. I see a State Park in South Dakota, that's where we are now, named after that particular gringo, it's called Custer State Park, and Polly says she likes Tapioca State Pudding. The radio says blessed are the pure for they shall inhibit the earth. I'm filling the tank again. We're making 700 miles today. We're getting closer to civil-eye-zation. We can get Little Joanie Collins on the AM radio. The FM is broadcasting "Hercules" by Handel. I don't like it. That was before he went to England to write for the King. But we love Judy and Joanie. Also John and Yoko on the cover of Look. I see it in a Holiday Inn. This trip is either a continuous holiday or the Perils of Pauline, who is still hanging around my neck and I knew a Polly Hunter in Minnesota way back when, but on my vacations I saw my grandma Pauline in New York and my dancing teacher Pauline in Boston, who was a girl friend in the thirties to Sol Hurok. I had it real good. I'm happy about John and Yoko because Yoko was not happy in London. The British have this awful hang up about divorce dating from the Duke and the Duchess. The Windsor people. They made her feel just as bad as the King whom they excommunicated for life. I hope Tony is okay too. The third party feels just as bad. Tony called me in Houston. He's making a movie. I've got these movies in my head. I see cattle out the window. And horses standing still. Palaminos. Wish I had my chaps with me. The cattle graze, heads to the grass all the time. The horses don't move. Look like statues. No that's a Dinosaur. Huge! Adorning a gas station on route blankety blank, going through the Badlands. What happened there? I'm not looking. I'm not looking no more. Shit we saw Pine Ridge and then Oglala, the town what's named after the tribe of Black Elk and Crazy Horse, whose namesake is also a Paris strip joint I went to. Pine Ridge is a nothing place a nowhere town. It's worse than the Appalachian whites. It's worse than the white trash south of the border of North

Carolina. Drove through very fast. They wouldn't like us at all. We got the Pueblo beads Jerry's beads down damn fast. We cowered under our cowboy jackets. We put our darkest shades on. We stepped on the gas. What's all this about a population explosion? I never saw so much snow. And the white of the hills of the uppies and the downies or the plain middle the entire geography all white is blending into a gray white sky. Bad Day at Black Rock. You bring your weather with you. I'm doing 70 on an ancient road. Now we're speculating about the climate again. Polly says the rich are always near the water. I say the computers are handling the whole thing. Nebraska north of Pine Ridge is a mess from the bad vibrations of its unhappy Indians and its guilty white slave owners. Right now I'm drinking coffee in another Holiday Inn in Rochester Minnesota where the Mayo Clinic is which I don't believe in either. Modern. Medicine. Acht Schtung! When Adam's son returned from the war in Korea Adam asked Mr. Vallier to help him and so far as I could understand from Mr. Vallier they kept off the white medicine man and got their own Indian healers, the guys like Black Elk, to work on him to make him all better. Probably prayed hard like the Christian Scientists. But Adam's son returned to Korea. Whattya gonna do. In Taos I always said when in Rome do as the Indians. Now I'm in Minnesota, named after De Soto or Minnehaha I suppose, and I'm looking as English as possible cuz they call themselves American here. Very proud of it. Nationalists to the bone. In 1952 in Minnesota sex was something you did behind locked doors if you were lucky. But we're still traveling. We've got a lucky bone, a bleached jaw from a sheep from Texas, in the glove compartment. We put Jerry's beads back up again, hanging with the rosary. We cleaned the car, got completely drenched by some young bucks, near Northfield where that college is I once taught at, a girl prodigy. We've got 10,000 miles on the gauge. That's plenty for a coupl' of innocent globe trotters. Polly has a back ache. I've got a hand ache. So long. I love everybody looking out the car window. In Mankato a blond chick in a Swiss dress at the desk of the Holiday Inn said her daddy saw us at the same Inn very far south of here in Kingman Arizona. Wow. Busted our heads. Now we're leaving, going to Chicago, buy a belt to replace what I lost, going to Michigan why not why

can't we. Go see Mary and Bob, Anne and Joe, and George
and Cindy and also at all them underground movies after
they're paying me to do it. See youse later. Around the campus.

March 13, 1969

NON NOTO

Keep me abreast of your plans I'll keep you ajar of mine,
somebody said before I left. Oscar Wilde's definition of a gentleman was one who is never rude unintentionally. In Paris I'd
be walking down the Champs Elysées and some old bloke, a
working man, would yell a question une femme ou garçon and
I'd yell back laughing je suis cheval, naturellement. I'm writing
in a Holiday Inn twenty-three miles south of Detroit. I like the
Muzak. Also the gold-button leather brown chairs and a bunch
of businessmen paying no attention to me. Is this to conceal the
fact they're unlike anybody else? Does the outside world definitely not seem to agree with them? Is their only desire to ex-
plain absolutely everything? Is it quite clear that people are entering and leaving my brain at random? Is the cripple the only
one who beholds the fabulous? Does each community maintain
a secret language in order to protect itself? If so what'm I doing
here? They're mumbling. I left Ann Arbor. A failure to communicate. They said I was a judge and I insisted I was a char-
woman. Then they said I should look at them the films anyhow
and I said I would if I could eat guacamole salad. I really said
I couldn't possibly give away all that money to a filmmaker.
After all I'm living like a lord and loving to amaze everyone by
my lavish expenditures and the speed of my racing cars. Also
I'm still attractive although not unlike a flabby Rubens, but I
love her just the same. For him however the merciless distortion of the beloved who is seen as a sort of kangaroo in a hat
reveals the direction he was about to proceed. Isn't that a

dreadful story to know? When I saw *The Wanderer* I decided I don't see movies as stories anymore. Further I've decided money is the root of all pleasure. I made precisely ten dollars this trip. I had it all planned how I'd make enough money to pay for the gas. Really 12,000 miles means a lot of gas. So I was going around the whirld so to say to see what's up to make a stopover a business trip in Ann Arbor, the annual film festival, then give a lecture at the University of Illinois in Urbana where John Cage is hanging out, also George Manupelli, who invited me, but I'm like the little boy Polly told me about who said he wouldn't play Joseph in the Xmas play because "you should see what they picked out to be Mary" so he got to be an angel instead. I wanted to be an angel in boarding school but I broke all the rules so they made me a king (Wenceslas) instead, but I couldn't sing the part, I had a sore throat. At first I was the courtier's page. Later on I was in the Czech group. Did you know that the Czechs watched the invasion of their country on their TV sets? Who was sounding a few booms in the Marabar Caves of their souls? I'd like to keep you ajar of my soul but it isn't located in the plexus anymore. Besides, right now I'm in Pittsburgh, Pennsylvania, I've never been here before, I'm up on a big hill in a large old farmhouse maybe one hundred years ago full of beautiful junk talking to Benjamin Jackson aged six. His mum and dad are upstairs sleeping. So is Polly. So is a baby. Also a younger sister. Ben gave me one of his artworks. He's an artist besides a big brother. He goes to school also, he says. He's looking at Bugs Bunny. So am I. He's four years younger than Richard but they were born four days apart in the month of March. Sorry it was May. Because of all this, and another famous getaway yesterday, I'm not thinking proper about all my notes on the nature of the film. All I know is that Thomas Edison said there was no future in the film. I like them anyhow. And so far as I'm concerned the first movie was *Potemkin* by Eisenstein, or the flicks by Muybridge, or the *Prisoner of Zenda* by whom I forget, or the *Corsican Brothers* starring Douglas Fairbanks I think, and more recently, post-Warhol, some movies by David Bourdon who shot them with nothing better in mind that I know of except to look at them at home by himself (Benjamin is showing me a chicken called Bucket) in his own viewer. I happened to see them about two years ago. That's because I starred in one of them. David said I was Esther Williams. I was swimming all naked out at Bucks County. David was standing at the edge of the pool with his black viewer and I didn't care since the water was comfortable. He also took a movie of LaMonte and Marion, Frank Lilly, and Henry and Chris. Sam Shepard too. He tried to get Michael Smith but couldn't. David told me all this from Ann Arbor by phone. I used to call the library in my research. Now I call my friends. Benjamin is eating sugar-sparkled flakes. I'm boiling eggs. I time them in my head. I like the yokes kind of hard and the whites rather medium. Bugs Bunny is over. The Wacky Racers are on. I very often run into the conflict between autonomy and devotion. My themes are likely . . . to become more obscure . . . vague . . . of little interest to anyone except myself (or so I am projecting). I wonder if my transgressions are becoming ingratiating. Or if I'm projecting properly. My viewer is a pair of cat's eyes very green they say but sometimes blue if the sweater is royal not navy. (Where's Benjamin?) Where's everybody? Here's Sandy, aged four. She's pretty. They're all friends of Ann, who grew up in Pittsburgh. Ann said we had to see them on the way back. They've got two monkeys in a tremendous cage and a parrot or a canary, I recall *The Cat and the Canary* as a movie I couldn't look at or listen to I hid behind a post at the back of the movie house, this bird is okay it's in the bathroom and it keeps you company on the toilet. We're ready to drive back now, into our great city, and I'm looking forward to the movies. I saw a big whale on tellie last night. Mopy Dick is not a social disease. Is this an element of the great and polymorphous revolution against his sovereignty? Can I measure all of you, not just your shoulders? Can I be mechanical if my curriculum didn't call for Greek? Are you keeping abreast of your plans? Are you Czeching it out? I'm too tired. Benjamin Jackson is a great artist. He puts stickers onto his monster pictures like how Alfred Hitchcock presents stories that scared even me. And Sheindi tells me she learned her English history from the movies whereas I read it in a book which isn't kosher anymore, either. But I have to get my Jewish history by mouth from someone like her because my curriculum called for French. And not only do I not see the movies as stories anymore, it's all so dreadful, I turn off the sound and watch only the pictures. I like only the lullabys anyhow. If I look at it (Where's Ben again?) outside my coffee, it's sunny here too, but we have to get going soon, I read the gestures the expressions like the good dance critic I am and I see then the true cinéma vérité of the Maysles, I haven't seen, of the mind my body actually reminding me I'd better close or open the door all according to the sound of the fox prowling into the flashback of my present location. No kidding, that's what the movies are all about I guess. A terrific responsibility. With all that cutting and splicing the underground film artist could ruin a good friend. I saw one like that in Ann Arbor. She was rolling around naked on the beach. Meanwhile, I was gloating over her charms, her beautiful arms. But Andy doesn't show me anymore, how nice. I was wearing a blue chiffon gown. I was dancing with Freddy on the roof. I think it went on for five minutes. (Here's Ben's father into the icebox.) He showed it at Gramercy in 1963 I think. I thought it was funny. So did they. I'm really a comedian even if David thinks I'm Esther Williams, I think I'm Bea Lillie. Andy is okay too. I saw *VivaFucks* before I left New York at MOMA. Andy isn't a big cut 'n' splice man. He did portraits because he was a painter, or he liked the faces of the sitters. He did the *Sleep* because the man slept. He did the *Empire State* because it happened to be there. He did me dancing because I like to dance. He did the *Lonesome Cowboys* because they must be lonesome. But why he did *The Chelsea Girls* I don't know cuz I didn't see it. I saw thirty films or more at Ann Arbor and it hurt my eyes, I see better in the daytime, so I said I'd have to leave, I couldn't do it. Besides, God respects us when we work but he loves us when we dance. And they say my writing isn't unlike a method of intercutting. What I say is the mind of the hero the Director is all about the director's present reality which is the actor in front of him and the viewer his camera his gray-blue eyes, and in his mind's eye his fantasies or his past tense or in the case of *2001* his future tense is making him an autobiographical man in search of an author an identity. NON NOTO. Thus I like Andy's movies I do I don't see a tense in them. I like the Maysles also just from reading about it. (Mitch is feeding the baby, Charlie tells me the only thing he worries about is that they're having more fun playing money games than he is just playing.)

I guess you can pick your nose but you can't pick your friends. Isn't this a brilliant article about the movies? Shoot me friendly. Ach die Lieber Auberstein! They call you an argh or an ugh if you use the words too much. Bradshaw used to say thonk. I never use another man's words. It's sacrilegious. I have to get William Penn in here now. I'm still in Pittsburgh after all. The Liberty Bell is due directly East. It's cracked. They're making some new ones, in England. Mitch says I should Czech it out. That's her expression not mine. In order to call Charlie and Mitch when we passed through here Polly and I stopped at the William Penn Hotel for a drink. They didn't like it, it's the Waldorf of the West, but I said we were cowgirls in disguise, we loved their palace gone wrong. That's what Sam Wagstaff said to me in Detroit a few days ago after our elaborate escape from Ann Arbor and a night in our last Holiday Inn to celebrate all holidays and Sam took us to lunch at his Museum the Detroit Institute of Art a grand place. I had salad and we took some milk to go. Sam showed us some postcards. He collects them. He's got brown paper bags of the stuff. Thousands. They're in five categories: night, sunsets, waterfalls, phallic monuments, hotels, and motels. For lunch he brought along the hotels and motels. He gave me one dated 1951 addressed to Mrs. Winn Richard. I copied the info off one postmarked Habana Cuba Mar. 10 8:00 P.M. 1929 to Mrs. Rob Eveland in Detroit saying "Just arrived this is our hotel had a lovely trip mother all feeling fine." I copied another one dated 1916 and also I wrote down the whole message that Sam got recently from Agnes Martin in Cuba, New Mexico. She says she's building a small log house there not knowing what it was for till she decided that it is a guest house-landscape like Chinese painting—open range (no fences) on the other side Jemez Mountains . . . she sends best wishes to all. She tells Sam he'll have much difficulty getting enough of her paintings for a retrospect, and doesn't know what she can do about the drawings.—You can go a long way baby . . . even if there aren't two of you. Art may be historically more important than dancing but now they've got me out here looking at the movies. Next life I'm going into the listening business. Maybe I got Sam interested in the writing on the backs of postcards. He loves the pictures. So do I. I'm into the dates too etc. Anyhow I'm strictly an invitation person. That's why I wouldn't carry a sign on a street. I wasn't invited. And I like my head, now that it's linked up to my body again. Hi I'm back. Walter said he used to go to the burlesque because of his prick; now his daughters go as a sort of sociological visit. But I'm thinking now what Cocteau another moviemaker said about how you could put a commonplace in place, clean it, rub it, light it so that it will give forth with its youth and freshness the same purity it had in the beginning and you will be doing the work of a poet. By the way I called John Cage from Ann Arbor at Ben Johnston's in Urbana and asked him hey what's the situation down there and John said hi how am I he didn't know what's going on there but glad to I don't know what could he do something for me I said no thanks a lot I just wanted to know if I should drive home and I think I should. So long.

March 20, 1969

COME SEVEN

What he did behind the scenes was as much a part of his life as what he did on the stage the man says. And a photographer tells me his work is a search which I think is a secret. I'm not generally interested in the secret code of a man's work. The code it seems to me is how we don't know our secrets. Yet give me strength to go on but most of all give me a companion to ride with at least part way is a line by my collaborator as of October, 1968. In our journey between collaborations there are no secrets, hardly. They become as one. Every week I dream up a new collation always mindful of the limitations they gave us to unite as one with another while imagining the world is so perfect as to make it possible I could walk out the door any old week and embrace a man who remains unconscious. It looks like they want to move but their feet are tacked to the ground. The reason why two can do it is that each pretends for the other. My entries for February 22 are out of sight. For today as well. For May 7 is a lucky number day. And now it's gone. But at George Segal's we discuss the seven-year cycle of Joseph who according to George was the original Freud. He says since Joseph successfully interpreted the dreams of two fellow prisoners and the Pharoah heard about it he wound up a Prime Minister who set up a Henry Wallace ever-normal granary program where they store surplus in Goodyears agricultural something . . . anyhow he relieves everybody including the oppression of his brothers who originally did the poor guy in. I say better the seven-year plan to the neck at the end of the reign of the same as Frazer put it in the hands of a golden bough. The stories are good at least. We used to sing We Are Climbing Jacob's Ladder as Christian Soldiers of the Cross. I didn't comprehend the collaboration but the ritual I never questioned. The mileage on the VW for February 22 reads 7,777. In 1966 the mileage busted at 036 a number a lady psychiatrist pointed out to me as relevant to my age at the time of a broken head which initially assured me to have gotten very high on a sort of a seven-year plan also. My mouth fell open. She said what I knew already however. The creation of the world in seven days. It was reassuring to be corroborated. But on February 22 Polly says she felt too close to death at the Grand Canyon in 1966. We decide not to go by it. Later on she says oh shit we just missed the Grand Canyon (to our left). Looking down at the Hooever dam or the Boulder whatever they're calling it these times was enough for me. We're not any further away from home than they are. And we just broke the Genius machine back in Arizona. You're a genius if you score 700 and we left it all fouled up at 843. Now we're talking about birth dates while she might be thinking about the mountains to the right looking like piles of pebbles, one on top of the other my own thoughts she must be incubating again or upset about the collaboration in the record book I have her writing away furiously as I'm driving through a hailstorm and she says very old wood turns to stone in a million years or the hail is coming down in one special place and it looks like a geyser which is not interrupting my own excitement about the fact that Jeannie's birthday, she said, write it down hurry up, was June 15, so I'm now over the thoughts of even the trees historically raving about the Magna Charta signed in 1215 on June 15. June could be as wild a month as August. In August we all flip out. Or in. But on our way out of Las Vegas Polly says we shouldn't look back, at the burning city, and reminds me of the Sodom and Gomorrah story which George Segal now May 7, or later, is also insisting upon, I prefer it in its Orpheus form, but George did that sculpture of Lot the cousin of Abraham who might not've known how his cousin got screwed by his own daughters after his Lot's wife was turned to stone by looking back at the burning city of Sodom or Gomorrah. How come I'd like to know. George doesn't answer. He sculpted himself with the help of his wife into the form of Lot sprawled on the studio floor about to be raped by a hovering girl friend belonging to his best pal while his wife or Lot's looks on in a big stony silence completely out of it. But Lot was chosen by three angels the Lord he says. Yeah uh huh. And he gets advance warning to flee with his wife and two daughters. Yeah go on. To the mountain caves against angelic orders. Now you're talking. Go on. They were to run to save their lives, to not look back. I see. Okay then what daddy and now she's just a lousy old pillar of salt and who tolerated such incest and who wanted who and who decided they were the last people on earth to have such a ball and murder the mommie to do it and so on. I'm really appalled by now. But they bore two sons. Great, a happy ending. As a critic I was unconscious myself of how I'd been writing love letters in the sand in my dreams to the seven bags a-piping and the ten ladies dancing and the five gold rings for at least six years. And the only man I unequivocally adored was Merce Cunningham. The ritual of the others eluded me. Except for José Limón when I dreamt he was a king in a Maidenform bra. Or Alvin Ailey when I was beginning to get the African message. I didn't enjoy my role. Fortunately however I escaped my would-be captors, but he was killed by want of feelings in those who ought above all to have felt for him. Nijinsky say thank god there are a great many who will sacrifice their worldly interest for a friend: I wish there were more who would sacrifice their passions. The reason why two can do it is that each pretends for the other. This affair has long been a subject of gossip among magicians. Nobody even knows what virtuosos of imposture we are. We should marry our grown-up dreams and stay behind the youngest still and sail our memories of home like boats across the Seine. These are the colors of my father's dreams says Judy Collins whose words Polly writes out to play also about the father who promised somebody according to Judy that we would live in France. The secret of the collaboration is out of the bag but Peter Hujar my photographer friend who tells me his work is a search is not answering my query as a statement for the press about the media problems, so I'll have to do a solo trip this time, here it is: People say Gertrude Stein was a big dyke because of those latter-day images of her in the papers the books and I say nobody got into her bedroom to know for sure and further I saw a picture of her aged much younger by an Italian fountain with Alice and the pigeons and to me there she looked like any ordinary American buxom Jewish college girl, a wide brimmed hat a big smile a lots of hair all piled up, much in fact a similar appearance to a second cousin of mine Martha who lived with her sister Elsie, who cooked and made the beds while Martha went to work, and further that Teeny Duchamp over an April dinner tells me she knew the both of them in Paris at one time, both Alice and Gertrude and Teeny didn't like Alice whom she thought was quite masculine which is besides the point of my point here, although I say to Teeny I think if she Alice didn't care for her it was because they don't have much in common; and if Gertrude got aggressive later on in life according to the pictures since I don't know them in person either it was because the two of them probably didn't have a dog to ward off any would-be intruders who wouldn't understand the collaboration. Pictures aside, in Spain I say to Jean Lanier the reason they made it at all according to Gene Swenson is how they got all stashed away in that house in Paris before anybody could do anything about it and I'm sure Leo was a good pal for awhile, like Theo was to Vincent under pressure of a blood relationship. That wasn't a solo trip either. It's hopeless. More than one of us arrived at a time. There's no end to these collaboratories. For instance I have a very special letter here, actually a photostat with handwriting on the back from a Pennsylvanian who lets me know he's thinking not only of me (he says he shares my appetites etc.) but of Sidney Lanier's namesake, I "missed a beautiful reference" he says, who was a "very interesting poet, flutist and composer of So. Carolina origins . . . his creative life straddled the Civil War, which, as a sensitive and cultured man, pained him deeply." The photostat is of *The Marshes of Glynn* by Sidney's father. I'm sending it to Sidney who was a priest once. I used to saturate the vestments of the priest in perfume myself. I was bad but the priest was old fashioned. That was 1947. I don't recall the day. I didn't have to polish the chapel brass for it anyhow. They didn't catch me. But I'm catching George Segal May 7, I'm getting to the point now, or later, for some collabor of love he did which I didn't approve of. That's why I'm into George at all on this date whatever it is. I say lookee here man, on February 22, George Washington's birthday we're driving along and Polly says she hates the birds flying into the windshield, that's reasonable, and I say the world of people excluding the mountains is all about who wants who sexually and she says the horses went crazy then we hid under a tree, that was another earlier trip, and I say in 1966 I flew over here sleeping from Arizona to New York, and the sign says either 7 or 77, two sevens, or Route 66 east from Kingman to Flagstaff, or entering two guns or Behold the Lord Cometh soon Where Will You Be in Eternity and Polly says after that maybe once upon a mattress, which was not the way it felt on a trip with Jean when they withdrew into a room because "this city (Vegas) is the epitome of how peoples' minds in this country work and what their goals are, it can all be summed up in the word money" which is not the reason George made that sculpture of me and Polly New Year's Day, 1969, and I think George is a learned man, he's telling us all about Joseph and Jacob and Isaac and Abraham and Lot etc. and all such I dig the stories and what I'm doing for him I'm analyzing all the possible reasons Hilton Kramer might have for hating him and/or his sculpture (Helen is always concerned) and I'm even divulging my plans for the next seven years, the Gemini years, and making endless confessions about my own impossible ex-life as a critic as well as a present lover and so on so I say it right out I'm so frank George you have no guts, you didn't transcend your own psychology, it was an aborted collaboration, a breach of faith, a travesty on an idea that we agreed upon when with much initial embarrassment to four people mutually arriving upon a pose for me and Polly who thought it was a decadent scene as soon as it began and I was doing it to call George's bluff on being a voyeur about a girl he thought I'm sure of it was free white and single and older than seven, which was underestimating the sophistication of today's younger people, who know who wants their kicks for what, and who might also be nice enough to offer to pose not realizing they'd get murdered by the plaster into the hair the cunt the pores the mess of it the torture in the cause of art; so I have to emphasize again over this problem of consciousness to be conscious is to know your own unconscious which knows only its blind desire for to be truly animal as we go into the 1970's it requires a depth of knowing into our deepest even darkest desires that we may surface into a behavior of mutual trusting a conscious effort to transcend our particular needs even, if the needs of another are endangered in the transaction, to make the unconscious conscious, I keep insisting, it isn't too late, for those who can't if they are spiritually dead I close my eyes, for my friends like George become momentarily enraged, I've about two days of the Taurus in me, I say as the sentence began, see above, lookee at this goddam sculpture the final property as it turns out, who would buy it even, you falsified the pose by separating the intimacy of a simple gesture. You got me leaning away, which I wasn't, I was merely resting my hand my arm on the mattress. Otherwise I was looking straight at my partner. You got Polly looking stiffer than she felt even considering the technical difficulties of the situation. You took her hands off my thighs where she must've wanted them if she put them there. God knows where mine ended up, the right one that was free I mean, since I didn't stay long enough at the gallery to find out. Boy George. He says well Polly was a ramrod and resistant. So who wouldn't be. He says I'm his old friend and he wouldn't hurt me. Yeah sure. Tell it to Mr. Washington who only did it to a cherry tree they said. I'm adding sculpture to my list of questionable activities along with writing the movies the photos etc. I had no idea what a hassle it'd be to become immortal. I can't even axe the thing because it costs a lot of money. Maybe I'l procure a purchaser myself, I'll even raise the money for it, then we'll have the license of ownership, any old financial wizard the Oz of it, for in our fantasies the thing is already rearranged, its property value is nil nada, nodo nasta, I'm even into the wildest pornography which was the joke of the situation to begin with, how we'd do a 69 to celebrate our only New Year of that number in our rapidly deceasing century. It doesn't matter. It really doesn't matter. It really doesn't this time. We're arriving into the beautiful seventies. If you don't become conscious in this life it'll happen in the seventies. All the signs point to seven. I don't care what anybody says. George say the land of the lotus eaters could've been a tribe of junkies. Helen say she's given up explaining George's success to people. I say I was a name as a striving neurotic writer, when I became an artist a medium I ceased to have a name. Polly say to be nude in the muck of a swamp though crude is the bed I want. George agrees the closer you get to yourself the more you belong to yourself then he's only the medium for making the work. I constructed myself inside the secret seven. It came to me as a child. I played with the dice on a Persian rug, roll seven and eleven only. The original collaboration a rug and a number. Yet I would walk out the door any old day of the seasons and embrace a woman who's becoming conscious. We might like to think that, finally, late in his life, for the first time, he had a genuine and emotionally rewarding relationship with a real woman.

May 15, 1969

PUBIS EST VERITAS

TAOS, NEW MEXICO—This could be my true confessions. That's one title they didn't think up before I left. But I shall return as the old man said. The ladies who never die might also keep returning from one place to another. I'm in a Sagebrush Inn. I'm in the Pueblo Indian country. Also Spanish and Mexican. Also American. Also Hippie. Finding love letters in the sand and all such jazz. Being at least 2,000 miles away I feel pretty close to home. I even make phone calls like it was as far away as the

Bowery to the Battery. I miss the Bowery, our lady of the flowers an' such sentimentality. Genet was one up on the bums with a title for a book as good as D. H. Lawrence's *"St. Mawr,* after his, D. H.'s mum, I suppose who must've died a death as bad off as he was in a coal mining town, Nottingham?, after her various sons her lovers especially D. H. or him only took off to go up or down to London make out real good he wouldn't have to be he hoped I imagine a mean bastard like his dad, his dad pretty alcoholic as I recall from being unhappy among other things about suffocating in the guts of a mountain digging out a bunch of black soot to supply a richer man a wood stock up for a winter fireplace; therefore a man very hard on a wife trying to be a good lover to a talented son. Besides, who wants mommie that bad to get down into her bowels. Get all black doing it too. Who knows. D. H. must've been a spaced cat after a book like *The Plumed Serpent* so excited over Mexico a once desperate kid from Nottingham to write a thing a title *St. Mawr* which I haven't read. I read Mexican book long time ago. Very lush. Zzzzz. A bit much. Myself I'm just writing love letters in the sand. Last night par example I was reading a comic book "True Love" and I also like "Secret Hearts" and "Just Married" and "Heartbreak" and "Young Romance" all put out by the comic book people just for me to read in a bathtub in a Sagebrush Inn three miles south of Taos in New Mexico 72 miles north of Santa Fe, Atchison Topeka we didn't see cuz we stayed in a funny motel outside the town, anyway I prefer the B. & O. railroad or Reading or whatever I used to buy on my Monopoly board, also the damdest distance of only maybe five miles short of the D. H. Lawrence shrine, I didn't know he lived here, with Frieda, who married an Italian after her cock disappeared, just up the road a piece from Taos north of Taos, up a bloody dirt of a mud path a wide enough road actually but not that good without a jeep so you turn around if you don' wanna get stuck, we did, turn around, I don't need to see it, it's probably close to the fir spruce look of New England I know from a drawing a "beautiful Jesus" (Ann calls them), Paul, a disciple of Christ, a Taos Hippie, a tall lanky lean one his eyes a desert bleached blue, wearing a dirty blanket, made this drawing in my record book I asked him to tell us about the shrine which was a ranch originally, a hang-out a get-away for D. H. and Frieda, the former at last resting his bones (Simone told me) in Europe, home again, because the Americans ho ho said he couldn't stay around here with tuberculosis; five miles south of the shrine I'm staying, possibly ten, liking these comic books I used to dig "Popeye and Olive" and "Smilin' Jack" even "Dick Tracy" especially "Little Lulu" and "The Little King" also "Mr. and Mrs. Gary Cooper," and I never read *St. Mawr* I prefer these teen-age comics, I'd like them even better, take them more seriously, forget it, if they got to be a subject matter lesbian and/or male homosexual exclusive just for a change from reading about how I'd have to pretend to marry the nice kid next door and after or hopefully before that under dad's or mum's suggestion a Tennessee gamblin' man or a man from Las Vegas, a place we also stopped at, having crossed the Rocky Mountains west of Albuquerque not even knowing it, a rich town Las Vegas but we didn't play the one-armed bandits cuz Polly only put a quarter in, I told her how many quarters out of five dollars she'd have to play in order to win by the mathematical odds based on my knowledge of the Table of Random Numbers, but shit you could never get outa there so I think I was glad she stopped at a quarter, I didn't wanna play myself, I was only interested in the situation mathematically, and now I have to stop this sentence since I've lost track of its beginning, the bathtub and comic idea, plus the Paul and the Christ idea, plus the spatial relationship idea, plus my true confessions and D. H. and Frieda. Etcetera.

Well I'm typing right now but yesterday I was sitting by the fire in the Inn here and happened to see Ronald Forsythe's article in the *Times*. It's about time. He's a brave Indian to say that stuff, pseudonym and all about how forinstance D. H. Lawrence, and this is my own intrapolation, wrote a story called "The Fox," I read it in London, and had a chick called Jill a poor chick dependent on a dyke called March big deal but very handsome pretty with a gun after the fox the would be intruder, corny symbolism, the intruder who of course naturally intrudes, both chicks puritan anglo types living on a farm in Vermont, but nothing happened sexually, and he D. H. had this Jill murdered the axe the tree cuz D. H. or the intruder the bad handsome cat the fox who played the part in the movie it doesn't matter they're all the same (although D. H. wrote it didn't he) a big cock a nice guy who loved March the dykie one for some reason, and seduced her, she liked it okay too, but Jill was unhappy, Jill didn't know yet (according to the movie) she sexually wanted March, and March was unhappy also torn as she was between the handsome fox and her Jill whom she wanted, being somewhat more hip, not as unconscious as Jill who was a social mess a rather psychological wreck according to the movie; although D. H. in his own story left the both of them in ignorance, maybe that was better, whereas the movie people were updated enough to make oneathem hip, but for Chrissake they gave old D. H. the benefit of the doubt by letting him win beat smash down the possible marriage of two youngish girls in retreat from a hopeless society, trying to work it out when old cockeroo comes along. Anyhow my point if I don't have one in relation to Forsythe's focsyle's article and I agree no kidding why doesn't some Cecil B. De-Mille make a movie where the two chicks or the two guys live happily ever after "I Do" etc. the way the books the movies the media the entire communications systems throughout the world do it all nice for a sweet teen-age public thinking about that kid next door and of course we do sometimes to keep the population going, why not, at least that's the biological idea they say. Why not if you like it. I did once. If this is a true confession I'd better not return from one place to another. I met a lotta chicks in a coupla weird hospitals once historically hospitable very whacked out messed up screwed for good from this man woman and/or racial problem Forsythe is tragically complaining about. Too bad the pseudonym by the bye. Walter Gutman told me once how Oscar Wilde was the first homosexual. Or Walter meant what he was saying I think that Oscar was the first gay boy he Walter ever heard about. And what I say is poor Oscar of the Man Was All For Being Ernest, about his own Importance if they'd just leave him along, poor Wilde Oscar was a helluva good writer for his time after all England just recovering from Victoria and/or Albert, and he a sad guy wound up dead in jail every historian of his own sex knows, just for somehow publicizing without meaning to, being a writer 'n all, a dreadful thing to be when under a Queen or a King necessarily incestuously interested in promoting their own kind through normal propagation meaning heter-ally speaking exclusive bang bang. Not to mention the Bloomsbury Circle. Not to mention Lawrence of Arabia a wreak of an Irishman who couldn't fuck anybody ever, I've read, since his dad had two wives, one after the other, he Lawrence being the product of the second one of about seven or ten other kids and allathem scared boneless over their illegitimacy, especially T. E. in some way, living in proximity the British Empire God save a pretty powerless present Queen, in proximity to their dad's first big family, what a drag. Not to mention Queen Elizabeth the I, about 1588 etc. who never married nobody, not even the Duke of Essex, no doubt the biggest dyke the history books won't ever record why should they since she's the girl who made the empire what it was, never mind her sex, by conning Mr. Drake Mr. Raleigh and so on such seaworthy fellows into cocking around the world, and all this after Elizabeth's dad (Henry VIII?) got rid of the Pope for good. Terrific story. Poor Mary got the axe though. Bloody Mary. Maybe Mary and Liz should've made out. That's life. Liz had smallpox anyhow so I guess even Mary wouldn't've wanted her too much if Mary had the sense to love somebody instead of pretending to the throne. I couldn't be further away from it myself. I didn't even look at the Crown Jewels at the Tower of London. And here I yam in Taos New Mexico breathing the good Spanish air.

What I've discovered crossing the country in a half moon shape cutting a pie out of the center (south from L. A. to Taos before Michigan) is that the architecture the mountains and gorges and rivers the chasms the stars the trees the architecture the incredible ancient adobe stuff I just saw west of Albuquerque and all around Taos here, the Mexican-Indian-Spanish buildings, especially the American Indian pueblo villages now called reservations but still preserved as to their architecture, that all this natural American land no matter what it once for us unhappily was, Indians from Alaska from Mongolia etc. I suppose, no matter what the land is fantastic and the people the people the people are a ship of a wreak. We need help. Not even Agnes Martin apparently can make it. She needs protection. And Taos is a beautiful town at the foot of the snow covered mountains, I don't know how old or their names, Polly took me driving all around a dangerous ride yesterday encircling the high places north of the town going up and down I spaced out completely from the air the trees the nothing the no

people etc.,—but even Taos so handsome a town of adobe and
Spaniards a town of adobe and cowboy and retired American
artists and Indians still surviving and Spaniards still proud and
Hippies still newcomers trying to change the world, forget it,
and even an old man originally from New Hampshire managing
this Sagebrush Inn. All these peoples are suspicious of each
other, sexually racially financially, I don't even go near the
town except to mail this to you seeking out of the postal mistress or the postal man at the desk the information as to which
sex will be most likely to send my message safely to *The VV,*
finding out instantly by X-ray survival vision that the mistress
hates her own sex and that the master must have a wife or
something and he'll at least be polite to a stranger (even) so the
devil take 'er until an angel saves 'er so I can mail myself all in
one piece.

Even Paul stalks around like a missionary. Five missionar-
ies in South Africa were eaten alive by the natives. Take, eat,
this is my body. You could say they were ideally suited to the
work they were doing. Paul whatisname in Taos, in a dirty
blanket, says he's becoming a disciple of Christ, I wouldn't
doubt it, and thinks it's a good idea to walk over hot coals transcending pain etc.,—and I said listen man I know all about
Christ, he was an okay guy, like you and me, why don't you become a disciple of yourself, why donchu leave me alone, Christ
must've been on 3000 milligrams of stuff a day out there in the
desert, walking on water and everything, turning fishies into
loavies or vice versa, and like the minister the priest or who is
he says recently in *Time* magazine Christ was actually a real
politico. I knew that all along, for two years anyhow. He got
the neck the axe cuz he wanted too bad to change something. I
say to Paul CHANGE YOURSELF. Do it yourself. Do yourself.
Know thyself. Have a ball, etc. Around the turn of this century
some hip psychologist types probably influenced by the new experiments in Paris (Charcot, pre-Freud) were trying to prove
how Jesus was a psychopath. Natch. He was spaced. Too powerful. At least old D. H. wrote a story "The Man Who Dies"
making Jesus into a sex maniac or a guy who could fall for
somebody besides Mary. Maybe he'd have been better off with
Paul, but I mean didn't Paul come later? Too bad. Clearly he
had a mother problem in any case. Too much mother not

enough sex. Anyhow the Western religions are a mess by their father exclusive orientation. Freud said that himself. Before Gran'daddy Moses and Abraham and Jesus and so on there was a more primitive situation, as in pre-Olympian (Homeric) Greece where the mums and dads reigned equally supreme, a Gemini androgynous homohetero-arrangement. And for sure I don't mean the mythologies. Because before the mythologies, and read Jane Harrison the great British scholar on Greece if you're ever interested, the primitive peoples mostly had no gods or goddesses at all. Everybody participated in the life the rites the whole thing equally and somehow at some time as great Jane described it the god and/or the goddess was projected from the crowd to be a sacrifice, a real sacrifice instead of a totem animal sacrifice, much similar to our Mexican-Indian primitive ancestors who practiced both kinds, but mostly the animal kind thing not so kind either, whence the Roman virgin forinstance the vestal virgin much later on in history but not long after Jesus got the axe to pay for somebody's or everyman's sin by that time no one even knew whose exactly. My sentence structure is getting out of hand but I like it again. Freud's point about Moses was that the early Jews were guilty over his murder, if indeed he was murdered as Freud surmised. Jesus atoned for the sin, but Moses wasn't Moses either, he was just a father a church father a founding father a person with a penis with a dingle dangle (Aristophanes) and the crime always leads back to the myth the Adam and Eve business whereby the man or the woman, some silly biological animal, i.e., protozoa, got separated into a woman with an inverted penis a cavity a canal plus a vestigial penis, and a man with the sexual reproductive apparatus showing on the outside and two vestigial breasts in the form of a chest with or without hair but the nipples that look pretty and don't do anything functional as they say. Well, I'm all shook up over my own head telling me these things. I could blow my cool clear waters south of the border but I'm not into the comics. Man and woman are truly one, once were an animal unthinkingly reproducing itself. Causa Sui. Separated in two parts the animal must needs locate its missing half which Socrates was quite bright about. He even put it into the mouth of Plato or Alcibiades or Thaeatetus, probably the one in the middle his special lover according to Plato, the latter the T. was just a young

aspiring mathematician. The great search the grail the investigations (of a dog) the crusades the sleuthing the detective work
the explorations all this careening by peoples around the globe
and the oceans plus now the skies into space is this search to
locate the other half and the other half was lost in history.
Nope. I'm not interested, in changing the world either. I wanna
live on it peacefully my life span whatever it is. The split of an
animal into two separate sexes was the unfortunate crime nobody committed, the other crimes are mere fabrications, although they're too bad also, and this is my true confession I
like the comic books, TV, Indian rugs, mayonnaise, girls and
sisters and old ladies and little boys and old men and girls, the
mountains to look at, the water not to walk on, the trees to
watch anybody climb up if they dare, I like dancing myself not
much to look at these days, tennis badminton Ping-pong to play
but not to compete, swimming if the water is lukewarm, clothes
for the hell of it to appear straight or strange or a comedian according as the space accepts me, traveling for no good reason
although I still love to write thus you might be reading this, no
clothes in bed if I'm all alone or just absolutely exclusive with
someone I'm crazy about who digs me the same way, the architecture anyplace if it isn't caving in from a man-made oil well
or a neolithic earthquake or a mountain so upset as to pour its
shit its lava junk down to ruin its own village. In other wordlets
I don't want no more hear about a Virginia Woolf walking
1941 into a stream all suicidal with a walking cane after a life
that wasn't all tea and sympathy like we'd think of a merrie old
country of intellectuals descended from Ben and Sam living in a
quiet part of London a Bloomsbury section about to be bom-
barded from the east by the missiles the cockeroos making a
fragile ethereal spaced out lady mit big eyes gray and blue a
lovely dame crazy she really loved her country. She wasn't even
a mother. Not even about Gertrude and Alice who were also in
hiding. Nor about sensitive Oscar, nor the death of Camus died
like a Pollock although he Camus wasn't driving the car; nor
about the life of André Gide another cat who couldn't say what
he really liked, not outright, only in funny novel form. I'm into
the autobiographies in the first person singular, like Isadora's.
Now we have a brave in the U.S. us in the form of, by name
Ginsberg. Is he the only one? And who was driving the car in

the recent accident? I hope he's better. I'm drinking tea and
lemon American style foot on an Indian rug a bit heavy Spanish
in design, I prefer the light herb colors washed out and sun
baked of the Indian who exists no more, in spirit, as a peoples.

A fantistic knockout of an ancient, really old they're not
joking (they lie to tourists natch), pueblo village, tiers of adobe
mud and straw baked the light yellow pink tan etc. is right up
the road here from the Inn from Taos, only a mile, and there
many of them still live, they even have horses and buffalo, but
suffering all year round the tourists the government and the ig-
nominy of the slave jobs to the white Spaniards the white white
man whoever migrated here from Spain by way of Cortez or
another conquistador Don Diego De Vargas also crossed the
Atlantic I suppose (I'm just a gringo here myself, at home I'm
a goy); and somewhat northwest of this village is old D. H.'s
final refuge as an alien expatriot now a shrine a tourist joint for
gaping also at the man's ashes returned for Frieda who married
a Ravagli in 1934. I didn't look. Was it really a fine thing for
D. H. to concentrate on the almighty cock even when the Western world needed no doubt a man like him say it was okay
after a dry spell of a century or so in the Anglo type world
very up tight over any sex that wasn't a single fuck for a single
baby on a wedding night following a proper courtship approved
by the family folk etc. and behind a locked door? Maybe so.
For myself thirty years later now or so I guess the times've
changed. D. H.'s story "The Fox," after which the movie, the
story really is a pale nothing not hardly beginning to realisti-
cally announce the love of the two chicks Lawrence naturally
resented from a Mary type compie. He must've been eager to
please his mother why not. He was her lover. But the girls were
just pals, also why not, so I think the movie people did D. H. a
service by making that all that hush hush sweet Charlotte etc.
stuff explicit right up to date if you like I don't care much I'm
enjoying writing also a fire here at the Inn juiced up by a pail
of Magic Indian dust meaning old ashes soaked in gasoline to
make life easy indoor campfire wise, and beyond that the mov-
iemakers, excellent acting I thought aside were still thinking
Mr. D. H. had a point he did he had a gun in the form of a
cock and he was as unhappy about that although he was at least
making it with Frieda as the last lady to love besides his maw,

got the love plus the sex thing together I bet and so on. After all the Lover who screwed Mrs. Chatterley was just a handsome bastard not long up from Nottingham to be a slave a gardener in a rich man's casa blanca the rich man impotent or what the wife still raunchy randy pulsing for a handy worker who was deeper much deeper the lover of his own mother whom he wanted to save, then, for himself in another life. Everlasting. The only problem as I see it if you don't I don't care about the Jesus trip is how the church after Paul the Christian aspect of it the dominant Western world aspect continually paternalized the Bible into a wrathful righteous all knowing monotheistic overpowering in judgment here come the judge here come the hell to pay the purgatory if y'don't shut up sit down stand up drink yer milk eat yer wheaties don' pee in yer pants y'nervous kid idea and . . . Why use the names? The lesson of Christ as I take it or don't like it, take a look at 14 stations of the cross made by some Spanish Christians as a starter, if there is any lesson for a passing student, is how come a guy got so spaced and so political as to have to drag a heavy cross from one place to another. Jesus! What I mean I agree with Forsythe whoever he is, I didn't even read the article, very closely, also congratulate the *Times,* why not enjoy yer comics while y'got'em and silently applaud some other human animal for doing whatever it is he wants from one life to death and/or back again too, since we all got here by no choice of our own baking, but not applaud, this I wouldn't advise, but don't quote me, not even look or think about any other human animal who thinks his comics are better than yours. I like parsley. I like guacomole salad. The green stuff. How green was whose valley. God rest ye merrie gentle men and women. I'm still finding love letters in the sand, which doesn't exist around here. And this isn't my true confession. I'll never tell all. I don't know where I am. I'm not in Tahiti. I'm not a Mexican. Polly says she's a Spaniard. I don't believe it. I'm sad. I'm happy. I'm going to Denver. We're gonna see the Once Group in Ann Arbor. See their movies. See ya later. Copulator. After a while, Crocodile.

March 6, 1969

THE BELLES IN THE TOWERS

Many children call the blocks towers if they happen to build
them upward, which they usually do since space is at a prem-
ium on the school desk strewn with this kind of material. Ann
reminds me the Hunchback of Notre Dame died in the Tower.
Beyond that she says the end of her own novel was going to be
just tower after tower, every kind of tower she could lay her
hands on. Specific graphic descriptions. My own diagrams involve a quadrangle centered by a lily pool bounded by the brick
walls of two stories of corridors supporting two castellated towers rising above a mountain top overlooking a river. Stan Van-
DerBeek says the Empire State Building was built with two
hundred tons of extra structural steel to prevent it from swaying
so dirigibles could be moored to the top of it now realized in a
modern concession to common sense by a Pan Am flight from a
flat roof to a landing strip or vice versa from passport to heli-
copter. Whereas his wife Johanna has dreamt that she was interested in her husband's tower in which dream he replied that
he needed it to throw his weight around at the time. They had
to conserve their energy for a future purpose. The twin towers
are united by a garland of flowers arcing from spire to spire.
The staircase winds upward into a discovery of the unity in circles, for circularity is the common principle which characterizes
all instances that can be called circular. I rush down the staircase anyhow and yell at the top of my lungs. The metal echoes
the clang of an ancient boot. I carry a small wooden weight to
carry on its chain the three keys to the locks leading into a
tower of bells made in 1931 by Gillett and Johnston in Croydon, England. Later it was converted from a foundry into a
munitions factory. Johanna says that someplace in New York
an iron foundry was converted to buttons for Civil War uni-
forms. On two sides of the lower part of the tower were cut the
first verse of Psalm 127 in the Vulgate. The bells number
thirty. In 1932 Thomas Hayes Proctor went to the top of the
Notre Dame Cathedral with his wife Edith who was paralyzed
by the accelerating volume of the biggest bell ringing the noon

hour by the weight of a man falling onto a board extending from the bell to make the clapper bong against the insides of its metal supported by a wooden structure including an iron ring for the bellman to hold in his efforts to notify the country of its time. Tom says Edith was paralyzed she couldn't move at all he tried to get her down but afterward she made her first acquaintance with Vouvray wine on the Boulevard. Tom is eighty-four. Edith is gone. He lives with his sister Hilda. He gives me a book of essays about Whitehead inscribing the book to Jill with affection and with contrition for having inoculated her with the virus of philosophy, a disease from which she has never recovered. But I'm into psychology now Tom. And he says the power of God is the worship he inspires. And I say it's the separation of mind and body what created our civilized illnesses. And he says not nearly as much as the identification of the mind and the body and I'm thinking oh phooey it isn't a notion but a fact, since he's going on beautifully as usual, the same old lucidity, stringing garlands from Plato to Whitehead, the twin gods, the notion of union as a complexity reducing all differences to nonentity and discovering ways of unifying factors in differences which to him is Plato's great contribution to philosophy, yet he makes me promise to send it back to him, a paper he wrote in 1938, swearing I can only borrow it on my heart or whatever organ I consider most sacred. He waits in the car while I go up in the tower. He doesn't know who made them. How come if he taught there for about thirty-five years. He says his memory is fading. It isn't, but he cares more about the cello than the bells. Also he says he's learning a lot from reading *Sappho's Daughters*. You can't keep it though Tom and I try to give him another such book in the pornie line for the type he represents. But he wants to know the latest. He thinks it must be anatomically impossible to get two vaginas together. I'm inside the tower. We can be sure that if we put all the necessary mathematical bricks in front of them they will not only build their mathematics out of wooden bricks but build a truly abstract and yet personal mathematics in their minds out of the mental bricks they have fashioned for themselves during the play. I can't wait to see the bells but I won't. Can we look at the internal structure of what we have to divide? Is a tower in the middle of a modern city called a skyscraper for anybody to be impaled upon its spire? Am I opening the right doors to the kingdom of the keys? Is the possibility of an indefinite continuation of the process perhaps the first door opening toward the concept of infinity which they say the children find extremely exciting? I dunno. If the tower seldom falls in one piece and it breaks in two before it hits the ground because the part near the bottom is anxious to get there according to the principle that the taller it gets the bigger the base and the top will undo itself to crush and crumble down onto its bottom not being able to support its erected member I'm inside a structure that isn't working out as to its share of blocks which were the only ones left on my desk in any case, as an answer to the problem. So I dream as I did in 1965 I fly up against the roof of a vault and fall down into a coma from which I recover by awakening to discover my fist. Johanna says I'll never impress anybody ever again with my special abilities. And they used to watch me. I was the only one who could do it. But I don't care what they say anymore about saying it out loud, snickering as though Freud was the first who said it and you haven't read about it yourself. I can fly if I have a mind to. You lie down flat on your back all dead. You decide to fly so you tense up your stomach muscles and erect into a sitting position by straining at the neck and so on. Then you stand up. Then you take-off. You flap the appendages called the arms by beating them against your breasts and yelling Tarzan or Jane and grabbing a handy rope and swinging from bell to balcony to rescue a princess from a big bad witch. Ann says the bell in the tower is like the virgin in the garden and the architectural structure of the cloisters is based upon the medieval symbolism of the virgin as an unviolated woman in a garden of that description. But according to my diagram the cloisters forms only one side of a quadrangle centered by a lily pool bounded by a courtyard enclosed by the four walls of bricks enduring the birds in the singing vines away under the castellated towers rising above two arches known as sally ports through which you could walk or even drive a car into the courtyard bounded on one side by the cloisters a long narrow corridor where we kept the winter sleds. The French windows rattled from the sounds of the train below the mountain. The belles in the towers were the girls on our way to be burned by the sun in the spring of a sky blue year. I was a female Icarus in that dream I say and I'm complaining I can't appreciate the sensation of a melting arm. Not unless I'm ready to go to sleep. And I'm thinking damn damn where's the keys? O Judas Iscariot and all the priests I can't get out, or in. They're locking me out. The sheep are climbing out of the ground. The steps are spiraling into a dizzy spell. I can't breathe. I've got claustrophobia bad. My palms are clammy. From reading the information on the walls. From stealing a picture and stuffing it into my pocketbook. From climbing when I should be resting. I'm into a panic.

I yell up the tower up the stairs an echo of a hollow man all headpiece jammed with straw the metal the clapper in my head I'm falling again I'll take it into my own feet this time after all I'm awake I rush like crazy down the regular steps quite geometric and I don't have the keys, I knew it, I left them up at the top the two chicks can look at the bells I could care for them I can't right now a furious pace past the practice keyboard onto the real one or the pealing electrical towers, a melange of robots Polly says near a big dam, the two sets of keys in my left-hand pocket to the car where the bag is lying in which I found the set I lost in order to have another made into a duplicate set of four to open the door and here's Tom too, he's eighty-four and philosophical, I'm all a-steam out of my breath into a last wind, I throw the stolen goods in the back and we make a terrific getaway. Isn't it grand? Yes. Look at the crop of dandelions. Not now. Tell me about your history. While he does that I view the tower from across a river. I was born October 17, 1885. I didn't like my birthday. I came to New York in 1901 to go to a Bible college in Tennessee. We were a big family in Liverpool. Very poor. I was headed for the ministry. There was no education available in England past the age of fourteen if you didn't have any money. We belonged to the Church of Christ. Now he's upstairs with his cello and his books. His sister Hilda she's seventy-three. She's devoted to him. She says Tom borrowed the money and came to America by steerage. Then he went back, and forth. I'm saying if I wasn't bound financially I'd lie down in a field of daisies and screw the daffodils but you can die in a bed of endless pleasure as I'm imagining of Johanna after I hear for the third time her dream of the underwater, if it came true about her being a fish along with her daughter August and they could breathe in the water as she says and keep in touch by toe as well; for I see her other dream, which was a reality she claimed, she really went out and bought a pig shortly after her daughter was born in order to eat the pig, she had to do it, after setting it on a platter before her very eyes to consume her infant visually sprawled beyond the pig in a cradle or another platter, quite intact in proximity to the roasted suckling pig entering the mouth of the mother, whom I view as enacting the properly incredible ritual involving the symbolic incorporation of the child who has also suffered the trauma of the separation of a unified being: the single entity of a mother and child. What would Tom say about that? I'd ask him if I was being immodest. He'd say no it was a just appraisal. Then I'd ask him if I was being irreverent. And he'd reply no but the empirical side of philosophy is the inclusion of all the facts, the evidence, that any belief that you can only hold if you have to close your eyes to the evidence may be formally consistent but your premises are arbitrary and from purely arbitrary premises you cannot make any statement about the real world. Not again. I'll try another tack. I flank in on the Cartesian notion of mind as higher than body, once more. Tom says but you can't describe consciousness in terms that you describe body. I say why not. You're too rational. Clearly he still admires Descartes. And he's doing it beautifully again, his best English which is the admirable prose he mentions in reference to that great period of Hume, Locke, and Berkeley, philosophers whose thought should be read as English if the function of language is communication, he states with quiet authority. Moreover, passages in Whitehead are pure poetry, and I agree. In the forties over Mrs. Whitehead's dead body Tom persuaded Alfred North (he was so old at the time) to give six lectures at Wellesley in the fall and the spring and these became *Modes of Thought,* his last book, which he claimed wouldn't have been written without the stimulation of those lectures. I'm impressed. I always was. I don't even understand why Whitehead isn't buried in Westminster Abbey. Because he died here Tom says. Oh right. But listen, if Descartes makes man a supernatural being by defining nature as a body of substance extended and moving and mind as the substance that thinks where do you come off as a lover like Socrates whose chronicler transformed all particulars into a unified system of being and thought. It doesn't matter. It really doesn't. You can, of course, he says, put things together by making mush out of them in a Waring blender. Forget it let's talk about sex. All we have to do is to make a certain number of equal piles. I tend to regard the structure as an amorphous mass out of which, say, two equal towers must be built. I'd like to give a block to each tower until the pieces are exhausted. If you had a tower 22,000 miles high you could literally jump into orbit. If the corresponding structure of all the boxes has been understood, I wonder if the question can be raised what happens after the blocks? According to Polly the clumps of rock appear to be giant cow paddies. According to Ann she was at a play in a dream and they were cutting down an ancient old tree and I said stop stop it's blooming and started to cry and it caved in just like cork. According to Sari Dienes, the widow of a mathematician whose son is writing about the same subject, in traditional Japanese erotica both men and women are fully clothed in gorgeous array but the genitals are exposed and the male organ tremendously exaggerated such that a young girl just becoming a bride and presented with this stuff as a costumary wedding present could become either disappointed or terrified. One of Tom's new books is about Jack the Ripper who murdered his first on August 31, 1888. Ding Dong the witch is dead. And all the tribes of Israel got together to build a tower to heaven to God so God caused them all to speak different languages so they couldn't complete the tower. They're all in ruins. And the walls came tumbling down. And Gunga Din was shot in the body holding the bugle. It's very sad. But a tower is what you erect and there's a town in Italy filled with towers one for every day of the year although I might be mixing them up with the temples in Mexico. The pure tower must be a bell in the house of a dream. As a diagram the geometry is perfect, a circle within a square. The lily is round and its pool is a rectangle. The tree outside the sally port is obscured by the magnolia blossoms. The towers are cut out of paper in a sky falling up in the river. The train is a choo in a book on the lawn. The birds in the vines are the song I'm thinking as I say goodbye to Tom playing as good as possible a hymn to a theology he didn't really abandon under the influence of Samuel Alexander in England to become a great teacher of philosophy: *Jesu Joy of Man's Desiring*. For of all the men of his time whom I have known, he was the wisest, the justest, and the best.

May 22, and May 29, 1969

ERGO SUM

I've got Gregory Battcock's Retirement Message on my table. I'm surrounded by the debris of the trip including eight lemons recently bought for a Puerto Rican Rum drink although the bottle was awarded a medal by Philadelphia in 1876. We cannot hallow this ground, Lincoln said, but that was Gettysburg. I wonder why. I'm reading the fine print of the great man's address on this here postcard I picked up on the Pennsylvania Turnpike before coming through the Holland Tunnel to be stopped for the first time in 12,000 miles around the corner from my abode by a man in a navy blue costume mit a pistol of some sort I hope the water type asking my credentials for following three other cars through a red light I never heard of such a thing I like to play giant steps myself, or the umbrella ones I like where you don't know your directions at all, and there ain't no chase at the end; well there I was trapped and no fine print to guide me no song on the radio be my guide and I said okay, you, stick 'em up, I've got a sick person in the seat here with a backache from carrying suitcases and I live down the street, where where he asked, so please meet me there and I'll show you my license, never mind the postcard. Nor looking like this either at the Liberty Bell postcard upon which it does not identify the man who made it. Every American should know how their Liberty Bell was made by the British along with the statue by the French. I'll sue somebody for this. No identification. Although Yvonne asked me recently what I am myself now and I said NON NOTO. I guess I shouldn't be writing like that when I'm right down at sea level. I love it, the sea. So this poor guy the cop the man with a stick or what looked like a bloke on a heath stranded nothing left to do. He said you'd better get that person home. I said yeah thanks a lot, also for stopping the traffic, he did really, so's to facilitate the rest of the trip one whole block home. Boy. My language gets bad under the influence of a bad song. On the trip I tried writing a music piece for Mr. Battcock's new anthology my piece to be called "Gregory's Chant," I did it myself in Latin for six years (Ann says she had Latin twelve years but she's excited about the Greek in a treasure book I borrowed from John in Houston, a book of Sophocles in French and Greek dated 1917 a real oldie paperback it's no longer Greek to me since one of the plays is *Electra*), lucky Gregory, writing up his Retirement Message. I should be so batty, he'll be wearing roller skates when they open the pearly gates. The next morning my latest deadline Monday I walked into *The VV* in my Indian boots 'n' all feeling more New Yorkish than usual and Ed said or I said we agreed anyhow I made the Kerouac trip and that's a compliment so maybe I shouldn't feel so bad. What I should really do on anybody's advice is to write this thing in one swoop entire then I wouldn't be stylistically consistent or what it might be a solution to an old problem in asstheticks. But I won't be around long. Polly's back is better. Mine's a mess. I'm going to Houston to look at the Machine Show transplanted there, with a pillow at the lower vertebrae against an airplane seat. And my notebook today reads Shakespeare. My son found me the quotes then I found some more. I flam'd amazerment. Now I would give a thousand furlongs of sea for an acre of barren ground. And I saw Bob Indiana down at Moisha's on the corner and he told me up at my place over tea a great story about Marisol carving in wood a favorite son, maybe *the* favorite son, of Hawaii, cast in bronze, full body life-size a portrait thereof, the man called Father Damien who helped the lepers way back when but in that new state Hawaii, who is was the subject of a monograph on him by Robert Louis Stevenson, who was also (Damien) a favorite character of mine aged seven when I learned everything from the Encyclo-Brittanica and I loved Father Damien although I had these bad leper dreams, along with the awful story of Pompeii, my two best stories, who was old

Damien became a leper himself that I know and died there an émigré a sort of missionary from his native Ireland or someplace. All lost! To prayers! All lost! I didn't thank Bob but thanks and I showed him my notes on Sam's postcard from Agnes because he's an old friend to Agnes who told me once how my vision about what Gregory calls quiticism was definitely correct and that I'd have another such vision which I did and that I would then know what to do which I didn't. Yet the time of these absences of meaning might be marked by an approximate interval of one centimeter per second. I'm not worried. My present life is charming. One is tempted to the melancholy observation that the only thing as sad as having one's dreams unfulfilled is having them come true. Did I quote you? Sorry. The table the willows the bottled forsythia from Pittsburgh is now blooming. We're listening to Judy Collins again. She loved her dad. She makes the songs up herself about these matters whereas according to Polly Joan Baez changes the words on other peoples mostly guy's songs no doubt to suit her particular hang-up or perversion or basic interest, alters the sex of characters. I think she's write because in my own right I don't listen to the words only the sounds therefore how could I know I accept the authority of another guitarist like Polly who hears the words most careful in order to learn the right song for another occasion, I only get the sound of it to ride the wave of my own crest falling hand action on this here white paper, I'll write that music piece for Gregory yet. I'd also like to write up the history of dance criticism in New York City beginning about 1902 which I happen to know all about. But the cast of characters isn't dead yet. I'm back but I wouldn't stoop that low to conquer. A pox o' your throat, you bawling, blasphemous, incharitable dog. Life's but a walking shadow. Pick on somebody yer own seize. Kyoko is going to sleep now, that's what Tony says to me on the phone about Kyoko which must be the letter *k* with Yoko added. I'm a screwball right but he says he loves me just the same he loves a lot of people and I say sorry I can only love one person at a time it's my perversion. And I also love Edwin Denby who told me by phone yesterday he was on a dance panel in which a girl said to Edwin I wish you'd just said that dance criticism ought to be fun to read. That's what Edwin is famous for. After that we talked about

Théophile Gautier who made Taglioni famous around 1830. I get Théophile mixed up with Thoinot much earlier a tree man the last name Arbeau an interesting dance historian. I should tell somebody I care I wrote an article in the *Times* last August nobody read, it was summer time, and that I saw Clive Barnes in London the Royal Opera House a month earlier and the very sight of him during the intermission on the red carpet stopped me from jumping out of my box onto the stage to interrupt a royal performance at the bequest of Charlotte Victoria my friend who didn't even have her camera with her to immortalize the experience. Also I thought Clive would stop the *Times* article since I was wearing pants. But he's English basically and that might account for his tolerance on my behalf. But all this might be getting us to some no place. This A.M. Yvonne Rainer told me I could say something about shit and I told her John Cage explained to me once how he wondered or definitely believes, he put it into a question form, What's in a fuck that isn't in a good shit? I was shocked. Ima a nice girl. Ima whore. No, John said he was into the four letter words at the time, no dubito from studying his pal's stuff, N. O. Brown, who was into Martin Luther who sat on a privy to tell the world the truth. That's my line. Ima poet too. But lizzen, speaking of writing, again, Gene Swenson is now would like to be a war correspondent in Africa where all you have to do is to get there and eventually they'll say you can write these stories some any old place where a war is going on. Next time I see Gene I gotta tell him about how Malcolm X said the white man now is in Africa digging and searching, that an African elephant can't stumble without falling on some white man with a shovel. Moreover, how the rhinoceros is not the only nonhuman victim of the war and that name officials are now concerned about what they call the indiscriminate shooting of elephants from the air. Is every community in the world involved in the contrapuntal struggle between democracy and imperialism? If so what is it I'm in the light. As a dance critic I'm even falling apart. I'm too good to be true. I know I'm ideally suited to the work I'm not doing. I'm cogito. I like the musicals. I'm an Ergo. A Sum. I saw John Perreault for a beer after I saw the others among whom Ross told me last Xmas time how you can learn more about life reading Tolstoy than Tom Wolfe, why not, and I said I'd love to write about Nixon's political action as viewed by the peoples on the tellies, that first press conference I viewed in Louisiana where the media got him into the pleasant Ed Sullivan poses and I told John in Houston I thought he'd be a good President because of that because I think Ed Sullivan is a gracious man. But that was so long long ago. For now Deborah Hay tells me even if nobody wrote up her concert, it was okay since the following day, Wednesday, February 26, 1969, a notice appeared in *New York Times* under the heading Dial 911 for Police Ambulance Emergency, a citywide police number available for emergency calls. It is 911. The police department requests that emergency callers be brief explicit and calm. Under that Deborah said to me was a notice abut Fire, about dialing O for Operator and telling her you wish to report a fire and how she'll connect you with the fire department. Deborah's concert was entitled *911*. Isn't that beautiful? I always read *The Times*.

March 27, 1969

DOWN TO THE HILT

SPAIN—The moon is still an old-fashioned yellow ball when you're sitting on a whitewashed balcony fifty feet higher than a Spanish piece of the Mediterranean giving off a yellow path of its reflections as good as a romantic postcard. But my note of it says moonshine on water drink rum on terrace. The other day inside a cove arranged by a mountain of rocks rising up in such a way in semicircularity as to make a thing a cove all of a sudden I said I wondered what I was doing there and our hostess said I was sitting on a rock eating a lamb chop. It's true. Also the sun was burning me up and I wanted to be in bed but instead I was pretending to be a geologist stumbling about in stocking feet identifying a stone as a slab with lots of holes in it. Someplace in France a budding ornithologist handed me a

Jill Johnston and David Bourdon.

Gregory Battcock in Houston, Texas.

book of birds and a pair of binoculars through which I observed a dog and a tree. That was outside a twelfth-century abbey. Nothing but stone. Not pretending to be a historian I noted its Romanesque unadorned beauty as claimed but standing by its rough stone altar imagined a beast about to be slain and wondered why I never realized before that an altar is just for that. Fashion the stone into a slab of a table for cutting the meat. I ate the drum and drank the cymbal. A young girl is squealing very happy to receive the black hairy bloody ear of a bull flung up in the grandstand by a victorious matador. I suppose it's the same as baseball. Driving through Arles I thought of Van Gogh but I didn't see him. The cypress trees are slim and together they don't swirl around and the town has an arena I looked at by postcard where the sport is to somehow get the red ribbons off the horns of the bulls and that's all. Here in Spain the rain is falling on the ocean as well as on the plain and we went to see Salvador Dali whose house is very white beside the pink tile roofs much sloping in various directions and sprouting big white stone eggs. He shows me *Paris* magazine *Match*. Many pictures of Dali. Here's Dali hugging a column. Here's Dali enjoying a meal. Here's Dali with an anteater on a leash emerging from a subway in Barcelona. Enter three girls and a boy. They want an interview. They want twenty questions. Dali says only one. He settles against a side of a white wall, shrugs his shoulders into the collar of a dirty jacket, takes in all possible admirers in a few darting glances the black eyes in a brown head, tweaks one side of the handlebar of his moustache. Two of the girls take turns clicking pictures. They ask the question. What are you doing now? Painting the crown of the new Spanish king into my new picture. Fine. They're gone. They came from Italy. Dali say the monarchy much more important than the moon thing. I can't identify any of it. On the way out a huge polar bear appearing as though for cocktails wearing at least fifteen necklaces given as gifts for the purchase of wine. Next to bear a stuffed bird of prey its victim tumbled at its claws. I want to be on the rock at the foot of the mountain at Vallerauge burned up by the sun drinking cider eating the blue cheese or the goats cheese at the top of the same mountain looking down on a thousand valleys. I know the poor peasants at the top are nearer to nothing. Didn't they say that in order to become nothing you have to learn a great deal, like everything? No. Time in day out the old lady sits crocheting to the melodies of her bells on her goats brooding around her below the image of another old goat her husband bent over an ancient task the great load of hay on the back a turtle's pace down a stony path through an alley of goat shit to a bin of a section of French farm stone stashed together only for shelter. God is all over and there aren't any conveniences. Hooray. I saw nothing there that I can regret here. I don't know if they murder the goats or the chickens. I know there's a coincidence of animals from Britain to Spain. After the bullfight I notice the key chain for the car from London. It's a cheap medallion centered by a phony gold image of the bull and matador in relief on a white pearl ground set in a frame of the gold stuff the same as the center. So that was the thing that powered the car. Does anybody want to see his living meat become at one with the stones and machines. Dear Jove or somebody, I never saw Death before. This was the death in the afternoon I thought you just read about as a piece of sociological information. I'd like to call it a dance to claim an old source of identification but that would be a euphemism for the fancy step of a white horse under a proud Spaniard laced up in leather showing off a dazzling routine of high knobby knees to make a swinging ass go swish to the drum the trumpet heralding the death of the bull dripping blood and gore dead center the arena by now immobilized awaiting the next act in a brutal ritual to be consummated in the roar of the crowd as the torero having faced the beast has taken aim and driven the sword down to the hilt into the withers. Every Sunday six bulls. Bred to be brave. Bred to be dumb. Bred to be black. Bred to see red. Bred to be slaughtered. In perfect form. I can't superimpose the image of the bull charging out of its pen all heaving alive flank flying heel onto the same animal dead in the dust on its side its mouth gaping open in blood its eyes glazed in a fix its legs flopping on each other dragged out across the arena by the funeral team, the three small brown horses decorated with ribbons and bells. A troika. So now I see the bull on the altar. A small pig on a platter. A goblet of wine and a wafer. A priest in a brocaded vestment. And there fell showers of black rain and blood red hail together. And he smote his eyeballs with the pins and as he smote them the blood ran down his face. The crowd hates the picadors who deprive the bull of its first energy to fight. The picador is fat. He's got a long pole with a stabby thing on the end. His horse is blinded in cloth. His horse is old on its last legs. His horse is or is not protected by a drapery of padded stuff drooping to the ground along which the bull comes and rams at the padding to be stuck, stabbed, stalled in its whirl to escape the pike thrust in its back and twisted, twisted, to make the first blood flow. Then he's ready for six of these batons they call banderillas also thrust in the back, by a sprinting jumping assistant to the matador, to further weaken for the dance of the fancy passes preceding the kill. The red cape. The sword. The cheers. The people waving white handkerchiefs. The parade to accept the applause. The holding aloft of the trophy the bull's ear like a scalp to be thrown as a bouquet at a wedding. Or another trophy a fine woman tells me for years she's had a purse made from the balls of a bull of a fight long ago. When did the sacrifice become a sport and is the sport still viewed as a sacrifice? The finer points of the game don't interest me. The history of the characteristics of great matadors doesn't interest me. I see the blood on the altar. I see the sacred animal. I see the bull as a victorious hero. I see the bull as the god the great god, for having seen the fight, if the lamb is nothing now but a dinner and the tiger a stuffed head at the end of a rug, there is still a glorious death in a dumb beautiful animal who transcends his murderers in the sublime acceptance of his fate in a bath of his blood in the dirt. It was forever fixed for me in the one bull who staggered and buckled at the knees to languish in helpless magnificence at the moment when his action has ceased in the perfect identity of his will and his destiny.

August 7, 1969

LIKE A BOY IN A BOAT

You might want to get off here and join the world again. No I
didn't. But you do. And I take it all back. When she makes a
mistake a little girl aged four says she's been foolish and deluded. How do you define a mistake? A mistake is anything you
decide to regret. Therefore there are no mistakes. A regret is a
fantasy about the past accounting for a terrible present. A mistake is an accident of birth you imagine as a gift to grow up on.
If there's a mistake and surely you could've done otherwise,
what might have been done? If there's a regret and you might
be mistaken what should be done next? Or thought? How do
you report a death without sounding sorry? I could write a
classical obituary but Gene isn't a proper subject. Gene Swenson is dead. I thought it would be from flying off a rooftop but
it happened in Kansas in a car with his mother. The next to last
time I saw Gene was before leaving for Europe in June he was
yelling at me behind an extended arm and a pointed finger. I
don't know the content of his fury because I was making just as
much noise in my own distress while cowering toward the exit.
Before London a young pregnant near stranger read me an *I
Ching* reading which I interpreted as having succumbed to an
inferior element and having relinquished my inside power since
in any case according to this hexagram the principle of darkness had become ascendant at the summer solstice. The real true
story of Europe was Patrick whom I never mentioned. When
you crash-land in a foreign territory you need a priest if you
don't meet an undertaker. I never look for anything. Patrick appeared as a cloud taking shape of an angel the way the others
back home were rising up in steam out of the manhole covers.
One of them was trying to get his teeth fixed in order to land in
London to be an Orestes to rescue the Electra from the clutches
of the Clytemnestra who would somehow have to "pay" for a
murder in the family. Since my teeth were in good shape I had
nothing to worry about except a London looney bin if an assault on the fortress by a couple of mythomaniacs from the col-
onies was misunderstood. One of our own kind right now is

planning a land-mass translocation to move England south off the coast of Spain or North Africa or the Canaries, for a better climate and/or because the island is tipping upward and eventually London will slide into the water. That's George Brecht, whom I saw last on his way to obtain Admiralty maps of the depths in the North Atlantic. About that time James Byars was at Oxford as a self-appointed extraordinary student in philosophy for a week going about to the twenty-eight departments or colleges, asking everybody what questions they were asking themselves. Curious activities by Americans abroad. As it turned out I did nothing outstanding myself. I joined the world again after a year in orbit. I paid eight shillings for my birth certificate. I felt sorry for myself. I thought I should go in storage for a while until things blew over. I was traveling because the *I Ching* said it was a good idea. I had no notion of where I was going. I didn't care. I felt alarmingly normal. I had nothing much to say for a change. I didn't even think anyone was after me. My head was turning into a cemetery of deluded proclamations. My pace was changing from hare to snail to stone and stucco. Not being in control of all these alterations it seems I had only to accept them. Along the way Patrick said there was nothing to worry about. At eighteen Patrick is a natural saint. He doesn't mean to be much of anything but gentle. Very tall and skinny and blond, the hair straggling to shoulders and covering part of a baby face, the unironed shirt dripping at the unbuttoned cuffs below the knuckles, the soft refined British acent, the posture angled over appearing to wish for invisibility, the recurring story of "the big trip" to India, the peace inside around him that isn't a political issue, the respect for nothing but a presence, he's too young to project any formulas for grace and he practiced no discipline that I could see. Such was the real true story of Europe if I don't take it all back tomorrow. Driving to London airport I said I had a vague sense of mission accomplished. Jonathan thought it was selling a car to someone in Spain. Why not. I complained about returning to write my memoirs. I'm too young to write my memoirs. Besides, it'll be damaging and incriminating. But Charlotte said never mind you haven't been to jail, you don't so far as we know carry communicable syphilis, you're certainly acceptable in polite society. Great send-off. But I was crash-landing into Kennedy and there aren't any Patricks in America and naturally a week later I'm doing the comic or tragic routine of walking along a *Vogue* thing about myself under arm only two hours after my car and brief and all my clothes are stolen and I open a certain door to pick up some mail and hear a voice at the top of the stairs saying that Gene is dead. The next to next to last time I saw Gene was the day he was released from Bellevue in June and I drove him across a bridge into some trees and he hung a hand out the window like a boy in a boat having never felt the drag of the water before. I didn't know Gene well until over a year ago when the art world was deploring his rage on the steps at the doors of the various establishments. First time I saw him in 1963 or so I thought the spastic mannerisms and erratic speech and exploding blue eyes didn't go with the charcoal suit and ivy league good looks. Sometime in 1968 I wrote a thing called "Pieces of Gene." I had this image of Gene all splat in pieces outside the UN after applying for international citizenship. A better story might be how he appeared at a MOMA opening in bare feet holding a lantern aloft and replied when asked what he was doing that he was looking for one honest man. According to Basil, a friend, Gene was sent out of Kansas to be a genius. He went through Yale. He became an art critic and historian. He lived for eleven years in the same tenement. He had no money. His sexual interests were inclusive. He was politically obsessed. "People who aren't interested in politics aren't interested in anything." He had a Pan Am reservation to the moon. He upset everybody. Mostly he was upset himself. "My fingernails grow long and still I don't have a job."—"If only I had been allowed to put my pants back on after my performance and come back down to my apartment."—"The harvest is past, the summer is ended, and we are not yet saved."— "The last time I saw him he was Gene the Gentle, walking down the Bowery slow motion, fragile, transparent, not really there. And scared shitless. Trapped. Didn't know what to do. Leave New York and don't go back to Kansas, that was all I ever said, I dunno what the others said. Not that anyone could keep up with his roles. The Village Priest, Poet, and Philosopher. The hippie revolutionary. The scholar and art historian. The hometown boy from Kansas. And at last the reports would come in how he was barefoot on the streets with a Bible and getting the number messages off the radio and he was becoming his Crazy Gene self and he was beautiful but it wouldn't be long before they'd come to get him because he'd wreck his place or something considered unsociable and thus for the third time in June he was going into the recovery phase of a cycle that included being a prisoner of state and so forth the garbage everybody knows about. Maybe he's lucky now. I have no opinion really. I'm just recording a few impressions. I'm thinking how to end it. Excessive in all things, Gene wasn't much of a humorist, but here's a line he wrote I'd prefer to ponder over the endless political ravings I always claimed was nothing more nor less than his father. "Special to the *N.Y. Times:* The President of the U.S. clad only in scanty tribal costume, announced the resignation of the American Government last night."

September 11, 1969

JOTSAM & FLETCHUP

A friend told me she thinks she could do some good work with five months clear of tragedy. She goes on to say isn't it repulsive for anybody to eat that many olives and still be alive. I'll remember to quote James on Dostoyevsky who was sailing on a ship to an island in an enormous depression when suddenly he heard the bray of a white ass and wanted to live again. Right now I'm putting a dent in my thighs leaning on a railing out a window at the Architectural League to look at some blue Cheer soap powder that a girl in the other window is pouring streetwards. I have various types of news: a Ford Falcon I'm driving tends to make its fuel dumpage and exhaust drop out at the front end. A few years ago I got rid of a DeSoto which would only go in reverse. Completing the back end of things a lady informs me the best way of getting around France if anyone bothers you is to yell *Va te faire en couler par les Grecques* meaning go and get yourself fucked in the ass by the Greeks. I think I'd recognize this blue soap powder even if I didn't see the boxes. I go downstairs. Now I'm kissing Edwin Denby and remarking he looks younger handsomer than ever. The deep blue eyes are deeper and bluer. The white white hair is whiter and whiter. We don't discuss dancing but I have some dancing news that appeals to me. Yvonne Rainer is hastening the deterioration of *Trio A* by no longer teaching it, herself, and encouraging anyone who's learned the work to go out and teach it, unlike the Graham people who always deplore the bastardization of technique in the hinterlands. Bob Wilson wants to buy a lot of land in Texas and put up a wall. James Byars appeared as a desperado at Claes's opening. Wilson gave me a good luck stone and took me to a French restaurant which refused entrance on grounds of an incomprehensible assortment of ties pants shirts and jackets. Byars threatened me with a concealed weapon. Keep yer hands off me you worldwide weirdo, I just want to be noticed not attacked. And here's Peter Moore as a street Event outside the League telling me I look more like Joan of Arc than ever (more than whenever?). Strange, I don't feel like it a bit. More like Olive Oyl riding a shaggy white dog slipping on blue soap powder in search of a crown for Popeye. I'm looking around for something dangerous. There's a man handing one of Hannah Weiner's wieners with sauerkraut to a passing cab driver. And a girl in a car offering me a black paper hat. And John Perreault's people "mingling" in their white T-shirts stenciled a black letter of the alphabet. Guess I should look for a "word." See nothing but VEZ. They must be good pals. Nothing dangerous. What I saw last week on Spring Street was a roof Event of about ten very young children fooling about on a one-foot ledge over the parapet at least six stories up from street level. I'm not thinking about it as I exit the League, try not to slip on the blue powder mixed up in the rain, walk through Marjorie Strider's Minimal "frame" and see an unscheduled manhole and garbage can Event whereby a building attendant made his can appear to be taking root in the cement by sticking it up to the waist in a manhole exposed by a missing cover. So right now I'm telling my friend these silly things and how I'd also seen an old man down Avenue A or B, or C, and how last spring also on one of those avenues I dou-

ble-parked outside a restaurant for one second to dash in to
look for two people who said they'd be there and they weren't
when prestimo the car was gone but actually rolling backward
down the street along which I gave chase not in time to stop a
lady at the corner in another vehicle from coinciding with mine
since she couldn't recognize a driverless object when she saw
one and so on and my friend pays no attention, only remarks
isn't it repulsive for anybody to eat that many olives and still
be alive. Yes and you could pour a little jotsam and fletchup on
it too. By the way I can't resist asking why is your ass so big.
An enormous pelvis my dear. "When I went to the hospital
with the twins the bag of water was hanging between my legs."
I take it as the central image although I don't know yet what it
means. It isn't however what I'd like to put up on my wall
when I get one.

October 9, 1969

HORSES' TEETH

Thinking to write this letter to Meredith: Dear Meredith, how-
aryu?, I went to yr concert up there at 119th Street. I liked it a
lot and I'd give you some special attention if I was a dance
cricket. If you should have occasion to do that for me ever I'd
appreciate it up. I heard someone attacked me for finding my
own life enthralling. I mean as though I should find it some
other way, I suppose. Not that I don't where I am in the boondocks coughing up a remembrance of things possibly better forgotten. It's a good thing that all you have to do about your past
is to be a starving dancer and put on red makeup and red-dyed
clothes and red paratrooper boots and red-smeared skin and
pretend to be a freak. Listen Meredith I know you're just a regular regular from Connecticut. You may think you have an odd
shape. Thanksgiving day my friend Ann said she'd never been

called a whale before on Thanksgiving day. She also wants a ten-foot tall mother-father in a gold Buddha gown that she can crawl up into the arms of and cry. I've been signaling through the flames myself. My car is wounded. Its left side is bandaged up. It crashed into an onrushing parked truck. Then yesterday I'm driving alawn when snow white blued into my face. The day before that I took a train to Philadelphia with Les Levine and David Bourdon and John Perreault and Lucy Lippard in order to talk about something at the Institute of Contemporary Art. Les said he has a son so I bought him five milk chocolate cigars and someathat gold chocolate money. What was Dick Higgins eating or snuffing at in your concert? He was very good I thought. Everything he did was true in to about his great hulk. I got the Mutt and Jeff and Little King and Lulu and Abner body-type idea and screw the whole pretty bit but that can come out looking just perverse and what you put out there were a couple of extreme types you might not want to shack up with (which is irrelevant) but so much themselves in the space so much altogether phenomenominous. I tell Ann she better stop eating or start loving the way she looks. She says at our age people aren't supposed to fall in love anymore. A truck I saw along the hi-way read on its side "you never outgrow the need for milk." Did your mother get to this last concert? Do you think in order to return to the source of things you have to travel in the opposite direction and what does that mean any-how? I had no time for putting my affairs in order for a long journey. At Penn Station John said to David you never told me about Australia and David replied there wasn't time, he had to pack for Paris. David went to Paris with Gregory for Thanks-giving dinner. In Philadelphia we got a taxi to the museum. I sat in a lounge over chocolate milk while they went upstairs to look at Duchamp's last cunt. Les photographed it and you're not supposed to for twenty years. Les is talking about being lib-erated. A year ago he moralized at me for an hour after I con-fided in him as I was accustomed about a trio scene I'd made the night before. Now he's got a videotape he made himself of two friends of his fucking for five hours. I'm glad you kept ev-erybody dressed up in your concert. It's like you have to now, right? Anyway what's the difference? But Les is pleased with himself. Also he was trying to feel me up in the car on the way to the restaurant after the museum and he knows I don't like Irish Jewish boys or boys. We got to this restaurant and had a scene and a half there. It's a fancy joint combining an oil portrait gallery with cocktail lounge and dining room. I thought of your tall ongoing beanstalk of a girl Madelyn (is she six foot three?) as I looked at our pretty hostess. Where did you find her? She's a lanky gawky gorgeous thing. Well our hostess was a regular sort in the pretty category. We had a drink before getting to our table in an adjoining room. Then we ordered more drinks and suddenly there were some dreadful indications of a crisis. I didn't hear what I heard. Our hostess was putting a stop to our second order. She said she was responsible for the success of the panel we were going to give after dinner. Truly it is by not giving people their alcohol that you turn them into drunkards. I wanted to be home reading about the evolution of horses' teeth (Ann says I should read the holy books). The table went into a silent apoplexy. Then Lucy was quite brave. She groused and grumbled and refused to eat her dinner. So did David. And I said something boardingschoolish about mothers and Les told the lady she could get out of the predicament by just bringing on the booze and she then delivered the situation to her husband who wouldn't participate and she then had a real or simulated breakdown by rushing from the table to the powder room followed by her daughter and we ordered our double bloody thises and thats. The violence of raving thirst has no parallel in the catalogue of human calamities. Right now in the boondocks I'm looking at a George Brecht postcard of an orange and a white cane on a white chair and listening to *Holly Holy All My Bags Are Packed So Smile a Little Smile for Me Rosemarie I'm Not Scared of Dying Last Night As I Got Home Mary Hill Was Such A Thrill After Dark You Know That's Against the Rules* and alternating soup with milk with coffee with rum with lemon with V-8 juice. Don't know if I'll be able to make your third installment. This one I would remember as the red and orange guerrillas and very often I think the bleeding bums on the Bowery are holier than the holy Indians. Love, Jill.

December 11, 1969

UNTIL WE'RE 90

Thinking to write this letter to George Brecht: dear George, happy to receive yours. Are you staying on in Germany? Hope you're not still bleeding from the stomach. I wrote a letter like this to Meredith Monk a couple of weeks ago and enjoyed getting mixed up as to private-public, in my head so thought I'd write one this week to Yvonne but I'm angry at her and I owe you one anyhow. Damn, like I went out of my way I don't know how many miles to stop at that college Amherst on a Friday night to see a concert she said she was giving there, that night. I go into a great mausoleum administration building and have to hear one of those smug smooth and scrubbed all-American campus boys acting as operator and information clerk tell me that her concert isn't until the next night. There must be some mistake, I say. No-o-o. No mistake. And I know he's sneering beneath ten layers of baby fat but he wouldn't express an emotion on Judgment Day and he lets go of a law book to find a telephone number and I'm telling a Professor Piglet or Pigskin, or Pitkin, after he confirms the altered date, and in answer to his question what can he do, that he can give her a piece of my mind when she gets there. For not letting me know.—You know that personal theatre crisis I went through. It still isn't easy to spectate anything. I drove off extremely parannoyed. Cooled out in Springfield over a shrimp salad sandwich in a Friendly Ice Cream place. Sometimes my complaints fill up the universe. There's a line in a new song here: o daddy please don't cry—together we'll find a brand new mommie. Breaks me up. Tonight something is happening on TV that could only happen in America. Straight sturdy standard stud-happy America is going to gawk at Tiny Tim getting married on the Johnny Carson show. Anerica got its prize freak straightened out. Gregory told me he'd get married himself in order to be on nationwide TV. He's too much. And by the way George, who said "a tongue in the cunt is better than no friend at all." Sounds like some sort of sex consolation prize. Maybe you should rethink that one. Any other whizzy idea? Are you working on a translocation plan for Germany as well as for England? Gregory said he saw you in London and liked the whole thing. The best artwork I've seen here is my car. Fortunately it got into a mess and banged up its left side, meaning both windows upon impact crumbled onto the floor, and the street, and into the crack spaces where you roll them up from; and the center post around crunched backward, and other dislocations and of course the door seemed permanently locked—all this being the occasion for a piece of amazing handiwork by a saint posing as a country mechanic who saved me a few hundred by removing all my improvised bandaging of miles of masking tape and two lousy pieces of plastic, half of it blowing up outside like a ratty rumpled sail; then by taking a sheet of vinyl donated by Levine and cutting it to fit the two window spaces and I don't know a lot of miracle hammering and spitting in the right places so that it looks very interesting and it functions like new except for an immovable vinyl window. Levine, by the way, has another madcap scheme for which I'm partly responsible. He must dream every night that he's won a great prize for which the whole world has competed. I stopped in to see his new Irish-Jewish-Japanese-American-Canadian baby boy and there was a fellow there from the coast come to edit his newspaper called *Culture Hero*. With malice afterthought I remarked so this is the paper you didn't ask me to write for. Les said so would you write for it if I asked you?— No. Five minutes later,—would I like to take over the next issue.—Write a whole issue?—Too much work, I'm too busy. Then I'm thinking about it, and how if we got twenty or thirty people to contribute, each person have a page. . . . Now I'm writing to all these people, including you, requesting fifteen-hundred words about me if you can manage it, any style any thoughts, and with photo (s) of yourself, deadline January 15. I think it's very blatant and I don't care anymore. I mean what anybody else thinks. I dream by day and sleep by night. Les says not to go crazy before the issue comes out because I'm impossible when I get that way. Saw Robert Frank's movie about Peter Orlovsky and his brother Julius. I made it with Peter once. Never saw Julius before. He isn't crazy, he's different. And beautiful. Also saw the Viva movie. Arriving New York from Springfield I made up for missing Yvonne's concert straightaway. Viva's terrific. But the two walruses they picked up to be her roomies . . . —She was talking about a new religion called the cosmic climax, the last death, an end to fucking, etc., in her deadpan ennui. Do you think you're making up for your Puritan background? If you "can only imagine fucking heartily at eighty" I guess we'll have to put off the wedding until we're ninety. Maybe I'll try nationwide TV with Gregory. America should be happy to straighten out two at once. Never mind. Here's a radio joke for you: Aunt Margaret was trapped in a bagel factory for twenty-eight days and coming out she said she likes it with cream cheese herself. As always I miss your special clarity and wish you great happiness also. Merry Everything. Love, Jill.

December 25, 1969

ERE MIDSUMMER

FRANCE—Beginning backward this is a tower on top of a mountain where possibly she sang one of those old ballads full of melancholy and love which always tell of the sufferings of a princess confined in such a place by her father as a punishment for having fallen in love. I'm looking at the Mediterranean spread out 2,000 feet below a red tiled roof and a cat indulging its tongue over a gray white breast on a gravel walk. In a tea shop at Canterbury a lady of two purple bloated lips was swooning at the tellie upon the investiture of Charles whom I caught being led from the tower to be presented with a sword a crown a ring a golden rod and a mantle as the new Prince of Wales. A few hundred yards away in the cathedral lay Edward the Black Prince dead in 1376 under the emblems of war which occupied his life. "Thus the glory of this world passes away." Back in London an interviewer asks a child what a prince does when he wakes up and the child replies oh he'd have some royal bread and butter, then do some deeds. Always below from this tower of stone on top of the mountain west of Nice the old shiny black Ford rolled back down as we jumped out to say hello to the first English speaking people since Calais and the young bloke rushed after to stop it from being the end of a victorious ride. The day before was an inexpensive day, only a thousand francs for repairs on the car. They put a little thing in it and it started to go again. May the Lord grant me to lay down my sword and go back to my parents who would be so glad to see me again. So it said of Jeanne d'Arc at Orleans where I added a medallion of the girl in profile to my dingle dangle which was broken and instantly repaired in the toilet of a restaurant in Monte Carlo where the Princess Grace hangs out. In London I added a Sphinx costing tuppence in a Saturday market. That was from reading Oedipus in a foreign city. They didn't think they'd met anyone so determined to be foreign. Moreover, it's an embarrassment to see their colonial relatives. She had actually put on male clothing again and that was enough for the judges to reach the conclusion that she was an apostate and accordingly a witch and a heretic. I asked somebody about these types in the North of England. He thinks they burned the last one a hundred years ago. What was she doing to cause her demise? Nothing, they just decided they'd had enough of her. I see. And I suppose there was a ghastly squabble as to whether her feet were touching the ground before she was cut down. The English, not being a very spiritual people, have invented cricket to give them a sense of eternity. The French I don't understand at all excepting Nerval who paraded the gardens of the Palais-Royal with a lobster on a pale blue ribbon and knew a sculptor who brushed his hair into twin peaks to simulate the flames of genius. And now Ben Vautier the Southern French Fluxus exponent who lives in the middle of hundreds of objects including a dog a child a wife and a tank of goldfish and's writing a book or a pamphlet concerning twelve efficient methods of committing suicide as one of five solutions to the hopeless human condition. The practical realization of individual and collective suicide at all levels, he says. I note the great red rock cliffs hanging over the sea in between the various Coney Islands of baking bodies along the Riviera. But you can't tell about the slope of a cliff. So I'm thinking well all you need do is close your eyes with your hands on the wheel of an English Ford which you haven't yet developed any affection for and let the drunken mountains totter over the rivers of roads the width of a boa constrictor lashing itself around the rocks and pinnacles of your head imagining you might be sitting naked in somebody's garden waving gently in the breeze discussing the questions of the day. The cats have multiplied from one to three. The view is a fog. The rain is coming and the Prince of Bulgaria down the way built a chapel to marry a maiden who then flew off the top of the mountain in a heliocopter to where they don't know and I'm henna dye of her arms and eyelids, her richly tattooed chest, her brand marks, and her pierced left nostril. As with most literary suicides a theory sprang up that he didn't kill himself although actually few scholars tolerate the idea that he was murdered. At Canterbury I stand where Becket died on Tuesday, December 29, 1170. However, I might not be since "the pillar and floor soon after the murder were removed so that the spot might be better seen." Thus I turn round and regard the steps the archibishop was ascending when he came down to meet his murderers. Why are we going down? I don't remember going up. And why don't they make roads that go through the valleys? Because people like to go up and down the mountains. Yes I'd forgotten. At the foot of this mountain at Mayres hoping to reach Pont St. Espirt by midday we take the *café au lait* and no *petit déjeuner* ("this is how I think of France: sitting in a café and it's quiet and sunny and everybody lazy and everything happy") and there at the sharp turn of a bridge over a piece of water on its way somewhere a monument to the nineteen who died in a bus in 1953 crashing out of order into the river. *Connaissez-vous le grand catastrophe de Pont St. Esprit de 1951? Non.* So we're driving there now and there's nothing to see. On the way some trees linked overhead to form an arbor. Further on the horns of two oxen locked in burden as beasts hauling their masters. Is this the heavenly correspondence of things on earth? If so why is the car stopping again? Because all happens as it was meant to. Anyhow, better the car doesn't start at all, then a rescue squad will come. When you just lurch into a garage complaining about the loss of a gallon of oil in several hours they refuse to do anything. Also, we're sitting opposite a peach stand. Now we're not. I've decided since it won't start I'll throw it in second to which it responds and begins climbing of its own accord all the way for miles in second to the very top and a smiling mechanic who puts the umpteenth pair of black hands into her belly but fixes 'er up for good by removing a dead floater. So I surveyed the realm below and gave the orders to storm the ramparts. Stand by me all the time for I will have much to do and the blood shall gush forth above my breast. Help! Help! for the Holy Sepulchre! *Adoramus te Christe et benedicimus tibi.* The rhetoric is seductive. The truth is that while inspecting the ditches her voices were heard with the terrible news she'd be captured ere midsummer. Having built his castle he prowls the adjacent waters glaring about in search for intruders of his own species. Rubbish, what bunkum these people talk. France is very big and it sometimes resembles Vermont or Ohio or Nebraska where the Cathedrals of Orleans and Rouens could never've happened but the farming must all be the same. Or you might notice how at Canterbury behind the altar upon the most elevated area of the church are the signs of the Zodiac surrounding an abstract mosaic so you still don't have to know where you are nor do I think it matters. Except for Dover. That's where I am now although the cat is still licking itself and the fog rolled back and the Mediterranean is still an expanse afar below this gravel walk under an absurd stone tower a Roman fortress I suppose—somewhere around Monaco and Cannes and Nice. The thing is you drive into Dover and there's a castle on a hill naturally. Then they want money and identification and more money and answers to questions and more identification after which you drive up a pin nail narrow ramp onto a blue and white ferry which waits long enough for you to observe a huge hover-craft the size of a blimp beaching into the port you're about to leave as you hold a drink at the stern and gasp at the white cliffs of Dover all chalky steep as it was written or pictured to be besides I don't care I'm already watching the gulls and thinking it's a weird way we fly, right inside the body of a bird, which moves forward and backward and up or down according to no principle I can determine but the bread in the ocean or the wind on a wing, which I can't see now as the same wind blows my eyes shut and my hair into France before moving on to Spain. If the land becomes visible when the water recedes from it and all land masses are floating apart from each other and you can fit all these masses together like a puzzle we might do as well in a parlor with a box of such pieces to find out where anything is located although it doesn't matter does it since the object isn't to locate anything but to note the absence of the self in the midst of nothing which is my way of saying it's all the same the world over unless you're determined to be impressed by the names of things.

July 17, 1969

THREE AMERICAN PENNIES

What does it mean, I'm wailing the phrase into the hallway down the steps under an armful into another journey, what does it mean, I know it means something if a glass container and a plastic container go flying out of a cellophane bag into their glassy and plasticky fragments in pools of goo on the landings below my wailing complaining questioning what in the name of any great god goo is the present design in the total scheme. There is a design and I am not a free agent and I will to mine own self be true by not knowing and not pretending that I know whatever it is at the moment which is not to be known. Later. For now for what happened before I've unscrambled one image as an indicator which was registering its message at the time only as a strain on my resources to locate a friend in a scary altitude in a foreign terrain. It was Vallerauge in the south of France. I've bent quite a few ears over Patrick but I didn't see Patrick myself as the perfect standout until the night before that drugstore junk went into pieces and pools down the stairwell and the night after a big container of hot 'n' sour Chinese soup filled up the floor of my car from lurching off the front seat as I jammed on the brakes at a light, and right after watching Cousteau and his pals on the tellie rescue a baby whale marooned on a sandbar and thinking how great to be all beardy and salt washed and sun bleached cruising about making friends with whales and then I got the right image of Patrick, Patrick who wouldn't understand some of these scenes in the cement desert, like his tall American writer friend on stage at the New School sousing up on gin and vermouth out of a paper bag next to a chair where she was sitting playing "Monopoly" with three other writer pals all appearing at the request of Buddy W. to talk about words or something for his Intermedia class; or at the Met opening doing an old routine looking around before leaving how to make a spectacle of herself and finding a reliable soulmate our American Michelangelo Mark di Suvero the lion head welded into a turtle neck red sweater which he removed and roared and pitched up on his spindly legs under a massive torso and wielded a new-looking metal cane which was a live property in the ultimate tumble the floor spectacle the sprawl under all that verticalypso cocktail clinkerchief kertails kerchoo kerfooey she wanted to rip it all apart so she walked off with a trophy a piece of a dirty undershirt of di Suvero's stuck in the opening of a metal neckpiece. No, Patrick wouldn't get it. Patrick Cardwell Derham. Whattaname. Two days out of Dover near Rouens happens the first image. This bloody black British Ford doesn't respond to its ignition equipment. Early morning just out of a roadside hotel. Patrick and two French boys hitching to Scandinavia heave ho on the tail for a push-start as I sit at the wheel. No soap. Rest. Again. Nada. Rest. Third time and lots of panting, I'm sitting at a dead wheel, I look up and around, the French boys gone, where's Patrick, Uh oh, alarm, Patrick makes a beautiful anemic sight slumped against a tree trunk the exhausted long blond haired Buddha, I'm traveling with a Buddha but I don't know it yet. Alarm. Are you okay? Yes I'll be all right, weakly. I walk back to the hotel to phone for *mecanique*. Returning I find Patrick in the car bending intently over a pale blue tin box crammed with vials of pills. Holy Batman boy, whas that? Homeopathic medicines.—Ummm, one of those. Clearly he's looking for *the* pill to cure exhaustion from push-starting British Fords on early mornings in French countrysides. I never saw the tin box again. But I hear the story how four good Catholic children grew up to abandon Catholicism and to be sold on

Homeopathy. Even so, I tell Patrick, you're going to be a priest, I don't know what kind, but a priest neverthechurch-less. And you'll go to India again. And . . . And he asks me about Cage and the like and I'm imagining he thinks I'm older wiser I'll tell him what's whats, but I dump it right back on him, this somewhat unconscious eighteen year old Buddha who doesn't say much (no, he isn't withdrawn, he says, he's "inward"—of course), I hand him the credentials I hope he'll never have, for in his innocence and angel smiles and earnest but relaxed good nature he knows the way that I've recently lost and I never find the indicator on a credential card. At Pont St. Esprit we split cuz I want to go east toward Nice and he's hitching due west to a cottage in Vallerauge belongs to two English friends. He gives me instructions how to get there on the way back if I want to. I do. But it's an indeterminate altitude once you hit the town. Straight up to Cloud X. There's a road, Patrick said, across from the gendarmerie round back of a camping ground. Don't drive up the road. But I've got no gut for walking up a foreign mountain. The friendly gendarme says yes yes you can drive, and yes there's some weird looking kids up there some-where. Good. I drive. I shouldn't. Right off I see what he meant. The road is no wider than the car which is narrow. Pronto the drop on the left is precipitous. And the turns are bobby pins. And the pavement becomes dirt littered with small boulders. So I'm roaring up in second not looking right or left and thinking there's no turning back and where the hell is this "cottage"—I'm really in a lather—and there isn't a living soul etc. Then I cross a black hose, then the steepest incline in the middle of which my horse stops balks fumes refuses, so we roll back down to the hose Life, maybe. I get out. I see where I am. It's not real. I'm at the top of the world. I'll fly away and never be heard of again. I can't look. Endless chasms of light struck valleys. Really giddy from this. Scared out of my skull. Start yelling. HALLO HALLO HALLO. That hose does connect to some-thing. Up a high embankment, up up to a dilapidated looking stone structure. HAAAAALLOOOOOO. And I'm desperate, strug-gling up the embankment my voice echo bouncing off the god-dam mountains. Then it happens. The image. First there's an-other human voice. It yells JILL. Fantastic. Somebody up here knows me. Then a white thing is floating down the slope. It's got a flying blond mane. The rest of it is all white. It's Patrick in his indian cottons. It's Himself. Then we're sitting where the water is coming down the rest of the mountain in another black hose and I'm drinking all of it. All up. Never so happy. Relieved I should say. And Patrick is the Buddha, but I still don't know it. Later I notice what's around his neck. I recall the morning leaving a hotel someplace between Orleans and Pont St. Esprit he mentioned a charm he's been wearing for some time from India, from an Indian who meant something, and it was gone. I said let's go back for it. No, it was all right. I was impressed. I'd go back, and forth also, for my metal thing. Now I'm remarking on his new necklace. The feature is a tiny blue denim bag with a drawstring. He opens it and produces three American pennies. Too much. I really like it. They're the pennies I hadn't retrieved after he used them one night in some hotel, crouched over the *I Ching* to find out why he was traveling with me. And one day on top of the mountain at Vallerauge he says let's look at it, the *I Ching,* just as I'm thinking the same thing on my way to the chemical toilet, and he gives me the reading for the darkness changing to light at the winter solstice and I know later on it'll all come together.

November 13, 1969